SELF-HELP GROUPS AND MARGINALISED COMMUNITIES

ABOUT THE AUTHOR

Dr. A.A.A. Faizi, a postgraduate from Patna University, is an officer of Bihar Administrative Service. He has served the state in various capacities. He has also worked as Additional Private Secretary to the Minister for Rural Development, Government of India. He is advisor to the HARYALI Centre for the Rural Development, New Delhi.

Dr. Faizi has conducted several other studies including the NIRD sponsored study on 'Functional Status of Women PRI Members: Problems and Prospects—with Special Reference to Muzaffarpur District,' and 'Poverty Alleviation Programmes—Future Strategies.'

SELF-HELP GROUPS AND MARGINALISED COMMUNITIES

Dr. Amir Afaque Ahmad Faizi

CONCEPT PUBLISHING COMPANY, NEW DELHI-110059

ISBN-13: 978-81-8069-621-3 ISBN-10: 81-8069-621-9

First Published 2009

Published and Printed by

Concept Since 1974

Concept Publishing Company

Regd. Office:

A/15-16, Commercial Block, Mohan Garden

New Delhi-110059 (India)

Phones : 25351460, 25351794, *Fax* : 091-11-25357109

Email : publishing@conceptpub.com,

website: www.conceptpub.com

Editorial Office:

H-13, Bali Nagar, New Delhi-110 015, India.

Cataloging in Publication Data--*Courtesy:* D.K. Agencies (P) Ltd. <docinfo@dkagencies.com>

Faizi, Amir Afaque Ahmad.

Self-help groups and marginalised communities / Amir Afaque Ahmad Faizi.

p. cm.

Originally presented as the author's thesis.

Study conducted at Muzaffarpur District of Bihar, India.

Includes bibliographical references and index.

ISBN 13: 9788180696213 ISBN 10: 8180696219

1. Self-help groups--India--Muzaffarpur (District) 2. Microfinance--India--Muzaffarpur (District) 3. People with social disabilities--Employment--India--Muzaffarpur (District) 4. Rural poor--Employment--India--Muzaffarpur (District) 5. Rural women--Employment--India--Muzaffarpur (District) 6. Rural development projects--India--Muzaffarpur (District) I. Title.

DDC 307.14120954123 22

Foreword

Poverty and unemployment are two curse for rural India, to me the two are synonymous in character and closely related to each other. It can be alleviated through providing additional income to every family and this can be achieved through the instrument of Self-Help Group and self-employment. Rural poverty and unemployment has a wide variation between different regions as well as across various communities. About fifty per cent of the rural poor are concentrated in Bihar, Uttar Pradesh, Madhya Pradesh, Jharkhand, Orissa and Chhattisgarh. The NSSO 61st round gives the detail of the variation of poverty level amongst different communities and according to it, it is acute amongst Scheduled Caste (SC), Scheduled Tribes (ST) and Muslims on which the study focuses. The Socio-economic condition of women especially within the SC and the Muslim community of Bihar in general and Muzaffarpur in particular is the worst amongst all. The impact of the Self-Help Group movement for this segment of society as well its net effects has been examined on the group's, social and economic status. The emergence and rapid multiplication of Self-Help Groups (SHGs) based on micro credit is a phenomenon that is gaining increasing importance in the development scenario.

The present book attempts to explore the impact of SHGs on the marginalized communities. It deals with the concept and status of marginalised community in brief. The Scheduled Caste, Backward Caste, Muslims and women have been included among the marginalized communities on the basis of various studies on social exclusion and marginalised group and demography of the area i.e. Muzaffarpur district of Bihar. Also gives, a brief overview of the concept of SHGs which discusses the definition of Self-Help Group, its procedure for formation, its history, approaches, principles, norms and other such related issues and the level or mode of implementation at ground level at various levels.

Overall in the book, it has been observed after discussions with various groups and stakeholders, like members of SHG, NGO, bank and block officials, PRI members, social activist of the areas, higher officials like DDC and DM of the district along with and sampled population, that though economic impact is not much visible the social impact is loud in the area of study. The communities gained in good habits and confidence especially the women, now they could think positive and empower themselves. It has been suggested that to achieve desirable level of success, it is imperative to shed undue bureaucratic and mechanical approach and fix accountability of actions on the part of bank and block officials and other government or non-government official, moreover it is extremely important that Panchayats be linked with SHGs to have a better monitoring and guidance. The book also provides a comprehensive literature review on the theoretical and empherical research literature conducted in the area, especially on the concept and processes of SHGs and measures for strengthening of SHG movement in Bihar in particular and India as a whole for the up-liftment of Marginalized Communities.

I am sure this book will aid academia, policy makers, practitioners, banks, funding agencies, researchers and the government in getting a sense of the socio-economic returns of the SHG interventions in community-level institutions in India.

Dr. Raghuvansh Prasad Singh
Minister of Rural Development
Government of India

Preface

Despite sixty years of independence, constitutional commitments, planning, processes and various other schemes, plans and projects on poverty alleviation, it remains a major issue that persists to be dealt with by successive governments. Recently, promotion of Self-Help Groups has undoubtedly created confidence amongst marginalized communities and substantial self-employment opportunities. However, its coverage and functioning has serious limitations.

The emergence and rapid multiplication of Self-Help Groups (SHGs) based on micro credit is a phenomenon that is gaining increasing importance in the development scenario. Today, there are more than seven million SHGs in the country. Of that, nearly 90 per cent of the groups are women only groups. SHG are being viewed today, by the State as a strategy for both as tools for empowerment of marginalized communities including women as well as poverty eradication. SHGs are a conduit for routing a wide range of government sponsored development messages and schemes. NGOs have increasingly been adopting SHGs as a strategy to bring women together, at a faster pace and larger scale than the collective building process adopted by them earlier. In addition to the State and NGOs, banks, donors and corporations are some of the other powerful players, all of whom have a significant and growing interest in the SHG phenomenon, which centers on poor women. These concerns draw upon the understanding and inspiration to undertake this study and go into details about its impact on the marginalized group.

Bihar, the states with highest poverty ratio in India has been studied in the book. The NSSO 61st round gives the detail of the variation of poverty level amongst different communities and according to it; it is acute amongst Scheduled Caste (SC), Scheduled Tribes (ST) and Muslims on which the study focuses. The study has been conducted in five blocks (Kanti, Sahebganj, Madwan, Kudhni and Paru) of Muzaffarpur district and a sample of 500 self-help group members, from 47 villages were interviewed.

A sincere attempt in this book has been made to evaluate the socio-economic impact of SHGs on the marginalized communities. Highlighting how far Self-Help Groups have been successful in the social and economic up-liftment of the Marginalized Communities and tries to explore the changes that occurred in the respondents living condition and behaviour after becoming the member of the Group. The impact of the Self-Help Group movement on this section of the society as well and the net effects has been examined on the groups, social and economic status.

The present book has intrinsically gone into various issues, its approach and solutions for making the Self-Help Group scheme a phenomenal success. This will help the women think positive and empower themselves. The book highlights that how far Self-Help Groups have been successful in the social and economic upliftment of the Marginalised Communities i.e. what was the impact of SHGs on Marginalised Groups. The book is written with the objective to see that what transformation has been done in the respondents lives after becoming the member of the Group.

Hope this book will enrich the knowledge of academicians, policy makers, researchers and students on SHG, Micro-finance, poverty reduction and development mechanisms of the marginalised groups and communities in India.

Dr. A.A.A. Faizi

Acknowledgements

Prof. (Dr.) Mohammad Mujtaba Khan, Director Dr. K.R. Narayanan Centre for Dalit and Minorities Studies, and Provost, Jamia Millia Islamia, imbibed in me the intellectual and academic insights into the topic and transformed my initial skepticism into active involvement in the subject and the result is the modest thesis. Therefore, first and foremost I am highly indebted and grateful to Prof. Mujtaba Khan, my mentor who instilled the academic zeal to concretize and conceptualize the present study.

I am extremely thankful to Shri Mustaq Ahmed, Sr. Consultant and Advisor, HARAYALI Centre for Research Development, New Delhi for their valuable advice and support in conducting the study. I am very much obliged to Mr. Saurabh Shukla, Assistant Librarian and information officer, Ministry of Rural Development.

I fail in my duty if I do not mention the cooperation and support of Mr. Mohammad Yusuf, Director HARAYALI Centre for Research Development, New Delhi and their entire staff for their kind cooperation.

In all oddities, the help provided by Mr. Gopinath Iyengar whose valuable cooperation have helped me in bringing out the study to its final culmination.

I am also thankful to all those who collaborated with us during the process of data collection in the survey/field which includes the name of Mr. Maqbool Grameen Jan Kalyan Parishad of Sahebganj, Muzaffarpur. Mr. Satyender, Director NIRDESH (NGO), Mr. Ram Pravesh, Director, Hanuman Prasad Grameen Vikas Seva Samiti (NGO), Ms Shachi Sinha, Lady Extension Officer of Kudni Block, Muzaffarpur, and Mr. Abu Faizan (now Research Assistent JMI) and Mr. Subhash (Project Coordinator, HARAYALI Centre for Research Development, New Delhi) for their kind help for making this study a reality by their untiring efforts. Mr. Munna Khan has helped me in typing and formatting of the manuscript.

I am very much grateful to Dr. Raghuvansh Prasad Singh, Hon'ble Minister for Rural Development, Government of India, and Mr. Amrit Lal Meena IAS, P.S. to the Hon'ble Minister for extending his support and advice in conducting this study.

The task could not be completed without the silent support from my wife Nuzhat and my children Sobia, Aslah and Ikramah.

I dedicate my work to my parent Dr. Syed Mushtaque Ahmad and Ms. Taiyyaba Khatoon who always encouraged me for the study.

Dr. Amir Afaque Ahmad Faizi

Contents

List of Tables

Introduction

The Directive Principles of the State Policy of the Constitution of India give the direction to the State for the social and economic welfare of its citizen[1]. Unemployment and poverty are seen as the twin curse of India.[2] This is a major obstacle in the economic growth of the nation which has fixed a target of achieving a developed country status by 2020. About 260 million people in the country do not have a sufficient level of income to access the consumption basket. Of these, 75 per cent are in the rural areas. India is home to 22 per cent of the world's poor.

Such a high incidence of poverty is a matter of grave concern in view of the fact that poverty eradication has been one of the major objectives of the developmental planning process. The National Sample Survey Organization (NSSO) estimated that 22.15 per cent of the population was living below the poverty line in 2004-05, down

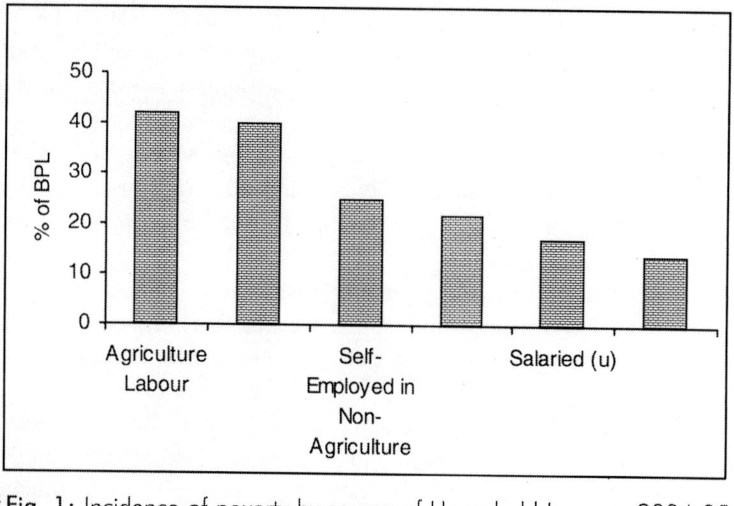

[4] Fig. 1: Incidence of poverty by source of Household Income, 2004-05

from 51.3 per cent in 1977-78 and 26 per cent in 2000. Out of the 75 per cent poor in rural areas most of them are daily wagers, self-employed households and landless labourers.[3] NSSO 61st round consumer expenditure survey report says that 44.1 per cent agriculture labour, 39.7 per cent casual labour, 25.3 per cent self-employed in agriculture, 21.4 per cent of self-employed in non-agriculture are living below the poverty line. This is shown in Figure 1.

Rural poverty and unemployment has a wide variation between different regions as well as across various communities.

About 50 per cent of the rural poor are concentrated in Bihar, Uttar Pradesh, Madhya Pradesh, Jharkhand, Orissa and Chhattisgarh[5] as shown in Fig. 2[6].

Eradication of poverty is the focus of policy makers. Most of them believe that employment generation is one of the means to achieve the goal of poverty eradication.

Rural unemployment is being targeted with more precision. Three groups have been selected to target three different classes of the poor unemployed rural population.

The first such group comprises of illiterate agricultural and casual labour. For this group, Government of India introduced and implemented various schemes through State Governments like Hard Manual Labour Scheme, Food for Work Scheme, SGRY, Employment Assurance Scheme and finally, in 2005, National Rural Employment Guarantee Act which was introduced and in 2006, NREGS was introduced in 200 districts. 130 districts were added to this scheme in 2007 in the rest will be included from 1st April, 2008.

The second group is that of educated unemployed youth. These youth seek employment in private or public organization. The Government facilitates appropriate job-oriented training and placement programmes to such youths.

The third group is that of unemployed traditional artisans, small and marginal farmers and semi-literates having courage for entrepreneureship. This group is the second largest segment of the rural poor. The Government of India and State Governments encourage and facilitate new enterprises for them through various programmes. Earlier it was through the Integrated Rural Development Programme which is now merged with Swarnjayanti Gram Swarozgar Yojana and such other schemes for minorities. Under IRDP, the

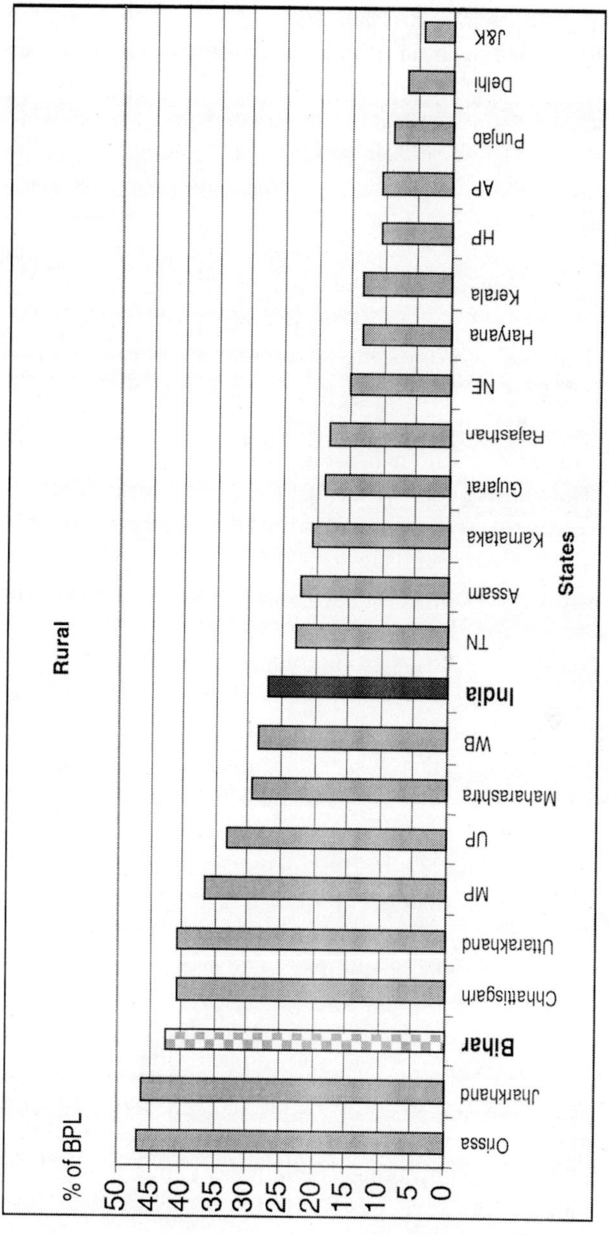

Fig. 2: Incidence of Poverty by State - 2004-05

bank officials were hesitant to finance the individual entrepreneurs in absence of any security. By 1970s a new experiment was underway in some corners of the world like Bangladesh and Brazil with Andhra Pradesh and Karnataka in India of lateral security for microfinance by providing loans to a group of people belonging to same profession or to varied groups from the village or town. Small groups were formed which is termed as Self Help Group in the country with the objective of encouraging collection of savings and providing loans for personal use and also to start new enterprises. These groups have become an institution where people develop the habit of saving, get training in group dynamism and book keeping. The institution also assists the members to solve many social and local problems. In 1999, Ministry of Rural Development, Government of India, gave importance to Self Help Groups in its new scheme of SGSY for providing capacity building, skill up-gradation, training, revolving fund, subsidy and loan to the beneficiary living below the poverty line. The Self Help Group concept has been accepted as the best way for providing productive self-employment and eradication of poverty.

It seems to be the best method to achieve the social, psychological, behavioural and economical upward change of the leftout communities.

Bihar is one of the states with the highest poverty ratio, this is why I have selected this state for my study. The NSSO 61st round gives the detail of the variation of poverty level amongst different communities and according to it, it is acute amongst Scheduled Castes (SC), Scheduled Tribes (ST) and Muslims[7] on which the study focuses.

The Socio-economic condition of women especially within the SC and the Muslim community of Bihar in general and Muzaffarpur in particular is the worst amongst all. The impact of the Self Help Group movement on this section of the society as well and its net effects has been examined on the group's social and economic status.

The Government of India and the State Governments started a number of programmes for employment generation which include (wage employment and self-employment), health and education, rural housing and sanitation etc. to improve the living condition of the deprived section of the society. By the end of 1970s, a new movement gained momentum in the subcontinent, commonly known as Self Help Group and Grameen Bank. When NABARD and SGSY[8] in 1999 started schemes of bank credit for micro enterprises on collateral security basis through small groups of people it was popularly referred to as Self Help Group.

The emergence and rapid multiplication of Self Help Groups (SHGs) based on microcredit is a phenomenon that is gaining increasing importance in the development scenario. Today, there are seven million SHGs that exist in the country, of that, nearly 90 per cent are the women only groups.

SHGs are being viewed today, by the State as a strategy for both women's empowerment as well as poverty eradication. SHGs are a conduit for routing a wide range of government sponsored development messages and schemes. NGOs have increasingly been adopting SHGs as a strategy to bring women together, at a faster pace and larger scale than the collective building process adopted by them earlier. In addition to the State and NGOs, banks, donors and corporations are some other powerful players, all of whom have a significant and growing interest in the SHG phenomenon, which centres on poor women. These inspired me to undertake this study and examine in depth the impact of SHG institution on the marginalised group.

The present piece of work aims to study the impact of SHGs on the marginalized communities. The study highlights how far Self Help Groups have been successful in the social and economic upliftment of the Marginalised Communities. The study tries to explore what changes have occurred in the respondents' living condition and behaviour after becoming the member of the Group.

The study is divided in seven different chapters. The first chapter deals with the objectives, coverage and methodology of the study and the profile of the area concerned that is Muzaffarpur district of Bihar.

The second chapter gives a brief overview of the concept of SHGs which discusses the definition of Self Help Group, its procedure for formation, its history, approaches, principles, norms and other such related issues and the level or mode of implementation at ground level at various levels.

The third chapter deals with the concept and status of marginalised community in brief. The Scheduled Castes, Backward Castes, Muslims and women have been included among the marginalized communities on the basis of various studies on social exclusion and marginalised group and demography of the area, i.e. Muzaffarpur district of Bihar. This chapter provides a picture of the social and economic life of the communities in Muzaffarpur.

The fourth chapter is about the initiatives of the Government and the Non-Government Organisations in the field of social upliftment of the marginalised communities through the instrument of Self Help Group. This chapter describes in brief, various schemes of the Government that are operational in the rural areas and their impact on the area concerned with special reference to Muzaffarpur District of Bihar.

Various departments of Government of India, State Governments and organisations like National Bank for Agriculture and Rural Development (NABARD), Rashtriya Mahila Kosh, Scheduled Caste Finance and Development Corporation, National Backward Class Finance and Development Corporation (NBCFDC), Minorities Finance and Development Corporation are using this instrument for the economic and social development of Marginalised communities. This chapter also deals with Self Help Group Promotion Institutions (SHGPIs) and the activities and impact of NGOs.

The fifth chapter deals with the impact of Self Help Group on Social development of Marginalised communities. The parameters of the social development taken in this chapter are mainly education, health and hygiene level, awareness level, confidence level, living standard, decision making capacities etc. These are the areas which determine the social condition and start the process of social inclusion of any community and group of communities. It is appended by case studies which explain how women of socially excluded and marginalised group emerge as the leader of the area and even elected as local representative to Panchayat bodies.

Self Help Groups and economic development of Marginalised Communities is the area of discussion in chapter six. The parameter for economic development discussed here are mainly occupation of the respondents who are females and members of SHGs and subsequent transformation in their occupation. Income structure is another important parameter which is also the main determinant for poverty. Their saving nature, their loan repayment tendency and capacity, their attitude towards new entrepreneurship has also been discussed. This chapter also includes a few case studies which provide a picture of women of marginalised communities using the institution of Self Help Group got economic and social recognition in the area and became self-dependent and economically independent.

The findings of the study and personal observations are included in the last chapter with some suggestion based on the experience and discussion with various groups and stakeholders like members of SHG, NGO, bank and block officials, PRI members, social activists of the areas, higher officials like DDC and DM of the district regarding efficient and transparent implementation of programmes with maximum output and total upliftment of the marginalised groups.

Notes

1. Article 38(1) The state shall strive to promote the welfare of the people by securing and protecting as effectively as it may a social order in which justice, social, economic and political, shall inform all the institutions of the national life.
   (2) The state shall, in particular, strive to minimize the inequalities in income, and endeavour to eliminate inequalities in status, facilities and opportunities, not only amongst individuals but also amongst groups of people residing in different areas or engaged in different vocations.
2. T.K. Manoj Kumar and Jai Singh Shekhawat, Poverty, Unemployment and Rural Development Programme—Background paper, National Workshop on Poverty, Unemployment & Rural Development Programmes (6-7 April 2007)
3. *Ibid.*
4. Abusaleh Shariff, Poverty and Equity at the Turn of the 20th Century in India, seminar on Poverty, unemployment and Rural Development Programmes, LBSNAA, 2007.
5. Amita Shah and Baidyanath Guru. Poverty in Remote Rural Area in India : A Review of Evidence and Issues, working paper 21, IIPA, Delhi, 2004.
6. Abusaleh Shariff, Poverty and Equity at the Turn of the 20th Century in India, seminar on Poverty, Unemployment and Rural Development Programmes, LBSNAA, 2007.
7. *Ibid.*
8. Guidelines of SGSY, Ministry of Rural Development, Government of India, 2006.

Chapter One

Approach and Coverage

A. METHODOLOGY

1. Objectives

The present research has six major objectives to examine the role of the newly formed movement of Self-Help Group for the socio-economic empowerment of marginalized communities especially in the backward region of the country. The following are some of the specific points of enquiry forming the focal points of the study:

(i) Description of the main principles and theory of Self-Help Group movement and the Government policies and programmes regarding SHGs.
(ii) To examine the status of SHG movement in Muzaffarpur district of Bihar.
(iii) To examine the impediments in its dynamics.
(iv) To examine the impacts of SHGs on marginalized communities in Muzaffarpur district of Bihar.
(v) To examine the role of Central and State Governments and NGOs in facilitation and strengthening of SHGs.
(vi) To draw conclusions and suggest measures for strengthening of SHG movement in Bihar in particular and India as a whole for the up-liftment of marginalized communities.

2. Hypothesis

(i) It is more likely that the members of the marginalized community of Bihar are illiterate and non-learner and having lack of entrepreneurial skills.

(ii) The members of the marginalized communities are less aware of the government policies and programmes.

(iii) The marginalized communities are denied the credit and banking facilities of the financial institutions, including nationalized banks.

(iv) The members of marginalized communities are less aware of the strength and weaknesses of the SHG movement.

(v) The NGOs of Bihar are not playing their role as facilitator.

(vi) There are impediments of internal dynamics of SHG movement.

3. Sampling

Muzaffarpur, a district situated in the centre of north Bihar, has been selected as it has diverse demographic economic and social condition in its different Panchayats of different blocks. Many of its Panchayats are dominated by Bhumihars and Rajputs whereas others are dominated politically and economically by Yadavas, Paswans, are dominated by Banias and even some Panchayats by Muslims.

To study the objective and test the hypothesis, randomly five hundred members of Self-Help Groups in forty seven villages of five blocks *i.e.* Kanti, Sahebganj, Madwan, Kudhni and Paru have been selected for the study and interview through schedule attached in the thesis and discussed with them. The list is shown in Table 1.1.

Many of the bank and block officials has been contacted discussed with them about the concept of SHG and problem in implementation of the various schemes having SHG as an instruments. The dynamic and implements of SHG has also been discussed. Moreover the problem of new enterprises, marketing, branding, quality problem has also been discussed.

Some twenty samples of interview scheduled have also taken from the Bank Official of different designation, out of which sixteen of Branch Managers, three of Field Officer concerned with the SHG formation and linkages and one that of Cashier. The officials of different banks are given in the above-mentioned Table 1.2.

Table 1.1: Village-wise Respondentes

Name of Block	Name of Village	Respondents	
		No.	%
Kanti	1 Mustfapur	26	5.20
	2 Narsanda	51	10.20
	3 Kolwa Dadar	27	5.40
Sahebganj	4 Pratappatti	13	2.60
	5 Vaidhnathpur	2	0.40
	6 Pahadpur	5	1.00
	7 Hussaypur	24	4.80
	8 Rampur Asli	4	0.80
	9 Madhupur Hazari	2	0.40
	10 Basudoopur	1	0.20
	11 Roopchada	1	0.20
	12 Devghada	4	0.80
	13 Bishanpurpatti	1	0.20
	14 Vaidhnathpur	4	0.80
	15 Rajwafa	13	2.60
	16 Ashapatti	6	1.20
	17 Haleempur	9	1.80
	18 Shahapur	9	1.80
	19 Pakdi Basharat	2	0.40
	20 Nawanagar Nizamat	6	1.20
Madwan	21 Paratap Patti	10	2.00
	22 Madwan Mauza	6	1.20
	23 Bangdi	14	2.80
	24 Chamarwa	10	2.00
	25 Fatehpur	4	0.80
	26 Pakdi Pakodi	23	4.60
Kudhni	27 Maniyari	89	17.80
	28 Madhaul	1	0.20
	29 Mahant Masimari	2	0.40
	30 Bhagwanpur	6	1.20
	31 Ghaus Khas	16	3.20
	32 Raghunathpur	1	0.20
	33 Sakri Saraiya	20	4.00
Paru	34 Ghariba	6	1.20
	35 Pasumat Tola	13	2.60
	36 Mojhaulia South	1	0.20
	37 Korria Nizamat	3	0.60
	38 Mehwadpur	4	0.80
	39 Lalchapra	3	0.60
	40 Jaleel Nagar	1	0.20
	41 Paru Chadhri Tola	7	1.40
	42 Gopalpur	1	0.20
	43 Lucknouri	1	0.20
	44 Firozpur	10	2.00
	45 Mohjamma	26	5.20
	46 Dadpur	10	2.00
	47 Chattarpatti	3	0.60
	Grand Total:	**501**	**100.00**

Table 1.2: Bank Official and their Designation

Name of Banks	*Manager*		*Cashier*		*Field Officer*		*Total*	
	No.	*%*	*No.*	*%*	*No.*	*%*	*No.*	*%*
Central Bank of India	1	100		0		0	1	100
Punjab National Bank	5	100		0		0	5	100
Bank of Baroda	1	100	1	100		0	1	100
Rigional Rural Bank	3	75		0		0	4	100
State Bank of India	1	33		0	2	67	3	100
U.B.K.G.B	3	75		0	1	25	4	100
United Bank of India	1	100		0		0	1	100
Canara Bank	1	100		0		0	1	100
Total	*16*	*80*	*1*	*5*	*3*	*15*	*20*	*100*

Table 1.3: Trained Bank Official about SHGs

Name of Banks	*Yes*		*No.*		*Total*	
	No.	*%*	*No.*	*%*	*No.*	*%*
Central Bank of India		0	1	100	1	100
Punjab National Bank	5	100		0	5	100
Bank of Baroda	1	100		0	1	100
Rigional Rural Bank	2	50	2	50	4	100
State Bank of India	3	100		0	3	100
U.B.K.G.B	4	100		0	4	100
United Bank of India	1	100		0	1	100
Canara Bank	1	100		0	1	100
Total	*17*	*85*	*3*	*15*	*20*	*100*

It is very remarkable feature, and against the general perception that the officer concerned with the SHG formation and linkages has not been trained, seventeen out of twenty *i.e.* 85 per cent is trained for this purpose.

4. Target Group

The focus of the study is on the marginalised community located in Muzaffarpur district of Bihar. Sociologists and demographers has given a detail list of caste and religious communities who are excluded or deprived or Marginalised by the society. Backward Caste, Scheduled Caste, Scheduled Tribes, Women and Muslim community are commonly accepted community by all the sociologists as marginalised or excluded groups. Scheduled Tribes communities are negligible in Muzaffarpur district therefore a balance composition of Scheduled Caste, Backward Caste, Women and Muslim community has been taken as the target group of the study. 211 of the respondents belonged to SC category, and 8 to ST category. 244 Backward Castes, including 102 are Muslims. Only 38 persons were interviewed from the general category for comparison purpose. Almost all the respondents are women.

5. Tools

Three sets of interview schedule were used one each for SHG members, bank officials and Government officials. The data collected through the schedule has been entered in SPSS software, and by the help of SPSS analysis has been done. Besides SPSS, SAS and Microsoft Excel and Word has also been used as a tool.

6. Data Collection

Primary data was collected through interview schedules. Secondary data has been collected from DRDA, State Report of the Department of Rural Development, Government of Bihar, Women Development Corporation, Patna, NABARD, Muzaffarpur; Mahila Samakhya Office, Red Cross Bhawan Patna; different NGOs active in the district and the Ministry of Rural Development, Government of India, Census Report, 2001, Village Census Report, 2001, and Human Development Report, World Bank Report and other reports published by various organizations and institutions.

7. Analytical Framework

The analysis of the collected data covers variables like caste, minority groups, field of economic activities of monthly/daily income; educational level, marital status etc. Simple statistical tools and services of the computer technology, especially SPSS software is utilized.

The Report of the Commission set up for study on credit bodies for poor and self-employed had recommended in 1988 various innovations in the credit mechanism to assist poor women who are unfamiliar with the complexities of institutional finance. The commission strongly recommended for setting up an exclusive credit body for poor and self-employed women, in recognition of their socio-economic realities.

B. A BRIEF PROFILE OF MUZAFFARPUR DISTRICT IN BIHAR

Muzaffarpur district in Bihar State referred to as: 'The land of *Leechi*' was created in **1875** for the administrative convenience by dividing the pre-existing district of **Tirhut** and was named after ***Muzaffar Khan,*** an Amil (Revenue Officer) under British rule. *Purbi Champaran* and *Sitamarhi* districts to the North, to the South *Vaishali* and *Saran* districts, to the East *Darbhanga* and *Samastipur* districts and to the West *Saran* and *Gopalganj* districts are the border districts of Muzaffarpur.

1. Geography of Muzaffarpur at a Glance

The name of the district has been derived from its principal city, *Muzaffarpur*. It has two sub-divisions (Muzaffarpur East and Muzaffarpur West) and the headquarters of both the sub-divisions are located in Muzaffarpur town which is the principal city and also the headquarter of the district. The total area of the district is 3172 sq. kms[1].

The district comprises of an extensive plain formed by the alluvial soil brought by the Gandak, the Bagmati and other rivers which flow through it. The ground is not marked by any high contour and at many places there are chains of shallow marshes which serve the purpose of drainage for excessive water due to rainfall and overflow of the streams. The alluvial plain is a tract of great fertility. A special feature of the district is that due to continuous deposit of silt, many of its river beds are higher than its adjoining areas. This leads to frequent floods during the rainy seasons particularly in north east and south-west parts of the district.

The Gandak, Bagmati, Burhi Gandak and Baya are the important rivers besides a few streams. The Gandak, which has its origin in the mountain of Nepal, enters the district near Karnaul in Sahebganj block and flows in the south-easterly direction. It is known as the Narayani and Saligram in the plains, while at the source it is known as Sapt Gandaki. Like the Gandak, the Bagmati also has its origin in Nepal. It enters the district in Minapur block. It flows along a serpentine course almost parallel to the Burhi Gandak and finally flows to Darbhanga district. The Burhi Gandak which is known as the *Sikrahna*, enters the district near the village Ghosaut in Minapur block. The river is navigable during greater part of the year. It had great importance before the introduction of the railways and was used as the main trade route. Even now, heavily loaded boats ply on it.

2. Operational Land-Holding

Muzaffarpur is primarily an agricultural based district which is why the operational land-holding is a key variable in determining socio-economic conditions within the district. The table given below gives an outline of this trend:

Table 1.4: Structure of Land-holding

Size of the Land-holding	*Number of Land-holders*	*Percentage of Land-holder*
10 ha >	759	0.27
4 to 10ha.	7058	2.50
2 to 4ha.	17125	6.06
1 to 2 ha.	74317	26.30
<1 ha.	183286	64.87
Total	*282545*	*100.00*

Land Use Pattern

The total area of the district 70 per cent is sown area and out of the sown area only 38 per cent is irrigated, inspite of numerous rivers flowing through the district. About 7 per cent is used for horticulture purposes, this means that out of the total cultivable area 59270 ha or 24 per cent is used for non-agricultural purposes[2]. Further, it is important to mention here that about 27 per cent of the total area is affected by flood every year, submerging quite a large area of land including dwellings. There is no forest in the district.

Table 1.5: Nature of Land

Total Area	*Cultivable Area*		*Net Sown Area*		*Irrigated Land*	
	Total area in Ha	*%*	*Total area in Ha*	*%*	*Total area in Ha*	*%*
317591 Ha	247721	70	219963	81	82964	30

3. Demography of Muzaffarpur

Muzaffarpur district represents a typically Indian mosaic in its demographic profile with a multi-cultural, multi-religious and heterogeneous population. The total population[3] of the Muzaffarpur district is 3,746,714 with 3,398,361 in rural areas and 348,353 in urban areas. Scheduled Caste in the district according to Census Report 2001 it is 594,577 (15%) and the same in rural areas is 561,354 (16.5%) and the Scheduled Tribe is just 3,472 (0.1%) and the same in rural areas is 2,942 (0.1%). The Minorities population are 5,73,951 (15.32%) Muslims Christians (1260), Sikhs (679), Buddhists (247) and Jains (177) which are negligible in terms of percentage.

Total literacy rate in Muzaffarpur is 48 per cent, it is 59.1 per cent amongst male and just 35.8 per cent amongst females, the case is worst for the rural areas. In rural areas of Muzaffarpur total literacy rate is 44.7 per cent and it is 56.4 per cent for male and 32.1 per cent for female.[4]

Chart 1.1: Pattern of Working Population

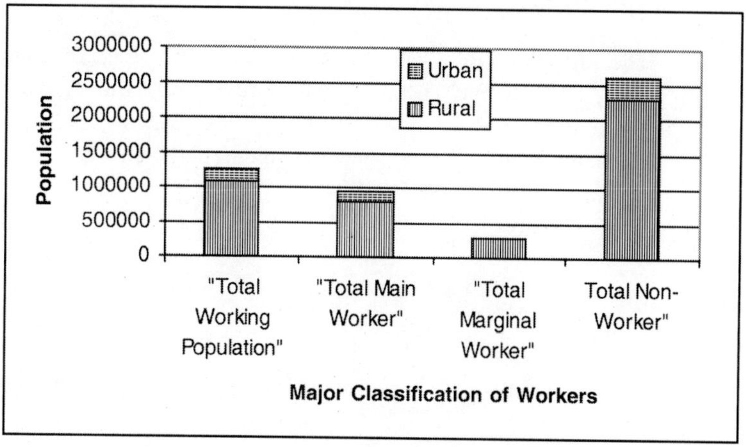

The population of non-Worker in Rural and urban areas is very high, main workers and marginal workers and even working population is low.

Chart 1.2: Classification of Labour

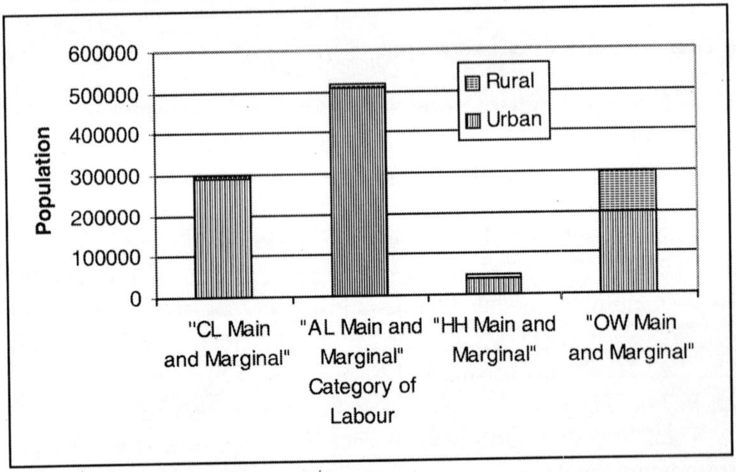

The casual labour and agricultural labour comprises more than three-fourth of the total worker group and most of them are living below poverty line.

Notes

1. The Encyclopaedic District Gazetteers of India, Eastern Zone (vol. 8), Ed. S.C. Bhatt, Gyan Publishing House, New Delhi, 2000.
2. Website of Muzaffarpur www.muz.nic.in dated 23-4-06.
3. Census Report, 2001.
4. Census Report, 2001.

Chapter Two

Marginalised Communities: Concept and Status

CONCEPT OF MARGINALISATION

The evolution and conceptualisation of Marginalisation of the society into various groups is not a new phenomenon. It has been in existence and practiced in varied degrees since time immemorial. The earliest discrimination or division could be from the time when men started to live in heterogeneous groups. It is a practice that refers to the overt or covert tendencies and practices developed within several groups of societies. Marginalised persons can also be described as a group of the level or degree of Marginalisation varies from State to State and from community to community. It is apparently clear that marginalised persons belongs to a distinctive social group and who have their own characteristic features and then they are singled out or victimised by the more numerically dominant members of the society. This act by the members of the society leads to social discrimination and is followed by social ostracism of individual or family or the entire community.

The socio-psychological impact on the individual or the community, when treated like an outsider from the society may lead to negative feelings and thus may drift into sub-criminal social groups or even become socially isolated.

Within the Developing World, racial, or ethnic minority groups, stand out as being the most marginalized social groups. In the Indian context, it also includes the scheduled castes, scheduled tribes, poor, the elderly, the minorities, the women, the sick, and the disabled. All these groups tend to suffer from some forms of marginalization and a typical host of social ills like poverty, unemployment, poor education and poor health. They each tend to be ostracised and so suffer various forms of social exclusion.

Marginalisation[1] is a mode of creating and maintaining social identities and individual self-definitions affecting individuals at all levels of society, which involves constructing a dominant social identity against the background of excluded individuals and social groups. This process can become counter-productive for the dominant society as well as for alienated individuals or groups. Marginalization is conceptually the alienation of individuals from the ability to access culturally held goods because of the individuals' minority status.

The Marginalised Group

It is not possible to provide a simple answer to the question of who are economically or socially marginalised. Marginalization can be viewed as a social construction, i.e., there are social definition processes which define what it means to be marginalised and what consequences this ought to have. This entails ambivalence, which is a central part of the research programme. On the one hand, marginalization is a social construction and must be studied as such. On the other hand, the existing data on so-called "marginalised groups" is accepted at its face value in connection with statistical analyses of marginalization and its individual causes.

In order to understand the manifestations of marginalization and possible solutions, and in order to avoid an idealization of the dominant norms and values and thereby normalization/disciplining of what is different, it is therefore important to incorporate socio-cultural factors (and not only economic and political) ones in marginalization research. Implicitly and explicitly, we neglect the possible qualities which can be located within the Marginalised persons' activities and lives outside the labour market. This is a part of the definitional process, which idealises the norms and values linked to the individual on the labour market, and these norms and values become the axis around which efforts at integration revolve. Even though the life spheres are social constructions and as such contextual and dynamic, the dominant set of norms will be maintained as general norms, and norms held by "the others/the Marginalised" therefore continue to be discursively articulated and treated as deviant/the other/ the foreign.

In a realistic approach, the question of who the marginalised are is simpler. Here one often builds from the dominant discourse, especially because data for such an analysis build mainly upon data from public registers. Here the question of who the marginalised are is linked to such general publicly determined definitions. These categories are used as a basis for statistical studies.

The structuring of interpersonal relations leads to various forms of inequality, *e.g.* between men and women, between ethnic groups, etc., and these unequal relations build on unequal power relations. Via symbolic power and violence and via different forms of power discourses, determinations are made of what is right and wrong, what is normal and deviant, and these distinctions and forms of practice are incorporated into the individuals' habitus dispositions, functioning as a part of the mechanisms and processes which determine what is marginal and who are marginals. They are a part of the underlying structures and forms of practice that can result in marginalization, but they cannot as such be labelled as areas toward which one can be marginalised. Marginalization will often be an expression of a complicated and not necessarily causal interaction between the mechanisms and processes that operate within the spheres within which individuals or groups are marginalised.

The present study primarily focuses on the Marginalised Communities and their socio-economic problems and in this process four major social groups have been identified and these are Muslims, Scheduled Castes (SCs), Scheduled Tribes (STs) and Backward Classes (OBCs). The study was conducted with a view to analyze impact of various developmental indicators of SHGs on these social groups. Some of the major findings, which have emerged from the investigations, are presented in the following section.

A. SOCIO-ECONOMIC STATUS OF MUSLIMS

Population

The total population of India is 1,028,610,328 and Muslims constitute nearly 13.43 per cent (138,188,240/1,028,610,328) of the total population of India.[2] Of these, 13,722,048 resides in Bihar. The overall sex ratio of Muslims is 943 and the sex ratio between the age group of 0-6 is 958.

Muzaffarpur District in Bihar comprises of 5,73,951 Muslims population out of a total population of 37,46,714 (according to 2001 Census), and is 15.32 per cent. The population of other minority groups like, Christians (1260), Sikhs (679), Buddhists (247) and Jains (177) are negligible in percentage terms.

Educational Level

The overall literacy rate of Muslim Community in Bihar is 42 per cent while the female literacy rate of the community in the State is 31.5 per cent.

According to the Muslim Women's Survey (MWS)[3] conducted by ORG-Marg carried out in 2000-2001 in 40 districts of 12 States the following findings were observed:

(i) Close to 60 per cent of Muslim women report themselves to be illiterate while the school enrolment rate for Muslim girls is 40.66 per cent. The proportion of illiterate Muslim women is substantially higher for the rural north than it is for the rest of India—more than 85 per cent report themselves to be illiterate.

(ii) Less than 17 per cent of Muslim women (enrolled in schools) completed eight years of schooling; less than 10 per cent completed higher secondary schooling, which is below the national average.

(iii) The educational status in the north is abysmal, resulting in substantially fewer numbers in middle school and higher secondary school (4.58 and 4.75 respectively) as opposed to the national average of 17.86 and 11.42.

(iv) The proportion of Muslim women in higher education is only 3.56 per cent. That's lower even than that of scheduled castes, which is 4.25 per cent.

(v) Urban location, which has a generally positive association with female education, has no great impact on Muslim women's educational attainment. This points to poverty as the foremost constraint on access to education, notwithstanding the noticeably greater educational opportunities in urban areas.

(vi) Of the women who completed their studies, 26 per cent felt that they had to overcome obstacles in order to continue. On the whole, a slightly higher proportion of Muslim women than Hindu women reported that they faced obstacles in their schooling.

(vii) A general devaluation of continuing education for girls is also linked to the desirability of early marriage, as indicated by the mean age of first marriage, which is a low 15.6 in the rural north it dips even further, to 15 years. Early marriage was cited as an important reason for dropping out of school.

Health Status

(i) The most common disease that prevails among Muslims is Tuberculosis, mainly due to occupational structure. A major proportion of the population is engaged in manual works and in bidi making or in textile sector.

(ii) Women reported that they have least access to basic health-care facilities not only at home but also by the Government in the village. The Primary Health Centres (PHCs) are either not existing, or if existing, they are inaccessible to the women. Auxiliary Nurse Midwife (ANM) rarely visits the village and sub-health centres lack basic infrastructure, medicines as well as manpower.

Family Size

The average family size of the Muslims is 5-7, according to a study conducted in Rural Bihar[4]. This has support of various official reports like District Gazetteer, Census etc.

Work Participation Rate

Workforce is defined as those able-bodied men and women between the age group of 15-64 who are employed as full-time or part-time for earning wages or income on monthly or weekly or daily basis.

The workers are classified on the basis of Principal or Subsidiary Status. The Principal Status of the worker means that the worker has worked for most part of the year except for the period of illness or any social function or even casually without any reason.

Subsidiary Status means that a worker has not worked for most part of the year in a reporting year.

The report concerns more about the existing workforce and their employment in the present scenario. The ratio of the workforce for all classes and religions is much higher than expected from the society.

Table 2.1: Worker Population Ratio (WPR) of various Social Communities in the Country—2004-05.

Gender	*National Average*	*All Hindus*	*SC/ST*	*OBC*	*Hindu General*	*Other Minorities*	*Muslims*
Males	84.7	84.9	87.3	85.8	80.8	81.8	84.6
Females	43.6	46.9	54.9	48.3	33.1	47.2	25.2
All	**64.4**	**65.8**	**71.4**	**67.3**	**57.4**	**64.5**	**54.9**

All the data are in percentage.

Poor WPR among Muslims community is due to higher presence of females who are able bodied but do not contribute in the economic activities.

If the Worker Population Ratio of female becomes 50 per cent instead of 25 per cent then, Worker Population Ratio of Muslims would have been more than National Average and almost equal to that of OBCs.

As far as workforce is concerned, only 18 per cent of Urban Muslim women are in workforce.

Majority of women reported themselves as not working. This low work participation rate pattern holds good for all regions of the country. Among all social groups, the least participation is by Muslim Women as compared that of to SCs and OBCs.

- The average rate of participation of Muslim Women is 14 per cent.
- Their work participation rate in Bihar State is 30.9 per cent.
- Rural work participation rate is 20 per cent.

➢ Of those, who reported work participation, the largest proportions of persons are in the wage/employee category, followed by self-employed women.

Table 2.2: Status of Self-Employed Persons in India.

Class	*SC/STs*	*Hindu-OBC*	*Hindu-UC*	*Muslims*	*Other Minorities*
Urban	37	50	43	57	40
Rural	45	60	70	61	57
Male	40	58	60	57	50
Female	45	60	68	73	58

Source: There is relatively higher share of Muslim workers in self-employed activities. This is particularly true for urban-based female workers.

Regular Workers

Hindu Upper Caste	13 per cent
Muslims	25 per cent
	(Urban and rural both)

Only 13 per cent of total regular workers are Muslims. It's poorest among all the SRCs[6].

Out of these, Muslims as regular workers are only 24 per cent in PSUs. The same data for SC/ST is 39 per cent. It's lowest among all the SRCs. Even when divided into Urban/Rural, Male/Female—Muslims show poorest participation in regular Government jobs.

Even in that, Muslims, SC/STs and OBCs are concentrated in lower positioned jobs. Higher positioned jobs are being filled with Hindu Upper Caste (H-UCs).

Formal and Informal Sector

The workforce is divided in these two broad parts based on nature of enterprises—

Formal and Informal Sectors base Workforce

❖ The rate of employment in formal sector is very low among Muslims. (6% for Males in urban areas).

- Almost 90 per cent of the workers are employed in informal sector.
- The Street Vending Muslims are very high then other SRCs—12 per cent Male workers (against 8% of the National average).[7]
- In Urban and Rural areas, the share of Muslim workers as Street Vendors is the highest.
- Females working from their own homes—about 70 per cent Muslim Women is the highest in all the SRCs
- Street vending shows their vulnerability.
- Working in own dwelling shows immobility of women due to various social customs and economic constraints.
- Only 40 per cent of Muslim workforce are employed in agriculture because comparatively Muslims have less land than other/religious groups/castes/classes[8].
- 14 per cent males and 34 per cent female Muslims are engaged in manufacturing sector. Out of which maximum are engaged in Tobacco and Textile production industries.
- 20 per cent males and 5 per cent female Muslims are engaged in the trade sector.

Income/Poverty Level: There has been sharp decline in the proportion of people living below poverty line. While in the year 1990, it was 37.5 per cent; it is targeted that this percentage will reduce to 18.75 per cent by 2015. During the year 1999-2000, the poverty head count ratio was 26.1 per cent with poverty gap ratio of 5.2 per cent, share of poorest quintile in national consumption is 10.1 per cent for Rural Sector and 7.9 per cent for Urban Sector and the prevalence of under-weight children to the order of 47 per cent.

Change in Incidence of Poverty

Table 2.3: Incidence of Poverty in Rural Area

Social Groups	*1987-88*	*1993-94*	*2004-05*
Muslims	43	45	33
SC/ST	54	50	41
Other Hindus	33	29	21
Others	25	27	18

(All the data are in percentage.)

Table 2.4: Incidence of Poverty in Urban Area

Social Groups	*1987-88*	*1993-94*	*2004-05*
Muslims	53	47	44
SC/ST	55	51	46
Other Hindus	32	26	22
Others	27	23	16

(All the data are in percentage.)

The poverty rate among Muslims has considerably fallen in both rural and urban areas during the decade 1993-2003. This is due to the efforts made by the Central Government in coordination with State Governments and various other agencies for initiating several developmental schemes in the area for reducing the poverty level of the Muslims in both urban and rural areas during the decade 1993-94 to 2004-05. There has been substantial decline in the poverty ratio in rural areas especially during the year 2004-05.

A comparative analysis of the poverty figures of various States is presented below. This table shows most poor states of the country in terms of manpower development and employment ratios of various social groups. After SC/ST, the percentage of Muslims in various States who are below poverty line is substantially quite high. The rest of groups show varied percentages in terms of the ratios.

Most Poor States[9]

Table 2.5: Poverty Ratio in States

States	*Muslims*	*SC/ST*	*Other Hindus*	*Other Minorities*
Orissa	48	69	22	49
Madhya Pradesh	58	64	13	6
Karnataka	45	52	13	9
Bihar	45	65	8	9
Chattisgarh	61	48	13	10
Uttar Pradesh	44	42	11	6

Growth Rates

Five broad categories of manufacturing industries where the concentration of Muslims is highest are—Tobacco, Textiles, Apparels, Motor Vehicles and its parts and Electrical Machinery. Growth rates (%) in these five industries in three parameters are as follows:

Table 2.6: Major Employment Sector for Muslims

Industries	*Value Added*	*Employment*	*Labour Productivity*
Tobacco	5.0	7.7	-2.7
Textiles	6.3	-0.2	6.4
Wearing Apparels	14.4	14.4	-0.1
Motor Vehicles and Parts	16.5	9.4	7.1
Electrical Machinery	21.7	18.6	3.1
All	6.9	2.2	3.1

Source: Social, Economic and Educational Status of the Muslim Community of India, report of Prime Minister's High Level Committee, Cabinet Secretariat, Government of India, Nov., 2006.

The above Trends are for the Year 1994-2001

The above parameters indicate that the overall employment has not increased in these sectors as far as value addition in all these industries is concerned. In this direction, the policy-makers, local and State level departments with the support from Central Government can play an important role in improvising the statistics.

Table 2.7: Type of Professional Skills.

Type of Work	*Muslims*	*SC/ST*	*Hindus-UC*	*OBC*
Professional and Technical Works	48	69	22	6
Administrative, Excusive and Managerial Works	58	64	13	6

(All the data are in percentage.)

The concentration of Muslims in the following occupations are more and are mostly undertaken with interest and enthusiasm and it has been found that almost all family members get involved and treat it as family's occupation, after the family member has learnt all the skills and technicalities of the job. Even women participate in some of the activities listed below:

- Shop keeping/General Merchants of various household items, grocery, and other daily needs and necessities.

- Tailoring (stitching new clothes or repair/alteration of dresses).
- Assistants to Dress-makers.
- Sale and purchase of transport equipments.
- Work as Sales Assistants for various products.
- Processing of raw tobacco preparation and preparing various end-products.
- Spinning and weaving of any fabric and carpets.

Access to Bank Credit

There are several dimensions to the rural poverty and too for people belonging to marginalized communities it is generally believed and accepted that it arises due to the lack of capital or lack of surplus. The rural poor is perpetuating poverty and is the victims of the "vicious cycle of poverty". Credit is a major necessity and liquid form of asset of the people for rural poverty alleviation. Lack of credit facilities by local *Mahajans* and other financial institutions results in high incidence of poverty among the people.

It was seen that the incidence of poverty among Minorities especially Muslims, has been much more than other groups. Total number of persons who are considered as poor by the various National and International Standards has been 251 million poor in the year 2004-05[10].

The Mean Per Capita Expenditure (MPCE) describes the expenditure and consumption pattern on individual basis and the following statistics gives a status of various social groups on All India Basis:

Mean Per Capita Expenditure (MPCE)-(average for each SRC)

All India average	-	712
Hindu-Upper Caste	-	1023
Hindu OBC	-	646
Muslims	-	635
SC/ST	-	520

In urban areas, the Mean Per Capita Expenditure is found to be lowest of Rs. 800 for Muslim and SC/ST.

- The proportionate growth of MPCE in relation to the growth of urban population has been quite low.

- Half of the Muslim population falls in the group of Rs. 300-600.
- Nearly 45 per cent of the Muslim population falls in the income bracket of Rs. 500-1000.
- On the other hand when compared with that of Upper Caste Population, it was found that almost 55 per cent of the Hindu-Upper Caste population falls under the bracket of 1000 and above as per MPCE.
- Similarly in rural areas 60 per cent of Muslim population fall under bracket of Rs. 0-500.

State-wise Comparison

State-wise comparison for the urban average of MPCE differs very much in on State level basis. On the one hand, West Bengal, Kerala and present a similar picture for all social groups but in Bihar and Uttar Pradesh it does not differ very much among SC/ST, Hindu Upper Caste, Hindu-OBC, Muslims and other minorities.

Land-Holding

87 per cent of rural households hold land of size more than one acre, but only 83 per cent Muslim households hold land of this size.

Incidence of Poverty

- 38.4 per cent of urban Muslims are below poverty line.
- 31 per cent of total Muslim population fall below poverty line.
- Only 8.7 per cent of total Hindu Upper Caste population are below poverty line.
- In small towns Muslims are the poorest. As size of towns increases condition of Muslims also improves.

B. SOCIO-ECONOMIC STATUS OF SCHEDULED CASTE (SC)

Population

According to the 2001 Census, the SC population in India (excluding Mao, Maram, Paomata and Purul sub-division of Senapati district of

Manipur) stand at 166,635,700 persons which constitute 16.2 per cent of the country's population. Out of this, women constitute 80,546,940 of this population. Their population in Bihar State is 13,048,608 (15.7%). Of the total SC population, 79.8 per cent (64,407,536) live in Rural areas and 20.2 per cent (16,139,404) live in urban areas. Their sex ratio is 936 females per thousand males, which is slightly higher than the national average of 933 sex ratios. Largest concentration of SC population[11] is found in Punjab where it is 28.9 per cent.

Scheduled Caste population in Muzaffarpur district is slightly more (15.87%) than that of the Muslims which is 15.32 per cent.

Educational Level

Literacy rate amongst this group is very poor and a matter of concern that it is just 22.55 per cent against 38.56 per cent. The average educational level for Muzaffarpur district which is itself very low in respect of the national average. Almost 4,60,514 persons belonging to Scheduled Caste group is illiterate. Out of total literate 12,093 (9.02 per cent of total literate SC and 2.03 per cent of total SC population) are barely literate without any formal education they just able to write their name etc. 37829 (28.22 per cent of total literate SC and 6.36 per cent of total SC population) are educated up to primary level only. 14921 (11.13 per cent of total literate SC and 2.50 per cent of total SC population) are middle class pass and 10585 (7.90 per cent of total literate SC and 1.78 per cent of total SC population) are Matriculate or secondary equivalent pass. Just 3973 (*i.e.* 2.96 per cent of total literate SC and 0.67 per cent of total SC population) did their Intermediate or pre university level. 5709 are graduate which is almost negligible (in abstract form 4.26 per cent of total literate SC and 0.96 per cent of total SC population). Likewise technical education is also minimal and neglected, 31 in number having non technical diploma or certificate it is 0.25 per cent of total literate SC and 0.005 per cent of total SC population. 202 are technical diploma or degree holder are in this community which constitute 0.15 per cent of total literate SC and 0.03 per cent of total SC population.5709 are graduate and above[12].

Fig. 2.1: Educational Level of Respondent

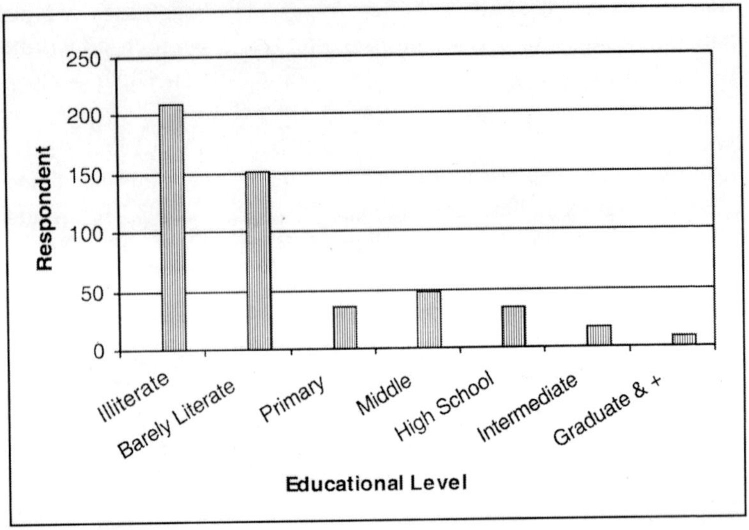

Dropouts of SC children at Primary Level of their education fell by 1.3 per cent.

Health Status

(i) Anaemia among SC women is more as compared to women of other communities mainly due to malnutrition.
(ii) At national level, full vaccination among SC infants is less compared to others.
(iii) The unmet need for limiting is more for SCs compared with others.
(iv) Unmet need with regard to spacing is more. There is high percentage of houseless, landless, and even homestead landless SCs
(v) Fertility Rate is 3.91.
(vi) Infant mortality rate is 83 per cent.
(vii) Incidence of tuberculosis is high.
(viii) Prevalence of HIV/AIDs is more.
(ix) 23.7 per cent households have latrine facility within premise.
(x) Least access to basic healthcare.
(xi) Suffer largely from hunger and malnutrition.

Income/Poverty Level

36 per cent of the population live below poverty line which declined by 25 per cent by the year 1999-2000.

Economic and Occupational Status of SC

Most of the persons belonging to Scheduled Caste category are living below the poverty line unable to meet even the minimum basic requirements of daily life. They are landless and even in certain cases homestead landless. In other words they do not have lands were to build shelter for themselves. Their main occupation or means of earning is wage labour, it includes agricultural labour as well as casual labour. They are the most valuable lot and their condition becomes more precarious during lean, drought and flood periods.

Marital Status

The tradition of child marriage still exists in this community. It may be due to high prevalence of illiteracy and poverty. The graphic given below shows that up to the age of 21, 4 per cent male and 12 per cent female were married. Early marriage leads to early responsibility and parenthood. The risk taking factor minimizes with the decrease in early marriage system.

Fig. 2.2: Martal Status Amongest SC of Muzaffarpur

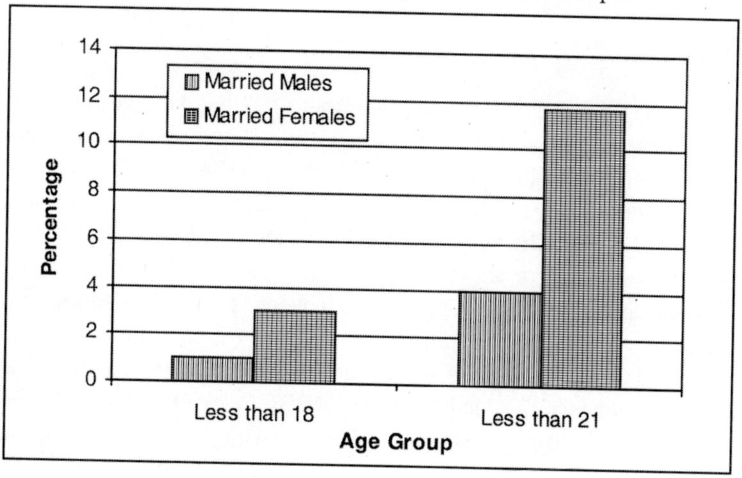

(i) Main occupation is Agriculture where 34 per cent of the population is engaged in it.

(ii) 85 per cent of the population is bonded labour.

(iii) Landless households among has increased from 12.62 per cent in 1982 to 13.34 per cent in 1992.

Fig. 2.3: Marital Status of SC Community in Muzaffarpur

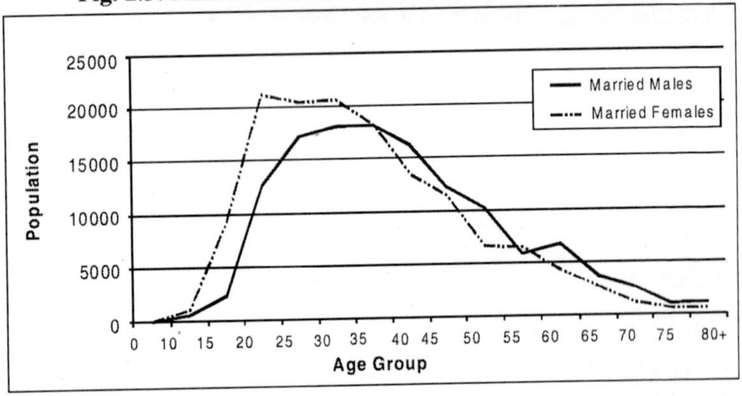

C. SOCIO-ECONOMIC STATUS OF SCHEDULED TRIBES (ST)

The number of scheduled tribes is negligible in the district. However, they belong to the poorest of the poor in the district.

Population

As per the Census 2001, the total number of Tribal women in India is 84,326,240 out of which 41,685,411 is the ST population. The total population of Scheduled Tribes in India stands at 84, 326, 240 persons. The women tribals number 38,292,947. In Bihar, their population is 758, 351 (0.9%). They constitute 8.2 per cent of the total population. Out of their total population, 91.7 per cent (77,338,597) were living in Rural areas while only 8.3 per cent were from Urban areas. The sex ratio was 978 females per thousand males (higher than that of the total population of the country as well as that of SCs). Their concentration is highest in Mizoram (94.5%). As per the Census 2001, the total population of Sheduled Tribe in Bihar is 758,351 out of which 3,472 ST population is residing in Muzaffarpur district of Bihar.

Educational Level

(i) Number of literates are 169, 895 and the literacy rate is same as that of SCs *i.e.* 28.2 per cent.
(ii) Dropouts of ST children at Primary Level of their education fell by 5.2 per cent.
(iii) Literacy rate less than 30 per cent.
(iv) Literacy rate of STs was more than SCs in the Bihar State.

Health Status

(i) Anaemia among ST women is more as compared to women of other communities.
(ii) At national level, full vaccination among ST infants is less compared to others.
(iii) The unmeet need for limiting is less for ST compared with others.
(iv) Unmeet need with regard to spacing is more.
(v) Fertility Rate is 2.45.
(vi) Infant mortality rate is 84.2 per cent
(vii) Prevalence of HIV/AIDs is more.
(viii) 17 per cent households have latrine facility.
(ix) Least access to basic healthcare.
(x) Suffer largely from malnutrition and hunger.

Income/Poverty Level

46 per cent of the population live below poverty line which reduced by 12 per cent by 1999-2000.

Employment Structure and Employment Rate

(i) 82 per cent of the population is engaged in agriculture.
(ii) Same proportion of ST population (85%) is bonded labour.

D. SOCIO-ECONOMIC STATUS OF OTHER BACKWARD CLASSES (OBC)

Population

As per the survey conducted by NSSO, the population of OBC

class has been estimated to be 41 per cent of the population in the country.

Moreover as per the report of NSSO, there are four States—Tamil Nadu, Bihar, Kerala and Uttar Pradesh are the States where OBCs constitute more than 50 per cent of the population. Bihar has the second largest concentration of OBC population with rural areas accounting for 59.94 per cent and urban areas 57.64 per cent.

E. SOCIO-ECONOMIC STATUS OF WOMEN IN INDIA

Population

At the last count of the Census of India 1991—there were 403 million women in India. Today out of India's total population of 1 billion and close to 481 million are women. By the year 2016, projections suggest that the population of women in India will rise to 615 million.

Scheduled Caste and Scheduled Tribes form an estimated 25 per cent of India's population, but another estimate drawn from the data compiled by the National Sample Survey Organisation places their number at 36 per cent of the population. If Muslims are excluded from the estimate, the proportion falls further to 32 per cent. However, these figures have changed and as per the survey conducted by NSSO, it puts SC population at 19.59 per cent, ST population at 8.63 per cent and the rest at 30.80 per cent.

Educational Level

Only 50 per cent of Indian women are found to be literate as compared to 65.5 per cent men.

School attendance in rural areas for Dalit girls was found to be 46.2 per cent as compared to Dalit boys where it is 64.3 per cent.

99 per cent of Dalit students come from Government School. It is usually understood that Government Schools lack the basic infrastructure facilities.

Health Status

In a survey conducted by ORG Marg[13], it was observed that:

(i) The average Indian women bear her first child before she is

22 years old and has little control over her fertility and reproductive health.

(ii) Census reveals that there is higher fertility rate and lower literacy rate among SC females.

(iii) A positive change that was seen in case of birth rate where the births of order three or higher have declined from 46 per cent in 1998-99 to 42 per cent in 2002-04.

(iv) Unmeet need for contraception has reduced from 25 per cent in 1998-99 to 21 per cent in 2002-04.

(v) Only 29 per cent of women were informed about other modern methods before getting sterilized.

(vi) 29 per cent of sterilized women and 23 per cent users of other modern methods reported side effects from the use of these methods.

(vii) Among sterilized women, only 31 per cent received follow-up visit by health workers.

(viii) Among women who adopted other methods, only 9 per cent received follow-up visit by health workers.

(ix) Only 125 of non-users were ever advised to adopt contraceptive methods.

(x) In the contraceptive prevalence rate state-wise, Bihar lies at the extreme bottom among all the other States where only 31 per cent of the women use contraceptive methods as compared to West Bengal where the rate is 74 pe r cent.

Work Participation Rate

There are far fewer women in the paid workforce than there are men. Women's work is undervalued and unrecognized. Women work for longer hours than men and carry the major share of household and community work which is unpaid and invisible.

Notes

1. The concept of marginalization contains at least four elements:
   (a) Marginalization is process and not a condition. An individual can be marginalised during some periods of his life and not in others. The concept of "exclusion", in contrast, denotes a situation in the absolute periphery of society's function systems.

(b) By definition marginalization is an undesirable situation for the individual. Marginalization relates to areas in society where there are normative expectations for the participation of the individual and these are of seen to be according to society's dominant system of norms and values. However, it can be difficult to distinguish between voluntary and involuntary marginalization. It might be a case of a coincidence of circumstances: a voluntary choice can involuntarily lead to types of exclusion or marginalization that are undesired by the individual. There can also be an adaptation to the marginalised situation so that the individual experiences it as acceptable or even positive. Here we might speak about the "social inheritance", "culture of poverty" or "underclass". These concepts also refer to the inertia, which exist in the social processes. The concept of "pattern breakers", in contrast, is applied to those individuals who break out of their social inheritance.

(c) Marginalization entails exclusion from participation in some areas of social life, which can be viewed as both essential in the given society and seen as important by the individual. Marginality is characterized by an involuntary, incomplete participation in one or more spheres of life, where there is an expectation of participation on the part of society as well as on the part of the individual: a situation of vulnerability with limited control over one's social and economic existence.

(d) Marginalization can be more or less extensive, in that it does not necessarily lead to complete exclusion from participation in one given sphere or all essential spheres of life. People can be marginalised in several spheres, but marginalization in one sphere does not automatically lead to marginalization in others. We find this emphasis on marginalization as partial or incomplete participation already in Simmel (1908), who points out that the poor are not necessarily marginalised. Because of their difficult economic situation they have a vulnerable or subordinate position, but they participate in social life and, when they become objects of the public or voluntary aid, discipline and normalization efforts, they are a part of the social relations and practice.

Marginalization can thus be defined as a process where there is a more or less comprehensive involuntary exclusion from participation in one or more spheres of life. A process where there is a normative expectation of participation both as regards the individual and in relation to the given socially dominant norms and practice

2. Social, Economic and Educational Status of the Muslim Community of India, a report of Prime Minister's High Level Committee, Cabinet Secretariat, Government of India, November, 2006.
3. http://www.infochangeindia.org/bookandreportsst22.jsp, dated October 9, 2007.

   A summary of the ORG-Marg Muslim Women's Survey (MWS) carried out in 2000-2001. It was carried out in 12 States, spread over 40 districts in India. Convend by Zoya Hasan and Ritu Menon, it surveyed 9,541 Muslim and Hindu women respondents—80 per cent Muslim and 20 per cent Hindu; and 60 per cent urban, 40 per cent rural.
4. Socio-economic Status of Minorities in Uttar Pradesh, 2002
6. Social, Economic and Educational Status of the Muslim Community of India, a report of Prime Minister's High Level Committee, Cabinet Secretariat, Government of India, November, 2006.
7 *Ibid*
8. *Ibid*
9. *Ibid*
10. *Ibid*
11. Millennium Development Goals and Dalits—A Status Report, April 2006, National Conference of Dalit Organisations (NACDOR)
12. Village Census Report of India, 2001.
13. ORG Marg, Muslim Women's Survey, (2002). Muslim Women's Survey. Retrieved on August 25, 2007.

Chapter Three

Self-Help Group and Microfinance: Concept and Status

1. Microfinance

The Microcredit Summit[1] defined Microcredit (mI-[*]Kro'kre-dit); noun; as, programmes extend small loans to very poor people for self employment projects that generate income, allowing them to care for themselves and their families[2].

Definitions of Microfinance differ, of course, from country to country. Some of the defining criteria used include—

- *Size*—loans are micro, or very small in size.
- *Target users*—micro-entrepreneurs and low income households.
- *Utilisation*—the use of funds–mainly for income generation, and enterprise development, but also for community use (health/education) etc.
- *Terms and Condition*—most terms and conditions for microcredit loans are flexible and easy to understand, and suited to local conditions of the community.

In other words Microfinance (mF) is a financial service of small quantity provided by Financial Institutions (FI) to the poor, These financial services may include savings, credit, insurance, leasing, money, transfer, equity transaction, etc., that is, any type of financial service, provided to customers to meet their normal financial needs: life cycle, economic opportunity and emergency with the only qualification that (i) transaction value is small and (ii) customers are 'poor'[3].

Wikipedia has also defined it as the extension of very small loans to the unemployed, to poor entrepreneurs and to others living in poverty that is not bankable. These individuals lack collateral, steady employment and a verifiable credit history and therefore cannot meet even the minimum conditions to avail of traditional credit. Microcredit is a part of microfinance, which is the provision of financial services to the very poor; apart from loans, it includes savings, micro-insurance and other financial innovations.

Besides, size and clientele group, what makes microcredit different from normal credit is that the latter is 'walk-in' and the former is 'walk-out' business for the FI. Unlike normal credit, microcredit is limited with collateral substitute and credit plus services. Microcredit thus becomes distinct from other regular credit where not only credit amount is small and clientele is poor, but also credit is provided with 'collateral substitute' instead of traditional collateral and non-financial services for increasing the productivity of credit.

2. Self-Help Group

Self-Help Groups are voluntary, small group structures for mutual aid and the accomplishment of a special purpose[4].

They are usually formed by peers who have come together for mutual assistance in satisfying a common need, overcoming a common handicap or life disrupting problem, and bringing about desired social and/or personal change. The indicators and members of such groups perceive that their needs are not, or cannot be met by or through existing social institutions. Self-Help Group emphasizes face to face social interactions and the assumptions of personal responsibility by members. They often provide material assistance, as well as emotional support. They are frequently "cause"-oriented and promulgate an ideology or values through which members may attain an enhanced sense of personal identity.

Self-Help Groups typically start from a condition of powerlessness, and then members spontaneously (*i.e.* not urged by an outside authority) agree on engaging in such actions in which they personally participate. Self-Help Group creates and acts within a purposefully organized setting.

According to NABARD, it is a group of 20 or less people from a homogenous class who are willing to come together for addressing their common problems[5]. They make regular savings and use the pooled savings to give interest bearing loans to their members. The process helps them imbibe the essentials of financial intermediation including prioritization of needs. Settings self determined terms of repayment, and keeping books and records. It builds such financial discipline and credit history that it encourages banks to lend to them in certain multiples of their savings and without any demand for collateral security.

In the other word we can say that Self Help Groups are voluntary unions of peers, formed for mutual assistance for economic gain and to change the quality of life. It is one of the means to achieve self employment.

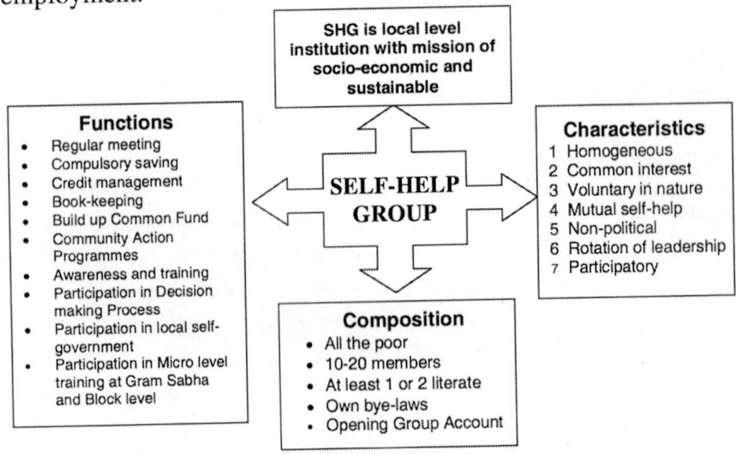

2.1 The basic principles on which the SHGs function are[6]:

(i) The members of the groups should be residents of the same area and must have an affinity and homogeneity of relationship could be in terms of caste/occupation/gender or economic status (which is critical).

(ii) Savings first, credit thereafter.

(iii) SHGs should hold regular meetings.

(iv) SHGs should maintain record of financial and other transactions.

(v) They should have norms regarding membership, meetings etc.

(vi) Group leaders should be elected by members and rotated periodically.

(vii) Transparency in operations of the group and participatory decision-making.

(viii) Rates of interest on loans should be decided by the group.

(ix) Group liability and peer pressure to act as substitutes for traditional collateral.

2.2 Brief History of SHG

Many authors trace the history of modern self-help groups to the foundation of Alcoholics Anonymous (AA) in the US in 1935. The 1960's civil rights movement gave people the confidence to trust in their collective power and empowerment and it became a core motive in the formation of Self-Help Groups.

The Self-Help Groups and micro-credit organizations have a long history. In Vietnam, Tontines or Hui with 10-15 members involved in financial activities in cash or in kind have been in existence for generations. In Indonesia, credit unions, fishermen groups, village based bank like institutions, irrigation groups etc. have been in existence since long[7].

In the 1970's some countries like Bangladesh and Brazil started a unique experiment in small lending[8]. Thus was born the concept of Microfinance or Micro-credit. Bangladesh became to the world the role model and the foremost and most successful proponent of this method of lending.

It is their model which is being largely replicated elsewhere in the world, including increasingly in India. In 1976, Muhammad Yunus, the noble laureate founded the Grameen Bank (Village Bank) to give loans to poor Bangladeshis. The Grameen Bank has issued more than US$ 5.1 billion to 5.3 million borrowers. To ensure repayment, the bank uses a system of "solidarity groups". These small informal groups apply together for loans and its member acts as co-guarantors of repayment and supports one another's efforts at economic self advancements[9]. As it has grown, the Grameen Bank has also developed other systems of alternate credit that serve the poor. In addition to micro-credit, it offers housing loans as well as finances for fisheries and irrigation projects, venture capital, textile, and other activities, along with other banking services such as savings.

The Self Employed Women's Association (SEWA) in Gujarat, India, is a combination of Self-Help Groups and co-operations of women workers in the informed sector. It followed a multi-faceted empowerment approach; in where all economic activities of the groups were linked with health and social issues.

The Mahavir Association of Literacy Awareness and Right (MALAR) was established in Kanyakumari District, Tamil Nadu, India, as a women's saving group with the purpose of mobilizing women belonging to the approved stratas of the society through a structure, independent of the Government. The MALAR experiment, which followed an empowerment approach, is an entirely self reliant movement without any external funding, but facilitated by external actors. Like SEWA, it has an organizational structure similar to co-operative with self-help groups forming the basis[10].

The Government of India has adopted the self-help approach and microfinance programmes as tools for employment generation, women's empowerment, and for achieving production oriented goals.

Subsequently, SHGs served as a platform for NGOs to implement numerous development programmes for social and economic empowerment. Some names commonly used for such groups or platforms are Gramsabha, Yuvak Mandali and Mahila Mandali. Many such groups were engaged in channelising development assistance to the villages. These bodies functioned as socially legitimate groups to help identify 'beneficiaries' for specific schemes, undertaking activities of common interest, assisting and following up on recoveries of loans made to members and revolving the recovered money for continuing assistance to the community. These can be considered the prototype of the SHG movement. Over a period of time, these forerunners of SHGs started managing their own savings and credit programmes.

It took the movement about two decades to gather momentum. In 1992 SHGs emerged as important players in the microfinance (mF) sector when NABARD introduced a pilot programme linking SHGs and banks (Self-Help Group Bank Linkage Programme) to enable poor households access the mainstream banking network and meet their financial needs. However, only 32,995 SHG bank linkages could take place during the period from 1992-99. The programme received a boost in the year 1997 at the World Micro Credit Summit in Washington D.C., US when a global target was set for supporting 100 million of the world's poorest families, especially women, with micro-credit by 2005.

Taking a cue from the targets set during the Summit, NABARD announced that the SHG bank linkage programme would be expanded to cover 20 million households by 2008. By 1999-2000, 1,14,775 SHGs were linked to mainstream banks. Meanwhile Ministry of Rural Development re-shaped its policy towards self-employment and incorporate SHG as an important vehicle under Swarna Jayanti Gram Swarozgar Yojana (SGSY) in 1999.

Thereafter the number escalated exponentially. By the end of March, 2004, 10,79,091 SHGs, with 90 per cent membership comprising women, were linked to the mainstream banking system with a 95 per cent repayment performance of loans from SHGs to bank branches. The credit flow went up from Rs. 571 million during the period 1992-99 to Rs. 11917.1 million by the end of March, 2004.

The phenomenal success of the SHG model in terms of outreach and repayment rate encouraged the Central and State Governments to use SHGs (as an entry point to reach the target population) as part of poverty reduction programmes. Today SHGs are increasingly being seen as an important vehicle for social and economic empowerment of marginalized communities, especially women. Banks other than NABARD have also begun to see the usefulness of SHGs in meeting their priority sector lending 'targets'.

The efforts of over 2,800 partner agencies have contributed to this growth of the SHG movement. Of the totals groups linked till the end of March, 2003, 72 per cent were facilitated by NGOs. Forty-eight participating banks, 19 Regional Rural Banks (RRBs) and 264 cooperative banks have partnered with the SHG movement so far.

3. Approaches Across India

The growth in SHG formations, sustenance and credit has been un-even. The Southern States are seen as SHG—developed States while Bihar and Madhya Pradesh are among those characterized as SHG-backward[11].

Self-Help Group concept been taken differently in different States of India. The objective, the methodology and the means of the Self-Help Groups are different, therefore their result or the impact is also different in different parts of the country. We broadly categorize it as Movement, Mission, and Programme approach.

SHG Movement	*Mission Approach*	*Programme Approach (SGSY)*
Andhra Pradesh	Andhra Pradesh (Velugu)	Assam
Kerala	Karnataka (Streeshakti and Swashakti)	Bihar
Tamil Nadu	Kerala (CDS)	Karnataka
	Orissa (Mission Shakti)	Madhya Pradesh
	Tamil Nadu (Mahalir Thittam)	Maharashtra
	Mizoram	
	Rajasthan	
	Tripura	
	Uttaranchal	
	Uttar Pradesh	
	West Bengal	

3.1 SHG Movement Approach

SHG movement approach has been largely confined to the three Southern States namely Andhra Pradesh, Tamil Nadu and Kerala. The SHG approach through campaign mode began in the 80s as an offshoot of poverty eradication programmes specially DWCRA initiated by the Government. This gradually expanded through the 90s and became a movement.

In the next phase, during the late 90s, these SHGs started to consolidate, building up their federations at the sub-district and district levels. This has spectacularly mainstreamed the marginalized, hitherto un-reached and under-represented in taking up their economic, social and political agendas. It is significant that the initial fillip for the SHG movement has come from banking and Government rural development sectors, as also the NGOs. Government agencies and NGOs continue to play a proactive role in consolidating the movement. Women's groups in these States have ably demonstrated marked improvement in their ownership and control of their household and community resources (saving, credit labour and income), accessing information and knowledge, leadership, and management of their Community Based Organisations (CBOs).

3.2 Mission Approach

Mission approach is a way of scaling up the SHG movement without diluting the objectives and the thrust. Andhra Pradesh [SAPAP (UNDP), Velugu: Poverty Mission Approach], Karnataka (Sreeshakti and Swashakti), Kerala (CDS) and Orissa (Mission Shakti) have taken the SHG movement to the mission approach in order to consolidate the gains as well as trigger further changes in the policy as well as implementation framework. This approach is gaining momentum and is facilitating an enabling environment for a pro-poor policy advocacy.

3.3 Programme Approach

The programme approach refers to following strictly prescribed programme guidelines of SGSY/other schemes and their implementation is overseen by the concerned Departments (DRDA/DWCD as the case may be).

States like Assam, Uttaranchal, Uttar Pradesh, Madhya Pradesh, West Bengal, Bihar, Maharashtra, Mizoram, Rajasthan and Tripura follow the programme approach. Some States have adopted both the approaches of mission and programme, but are integrating these to suit their specific contexts. This is largely true to those States which have had a strong SHG movement.

The three approaches are not mutually exclusive and there are considerable overlaps especially between the movement and the mission approaches. The following Table depicts some of the salient features in the three approaches. This is not an exhaustive list but only broad pointers.

Salient Features of the three Approaches[12]

Stages	*SHG Movement Approach*	*Mission Approach*	*Programme Approach*
Initial mobilization	Through building awareness about reasons for being poor.	Through intensive sensitization and capacity building of various stake-holders (Potential for mobilization is high)	More stress and emphasis on formation of groups. (Less scope for mobilization)
Social mobilization	Scope and emphasis on social mobilization in a campaign mode. Self-effort with minimum guidelines for formation of groups.	Mobilisation of more uncovered and unreached marginalized communities through motivated older groups.	Largely confined to the programme guidelines to form caste groups with members from BPL families to meet the targets.
Self-awareness	Bring about self-awareness, realize one's own hidden potentials and resources.	More potential for bringing about shifts in the attitudes, mindsets and more importantly in the organizations, systems and structures.	General awareness about activities and benefits of the programme (Might reinforce stereo-types and maintain the status-quo givers and receivers.)
Capacity-building	Building capacities and leadership among the community, which is largely exercised within the group.	Enabling the people to develop capacities to demand legitimate services from the various sectors.	Capacity-building to a large extent limited to providing information and skills related to the programme.
Entry point	Thrift and credit as an incentive for the group to remain cohesive	Thrift and Credit Savings, community based initiatives. (Offers opportunities for creating healthy inter-dependency and cohesiveness among the groups).	Savings to get more benefits—RF and subsidy. (May create dependency due to the approach subsidies etc.)
Collective interventions	Collective actions and interventions to address some social issues.	Bringing about social change through building partnerships, cooperation and collaboration.	The focus being largely on economic aspects. (Less concentration on coordination and partnerships to bring social change).
Convergence	Preparing the ground for consolidation and convergence. (In itself not sustainable)	Convergence of sectors resources and schemes of various organizations under one large umbrella for optimal utilization. (More sustainable).	Not much effort for convergence of resources and services from different sectors. (Setback for convergence is due to indifferent attitude and lack for inter-personal relationships among officials. Less sustainable).
Process/Activity	More process oriented.	Built on the process as well as activities oriented. (Inclusive)	More focus on time bound activities: grading, release of RF, link with bank loan, release of subsidy etc. (Structured and less inclusive).
Long-term objective	Setting a path towards empowerment.	Creating an enabling environment and providing opportunities for decision-making leading towards empowerment of the self and community.	No specific view on long-term objectives.

Highlights of Successful Experiences[13]

The analysis of the broad strategies adapted by the implementing agencies in the 15 study states reveals the following three major approaches, namely SHG movement, mission approach and programme approach. The three Southern States AP, Kerala and Tamil Nadu, which pioneered the SHG movement and consolidated these experiences and scaled up through mission approach offer valuable lessons.

3.3.1 Andhra Pradesh

- AP has had a history of strong SHG movement during the implementation of DWCRA programme which culminated into the SAPAP (UNDP) and 'Velugu' project.
- Identified and selected community resource persons at the village, mandal and district level. Intensively trained them in mobilization and capacity-building. This created a strong cadre of community-based resource facilitators for nurturing and stabilizing the existing SHGs.
- Learning from previous experience under UNDP, the Velugu mission made a conscious effort to focus on social issues such as girl child, child labour, gender, food security and natural resource management etc.
- The increased participation, mobility and visibility lead to institution-building (Federation) thereby building social capital.
- SGSY has been merged with the mission to converge the resources—revolving fund, subsidy, infrastructure and capacity-building.
- Indira Kranti Patham is a state-wide community demand driven rural poverty alleviation project. It aims to cover all rural poor households in the State (80 lakhs) with a special focus on 26.0 lakhs ultra poor households[14].
- It builds on the decade long statewide rural women's Self-Help Group movement in Andhra Pradesh. The focus is on deepening it, providing an institutional structure and develops a strategy for sustaining it for comprehensive poverty eradication.

- Institution-building—self managed institutions of the poor (SHGs village organization Mandal Samakhyas).
- Building and nurturing social capital grassroot women leadership, developing community activists and barefoot professionals responsible to the community.
- Knowledge dissemination—training and capacity-building of SHGs, paraprofessionals, project functionaries etc.
- Livelihood experiences—increase in incomes and employment, decrease in expenditure, costs and risks.
- Networking/linking institutions of poor with other institutions—public services, financial, markets, educational.
- Achievement[15] by 31-03-2007
  - 478891 Self-Help Group Formed
  - No. of groups linked to banks in 2005-06: 2,88,711
  - Own saving: Rs. 1500 crores
  - SHG bank linkages: Rs. 2001.42 crores
  - Target for 2006-07: Rs. 3000 Crores to 30,00,000 SHGs

4. Procedure for Group Formation

According to Tuckman and Jensen when people work in groups, there are two quite separate issues involved. The first is the task and the problems involved in getting the job done. Frequently this is the only issue that the group considers. The second is the process of the group work itself: the mechanisms by which the group acts as a unit and not as loose rabble. However, without due attention to this process the value of the group can be diminished or even destroyed; yet with a little explicit management of the process, it can enhance the worth of the group to be many times the sum of the worth of its individuals.

It is common to view the development of a group as having five stages:

- Forming
- Storming
- Norming
- Performing
- Adjourning

Forming is the stage when the group first comes together. Everybody is very polite and very dull. Conflict is seldom voiced directly and, if done, is mainly personal and definitely destructive. Since the grouping is new, the individuals will be guarded in their own opinions and generally reserved.

This is particularly so in terms of the more nervous and/or subordinate members who may never come to the forefront. The group tends to defer to a large extent to those who emerge as leaders.

Storming is the next stage, where factions form, personalities clash, no one concedes a single point without rigorous brain storming. Most importantly, very little communication occurs since no one is listening and some are still unwilling to talk openly. There may be instances of seething sarcasm, invective and innuendo.

Then comes the **Norming** stage. At this stage the sub-groups begin to recognize the merits of working together and the in-fighting subsides. Since a new spirit of cooperation is evident, every member begins to feel secure in expressing his or her own viewpoint and these are discussed openly with the whole group. The most significant improvement is that people start listening to each other. Work methods become established and are recognized by the group as a whole.

Next is the **Performing** stage where members work productively to achieve their goals and carry out their work. This stage is generally characterized by productivity: a sense of progress and achievement on the part of the teams develop, bonds are formed between members, enthusiasm and creativity for the team's work are high.

Finally comes the **Adjourning** stage in which members having completed their task, prepare to disband. This stage is generally characterized by reluctance to part.

The VOs where the team spirit is alive, after completion of one project, the team review their experiences together, evaluate their accomplishments, and restart the process for a new development project and also arrange to stay in touch.

Activities of an Organisation

The activities of an organisation of the poor can vary substantially depending on the nature of the socio-economic context in which it operates, the specific interests that a particular group seeks to pursue, and the level of consciousness attained by the members of the group concerned. According to Tilakaratna (2005), we may summarise the potential activities under 4 categories namely:

- **Defensive actions**
- **Assertive actions**
- **Constructive actions**
- **Transformative actions**

Defensive actions are basically aimed at protecting the existing sources, means and conditions of living against erosion or encroachment by actions of other interest groups or the Government. They represent collective actions initiated by the poor to prevent deterioration in their customary mode of living, which may result from a proposed project, policy shift or other external intervention.

Assertive actions refer to assertion by the poor of their economic and social rights available to them under governmental legislation, policies and programmes as well as what they collectively consider to be their legitimate entitlements.

Constructive actions refer to development projects of a self-help nature initiated by groups of poor using primarily their own resources. Instead of waiting for the Government to deliver their needs, organised groups could initiate actions to satisfy their group needs for certain services by mobilising their own resources with supplementary assistance from outside. The activities generated through such means can take a variety of forms such as:

- *Infrastructural Works*—Feeder roads, simple irrigation works, school buildings and similar physical structures.
- *Economic Projects*—Such as consumer goods stores, schemes for collective marketing, cultivation of new crops or animal husbandry, and diversification of economic activity by the setting up of small industries.
- *Social Development Activities*—Such as drinking water wells, housing improvements, health and sanitation programmes, pre-schools and community centres, and finally.
- *Cultural and other Activities*—Such as festivals, drama, sports and religious activities.

In this way, organisations can serve as an instrument to mobilise people's own resources for projects, which could satisfy a wide variety of people's needs.

Transformative Actions represent innovative and creative initiatives of organised groups of poor with a relatively high level of consciousness. Such groups will attempt to explore and experiment with development styles, which represent alternatives to the mainstream development processes.

The above listing of possible actions clearly shows the potential available for the poor to launch a process of self-development through organised initiatives. Organisations enable the poor to mobilise their own resources as well as assert their right to a legitimate share of social resources. The activities of any particular organisation may represent one or more of the above categories, often some combination of the above.

Community Organising: Methodological Characteristics

Community organising has four distinguishing process or methodological characteristics. These are:

- ***A progressive cycle of action-reflection*** begins with small, local and concrete issues identified by the people and the evaluation of and reflection on the action taken by them.
- ***Consciousness-raising through experimental learning*** is central to the community organising process because it places emphasis on the learning that emerges from concrete action and which enriches succeeding action. This dialectic relation between theory and practice progressively raises people's consciousness.
- ***Community organizing is participatory and mass-based*** because it is primarily directed towards, and biased in favour of the poor, the powerless and the oppressed. Through a participatory process, the whole community (as much as possible) must be involved in the organising experience.
- ***Community organising is group-centered and not leader-orientated***. Leaders are identified, emerge and are tested through action rather than appointed or selected by some

external force or entity. Thus community organising seeks democratic leadership where power resides in the people.

Roles and Functions of an Organisation

For people to become organized and act collectively, they need to have some recognized *roles*, formal or informal, along with supporting *rules, precedents and procedures* for enabling them to perform four basic functions that are essential for any organization and collective action:

- decision-making,
- resource mobilization and management,
- communication and coordination, and
- conflict resolution.

Collective action of any sort, whether through legally established local Government bodies, through formally constituted organizations such as cooperatives, or through informal sets of actors who have on-going social relationships and common purposes, will require performance of these four functions. To build up capacities of the poor to utilize their limited resources more effectively to achieve goals and benefits on their own behalf, one of the basic strategies for empowerment that goes beyond individual and household units and aims will be either (a) ***strengthening*** such roles, rules, precedents and procedures where they already exist, or (b) ***establishing*** them where they do not.

Levels of Collective Action

It should be understood that there are levels of decision-making and activity beyond the individual and household levels. Several levels often get grouped loosely (and un-usefully) as 'local'. This shows how three levels could be distinguished at which collective action is possible—and for the poor, desirable.

- The ***group*** level, at which people associate according to *common characteristics and interests* to promote common interests, as farmers or fishermen, as women or men, as youths, as members of an ethnic or religious group, as speakers of a common language, etc.

- The ***community*** level, determined by people's *residential patterns*, such that neighbours living in some proximity join together to protect and advance shared interests.
- The ***locality*** level, representing a set of communities that have ongoing patterns of interaction and cooperation, based on proximity, common-pool natural resources, exchange of labour, a central market, shared religion or ethnicity, or other interests.

For empowering the poor, the first level of collective action has many advantages because it is more *homogeneous*, based on members having shared characteristics. Organizations for the poor that are smaller and more homogeneous can be more easily utilized by the poor to advance their interests. It is an important question whether community and locality organizations be designed or given incentives so that they make *net contributions* to empowerment of the poor, not expecting them to be totally devoted to this purpose. If so, resources besides those of the poor will be mobilized to improve the livelihoods and help attain the needs and wants of the poor. This may not always be feasible, but as an empowerment strategy, it deserves consideration. How can the poor get community and locality organizations—through their decision-making, resource mobilization, communication, and conflict resolution—to take seriously the problems created by poverty and to redress these imbalances? Allies from higher levels, whether units of Government or external institutions like NGOs, can assist in encouraging such efforts, but they cannot dictate the internal dynamics of community or locality organizations (Ostrom, 1990). Possibly the poor will represent an important (swing) voting block, so that leadership from the richer majority will need to attend to problems of poorer members.

If voting power does not count, the latter can be more easily ignored; thus ballots can be one source of empowerment. The most reliable means to give the poor some leverage, even if they constitute a minority, is to have activities where the better-off majority benefit from the participation of the poor, or incur some costs from their non-participation.

Case studies of organisational form evolved by the poor in different socio-economic contexts reveal that organisations have operated best when they are rooted in small grassroots groups (as the base) which have as members persons with more or less similar economic interests and linked together to be able to operate as larger entities (a federation/association/forum) where necessary. The small groups at the base (generally not more than about 20 to 25 member households) are the operational entities dealing directly with matters relating to economic matters (savings, credit, production, employment, etc.) while the inter-group federations will deal with certain problems and issues common to all groups, which may be a larger issue, which no individual group can handle or simply co-ordination of activity. Small groups are organized first, for example on a block-by-block or small neighbourhood-by-small-neighbourhood basis. Once the small groups have met and worked successfully together on issues, they are brought together into a larger community-wide organization.

Community Organisation *versus* Organisations of the Poor

Many of the things needed to meet the needs and wants of the poor require *collective action* for:

- establishing and maintaining a clean village water supply;
- banding together to purchase raw materials in bulk at lower price for making handicrafts and to gain access to more favourable markets through group marketing, thereby also reducing the time spent on selling products individually;
- improving local sanitation to reduce diarrhoeal and other diseases that are unnecessarily endemic among the poor (improving hygiene would be more of an individual effort);
- deterring police, moneylenders and other local power figures from victimizing petty vendors, day labourers, unmarried women, lower castes and other vulnerable groups.

Many of the constraints, injustices and indignities identified as particular burdens of the poor require not just individual or public sector action but actions by the poor themselves. Empowerment of the poor thus can be promoted through some combination of:

(a) direct enhancement of their respective assets and capabilities so that they have a higher probability to achieve what they need and desire through their own efforts—a 'private' approach to empowerment of the poor, and

(b) establishing assets and capabilities at higher levels of decision-making and activity that lead to the same or similar outcomes, *i.e.*, enhancing the abilities of the poor to get what they need and want. This latter is a 'collective' strategy of empowerment, important because the first can never be sufficient to meet all of the needs and wants of the poor. Also, this is often needed to protect gains made through the first approach.

5. Norms for Functioning

The SHG should have developed some kind of norms for its functioning, covering its major areas as well as the decision-making processes, leadership etc. The Norms generally relate to:

(a) *Membership*—Homogeneous group, self motivated, one or two literate members.

(b) *Meetings*—The group decides the periodicity of the meetings *i.e.*, weekly, fortnightly or monthly. They also decide on the time of the meeting. Decision on time and periodicity helps in regular conduct of meetings. The regularity in holding the meetings and the attendance in them gives an indication about groups functioning. Therefore a financier sees whether.

- The meetings have been held regularly.
- Whether the meetings were well attended.
- The members were punctual and stayed till the end of the meeting.
- Are there any sanctions for the delinquent members?

In addition the financier takes into account the following facts:

(c) *Transparency*—Equal participation of all members.

(d) *Savings*—Amount, periodicity, rate of interest (return), profit sharing.

(e) *Credit*—Procedure for sanction, ceiling amount, purposes, rate of interest to be charged, repayment period etc.

(f) *Fines*—In case of default in attending meetings, savings and credit repayment. Group may also levy fines for any deviant behaviour.

(g) *Leadership*—Election or nomination of leaders, rotation of leaders.

(h) *Personal/Social improvement*—Minimum literacy level to be achieved, social work to be done etc.

The above norms may be written or oral. They may be decided in the initial meetings or they may evolve over a period of time depending upon the need of the group.

6. Grading System

6.1 Rating System of Self-Help Groups[16]

In general the following norms apply for rating them, but they are not compulsory. We understood that at several places the rating system has not been standardized and certain amount of subjectivity is there.

Sl. No.	*Category*	*Criteria*	*Mark*	*Key*
1.		Membership is homogeneous No homogeneity in membership	10 5	The rating is based on the judgment of assessing official
2.	Age of the group	One year and above Six months and above but less than a year	10 5	There is no need to evaluate an SHG if it is less than six month old (ignore marginal shortfalls upto 1 month)
3.	Weekly group meetings	Four meetings per month 2-3 meetings per month 1 meeting per month	10 8 5	The total number of meetings conducted during the last 3 months may be divided by 3 to arrive at average no. of group meetings.
4.	Attendance	More than 90% Between 70% and 90% Less than 70%	10 5 3	See explanation 1 at the end.
5.	Minutes book	Written in detail Maintained, but not in detail	10 5	Peruse of minutes book pertaining to meetings held during the last 3 months.

(*Contd.*)

(*Contd.*)

Sl. No.	*Category*	*Criteria*	*Mark*	*Key*
6.	Participation in group discussion	Participation by only a few members	5	Peruse minutes book (if rating is 10 for item 5)
		Participation by majority of members	10	Observe during a couple of group meeting Interact with members
7.	Savings (frequency)	4 times a month (by majority members)	10	*Step* 1: Take the average no. of members making saving during last 3 months.
		4 times a month (but not by majority)	8	
		2-3 times a month (by majority members)	8	*Step* 2: Compare this with the total no. of members
		2-3 times a month (but not by majority)	5	*Step* 3: Majority mean > 60% *Step* 4: For average no. of meeting, follow rating given for item 3 above.
		1 time a month day (by majority members)	3	
		1 time a month (but not by majority)	1	Note: Please see explanation 2 at the end.
8.	Savings and loan recovery (mode of collection)	Collected in group meetings	10	Ascertain from group leaders and members in this regard also, peruse minute's book.
		House-to house collection	5	
9.	Style of functioning and group decisions	Democratic and Transparent	10	Peruse minutes book, Interact with members, Observe in few group meetings, ascertain whether periodical elections are conducted for the leadership and whether all decisions are in group meetings and on democratic lines.
		Decisions taken by few dominant member/members/group leaders	0	
10.	Sanction and disburse-ment of loans	Selection of borrowers in group meetings	2	Ascertain the position from group leaders/members
		Sanction and disbursement of loans in group meetings	2	Peruse minutes book (Each item will get marks shown against it, if the conditions are satisfied)
		Loan terms and conditions discussed in group meetings and recorded in minutes	2	
		Utilisation of loans reviewed regularly in group meetings	2	
		Recovery of loans reviewed regularly in group meetings.	2	

(*Contd.*)

(Contd.)

Sl. No.	Category	Criteria	Mark	Key
11.	Interest on SHG loans	Uniform rate irrespective of source of funds	5	Peruse loan register. Ascertain from group leaders/members
		Different rates depending on source of funds	3	
		Interest rates vary according to the purpose of loan	5	
		Uniform interest rate for all purposes	3	
12.	Utilisation of saving for loaning	Above 80%	10	Compare savings outstanding on a given date with loans outstanding on the same date to obtain the percentage. Nil mark for utilisation of savings below 50%
		Above 50% and upto 80%	5	
13.	Recovery of loans	Dues not recovered in respect of 10% or less of total no. of loan accounts	10	Even one installment unpaid without authorisation by the group is treated as dues not recovered. Count such accounts and compare them with total no. of loan a/c. Also, peruse minutes book for authorisation for non-payment
		Dues not recovered between 10% to 30% of total no. of loan accounts.	5	
14.	Books of accounts	Attendance cum minutes book.	3	Each record/register, if maintained properly and upto date, will get marks shown against each.
		Savings Register Loan Ledger,	3	
		Bank Pass Book	1	
15.	Bylaws/ group rules	Known to all members	10	Ascertain from the member through interaction
		Known to most of the members.	5	
		Not known to many members	0	
		Total Marks	**150**	

SHG scoring more than 120 marks out of maximum of 150 marks will be regarded eligible for the credit linkage.

SHG scoring less than 120 marks will have to be further developed before linkage. The areas taken up after 3 months.

6.2 Maintenance of Books

Whether the group is maintaining the basic books that will give details of its functioning and accounts of the group is an important criterion to be judged. The books should give the details of number of meetings held, decisions taken in the meetings, amount of savings of the members and credit availed, the total savings of the group and repayments, who maintains these books is another important criterion for judging the group. Do members maintain it; if not, are they making efforts to achieve basic numeracy or literacy skills so that they can start doing it themselves.

6.3 Financier Verifies

- The details of meetings, proceedings, and attendance.
- Member-wise record of saving and credit.
- Whether the records are up to date?
- Whether all members are kept informed of their savings and credit balances from time to time?
- In case of illiterate groups what is the system followed, does the group gets verified the books maintained, by all NGO/ outsider.
- Whether systems have been developed to ensure safe custody of cash?

7. SHG—Federation

Under the federation a number of SHGs come together for achieving a common goal, without losing their individual identity and independence. It provides a platform for small SHGs to pool their resources to address the social and economic issues collectively.

The Self-Help Group (SHG) mode of generating self-employment has been an accepted mode of operationalising Poverty Alleviation and Social Intermediation programmes. Convergence of SHG based programmes at grassroots level by formation of Federation of SHGs at different levels was felt necessary for improving of their livelihood opportunities and for extending the basic services to the poor people. To ensure sustainability of SHGs, it is essential that Federation of SHGs are created to act as a forum for promotion of various activities related to SHGs in rural areas and dissemination of information at the grassroots level for the empowerment of the poor. Also as the number of SHGs grows it becomes more and more difficult for the promoting institution to supervise individual SHGs. In such a situation the best way is to create an apex body (federation/other similar bodies) having representative from all its member groups.

7.1 Objectives of the Federation

- Facilitates exchange of information and experience between groups.
- Strengthens the existing group by developing skills of members regarding savings and credit management and other economic programmes.
- Access and manages the external funds and inculcate sense of belongingness for facilitating income generating activities.
- Maintains linkages between the member groups and other agencies.
- Act as advocate for member group.

7.2 Functions of the Federation

- Monitoring of member groups.
- Managing flow of funds to the member group to ensure that there is no shortage of funds at group level.
- Planning and Organizing Training and other programmes for the members.
- Reviewing the progress made by the member groups.
- Liasioning with the funding/promoting organisation.

7.3 Model Structure of SHG-based Federation

- Existing SHGs are to be networked at village level.
- If no. of SHGs ranges from 50-60, informal cluster, association/union may be formed at village level. More than one cluster association/union may be formed at village level, if needed.
- Each cluster association/union will have a general body, a governing body. Every group members will be member of the general body.
- Governing body will consist of a chairperson, a vice chairperson and five committee members of SHGs through a process of majority decision.
- Village level monitoring committee will be formed having representatives of NGO, banks and 3/5 reputed persons of the locality as member of the committee. The President of

the committee shall be selected from among these members with unanimous consent.

- ❖ One or two representatives of SHGs may be co-opted into the village level sub-committees. The members of the SHGs in the committees would act as pressure groups in those committees and they could articulate their needs in different sectors and promote and protect their own interest. In this way, convergence between PRIs, CBOs (in form of SHGs) and the line departments would be ensured.
- ❖ The data base of SHGs formed within the village will be maintained by the monitoring committee.
- ❖ Federation of SHGs at block level if no. of groups exceeds 100 and thrift and credit co-operative society will be formed at block level to mobilize the savings of SHGs. For Federation of SHGs, only matured groups (at least 1 year old) should be considered.
- ❖ Block level society will be constituted of representatives of village level associations. This should be a registered body.
- ❖ Block level society will have a general body and a governing body.
- ❖ General body will consist of all the chairpersons and vice Chairpersons of village level cluster association/unions.
- ❖ Governing Body will consist of a Chairperson, vice Chairperson and seven committee members. Chairperson, vice Chairperson are to be elected from among the Chairpersons, vice Chairpersons of village level associations. All other members will be elected from members of village level societies.
- ❖ Specific working groups will be formed in each block level societies to co-ordinate government sponsored/other programmes; assess training and capacity building needs of primary groups, infrastructural and marketing facilities for primary groups.
- ❖ Block Level Society will monitor SHG programme which may be broad based to avoid duplication.
- ❖ The data base of SHGs at block level will be maintained in Block Level Society.

- District Level Society will be constituted of representatives of Block Level Societies. It will function as the store-house of information of SHGs as well as other relevant information. It need not be registered.
- District Level Society will have a general body and a governing body.
- General body will consist of all the Chairpersons and Vice Chairpersons of Block level societies.
- Governing Body will consist of a Chairperson, Vice Chairperson and seven committee members. Chairperson, Vice Chairperson is to be elected from among the Chairpersons, Vice Chairpersons of Block Level Societies. All other members will be elected from members of Block Level Societies.
- District Level Society will monitor SHG programme in the district which may be broad based to avoid duplication. NGO representatives may be inducted in society as co-opted members.
- The data base of SHGs will be maintained in Districts.
- State Level Steering Committee will monitor SHG programme in the State and will evolve policies, guidelines for promotional development of SHGs. State Level Committee will have members from Block Level and District Level Committees.

Societal Space for Organised Actions by the Poor

By space is meant the extent to which the right of association for the poor is respected and safeguarded by governmental legislation, policies and practices. In other words: What is the freedom available for the poor to form into independent organisations of their making without the fear of repression?

Currently, the most important method available for the poor to organise and enjoy legal status is to form co-operatives under Co-operative Law. However, the co-operative movement (with the possible exception of the thrift and credit co-operative societies) has in general failed to provide an effective organisational mechanism for the poor. At present most of the organised groups of the poor in the country operate informally—they lack legal status.

Hence, one positive action that the Government can take is the enactment of supportive legislation to facilitate the organisation of the poor and to give such organisation legal status. In regard to rural workers, the International Labour Organisation's ILO, Rural Workers Organisation Convention and Recommendation (Nos. 141 and 145 of 1975) provide the rationale and guidelines for the enactment of the necessary legislation. In this Convention, the term rural worker has been defined to include any person engaged in agriculture, handicrafts or related occupation in a rural area whether as a wage earner or as a self-employed person such as a tenant, sharecropper or small owner-occupier provided that they work the land themselves with the help of their family labour or with the help of occasional outside labour.

Besides legislation, Government policies and practices are a key determinant of the space available for the poor to form independent organisations of their own. The main issue here is whether there is a political will to permit free association for the poor. Organisation of the poor results in a diffusion of power.

Organised people operate as pressure groups on the political and administrative system. A conducive framework and an environment for the organisation of the poor can be created only if there is a political will and commitment at the highest levels.

Notes

1. World Micro Credit Summit, Washington DC.
2. Hari Srinivas, "So, what is 'microcredit'??", www.gdrc.org
3. Rajaram Dasgupta, "Microfinance in India, Empirical Evidence, Alternative Models and Policy Imperatives" Economic and Political Weekly March 19, 2005, p. 1229.
4. 'SHG Federation in India Emerging Structures and Practices', Sa-Dhan, the Association of Community Development Finance Institutions, July 2004.
5. NABARD Guidelines.
6. NABARD Guidelines.
7. C. Hemalatha Prasad, Social Mobilisation, Employment and Empowerment of Women through SHGs. National Institute of Rural Development, Hyderabad, 2006 quoted from Koch and Soetjipto, 1993.

8. Madhav Menon, Microfinance in India, Voice of Rural India, New Delhi, August 2006.
9. Ramon Magsaysay Award Citation.
10. 'SHG Federation in India Emerging Structures and Practices', Sa-Dhan. The Association of Community Development Finance Institutions, July 2004.
11. Rajaram Dasgupta, "Micro Finance in India, Empirical Evidence, Alternative Models and Policy Imperatives", Economic and Political Weekly Mar 19, 2005, p. 1229.
12. Madhav Menon, Microfinance in India, Voice of Rural India, New Delhi, August, 2006.
13. Madhav Menon, Microfinance in India, Voice of Rural India, New Delhi, August, 2006.
14. Indira Kranthi Patham Society for Elimination of Rural Poverty, Department of Rural Development, Government of Andhra Pradesh—A progress report folder.
15. *Ibid*
16. NABARD Guidelines.

Chapter Four

Government and Non-Government Initiatives

A. GOVERNMENT INITIATIVES

Government of India has been endeavouring for social equality of the marginalised communities through poverty eradication and other developmental programmes from Independence onwards. In this direction, planners, policy-makers, social scientists, educationists etc. were involved to identify the root causes of social and economic inequality in the society and also various solutions were suggested. The initial Governmental programme that was launched for overall development of the country was the five-year plans. Five-year plans were put into action in 1951 and a mechanism was devised to benefit all sections of the society particularly the socio-economically backward sections. Involvement of various Ministries dealing with rural poverty and rural unemployment, social justice and social development of marginalised communities was initiated various to address this issue.

Since then, Government has launched several developmental schemes for the welfare of the socio-economically backward sections of the society irrespective of their socio-religious affiliations. Some of the schemes are still continuing but most of them have been abandoned due to lack of support from society itself. In the 1990's, Ministry of Rural Development organized itself and launched series of developmental programmes keeping felt-needs of the people in mind.

For this an effective Management Group was formed with members from various sections of the society to identify the problem of the area, needs of the people and to regularly monitor the progress of the programme.

By 1990s, Self-Help Groups became the catchword and all the Ministries and associated agencies insisted upon setting up SHGs and entrusting them the task of carrying out the programmes for uplifting the status of socio-economically backward sections of the society. This was treated as a powerful tool in eliminating the backwardness of the society.

1. Swarnjayanti Gram Swarozgar Yojana

The Swarnjayanti Gram Swarozgar Yojana (SGSY) is the single self-employment programme for the rural poor. The Yojana which came into effect from 1-4-1999, has been conceived as a holistic programme covering all aspects of self employment like organization of rural poor into Self-Help Groups (SHGs) and their capacity-building, training, planning of activity clusters, infrastructure development, financial assistance through bank credit and subsidy and marketing support etc.

The objective[1] of SGSY is to bring the assisted poor families (Swarozgaris) above the Poverty Line by ensuring appreciable sustained level of income over a period of time. This objective is to be achieved by *inter-alia* organising the rural poor into Self-Help Groups (SHGs) through the process of social mobilization, their training and capacity-building and provision of income generating assets. The SHG approach helps the poor to build their self-confidence through community action. Interaction in group meetings and collective decision-making enables them in identification and prioritization of their needs and resources.

This process would ultimately lead to the strengthening and socio-economic empowerment of the rural poor as well as improve their collective bargaining power.

SGSY lays stress on the cluster approach. What this means is that instead of funding diverse activities, each block should concentrate on a few select activities (key activities) and attend to all aspects of these activities, so that the Swarozgaris can draw sustainable incomes from their investments. These key activities should preferably be taken up in clusters so that the backward and forward linkages can be effectively established. This would facilitate not only monitoring but also more importantly provision of various services required by the Swarozgaris.

Under SGSY, funds are released to the DRDAs and are utilized as per the decisions taken in the Committee formed at local level. Sometimes, the poverty reduction efforts require coordinated action by different departments and it may call for planning and coordination that may extend beyond the individual districts. There may also be occasions when the different departments or DRDAs or State Governments might want to try out new initiatives which are in the nature of pioneer projects, capable of triggering much needed growth impulses. Such projects would be indicators of possible alternative strategies. In order to take up such projects, 15 per cent of the funds under SGSY will be set apart by the Ministry for such initiatives in conjunction with other departments, semi-government organizations such as, the Khadi & Village Industries Commission, Development Commissioner, Handicrafts, Commodity Boards, etc., or international organizations. This would include initiatives to be taken in the individual districts or across the districts. If during the course of the year, such funds cannot be fully utilized, the balance funds will be distributed among the States along with the programme funds whose redistribution during the year will keep in view the absorption capacity of different States.

Till March 31, 2004, about 19 lakh SHGs have been organized under SGSY. Of these, 10 lakh SHGs have passed grade-I and 5 lakh grade-II and 2 lakh SHGs have taken up economic activity (Table 4.1). The percentage of SHGs taking up economic activity, out of SHGs that have passed grade-II, is around 40 per cent. Similarly, the number of SHG swarozgaris assisted has also increased from 3.4 lakh to 5.7 lakh during this period. Of course, the number of individual swarozgaris assisted has declined from 5.9 lakh to 3.2 lakh during the same period.

Target Groups

Under SGSY, the beneficiaries/target groups are known as Swarozgaris. The Swarozgaris can be either individuals or groups. However, the scheme lays emphasis on the group approach, under which the rural poor are organized into Self-Help Groups. In either case, the list of BPL households identified through BPL census, duly approved by the Gram Sabha will form the basis for identification of families for assistance under the SGSY. The Self-Help Groups should also be drawn from the BPL list approved by the Gram Sabha.

Self-Help Groups

SGSY will focus on organization of the poor at grassroots level through a process of social mobilization for poverty eradication. Social mobilization enables the poor build their own organizations (Self-Help Groups) in which they participate fully and directly and take decisions on all issues concerning poverty eradication. Simultaneously, SHGs have the advantage of the assistance—be it in terms of credit or technology or market guidance etc.—reaching the poor faster and more effectively.

Generally a self-help group may consist of 10 to 20 persons. However, in difficult areas like deserts, hills and areas with scattered and sparse population and in case of minor irrigation and disabled persons, this number may be from 5-20. Generally all members of the group should belong to families below the poverty line. However, if necessary, a maximum of 20 per cent and in exceptional cases, where essentially required, up to a maximum of 30 per cent of the members in a group may be taken from families marginally above the poverty line living contiguously with BPL families, if they are acceptable to the BPL members of the group. The group shall not consist of more than one member from the same family. A person should not be a member of more than one group. Further, APL members of the Self-Help Group shall not become office bearers (Group Leader, Assistant Group Leader or Treasurer) of the Group.

50 per cent of the groups formed in each block should be exclusively for women. In the case of disabled persons, the groups formed should ideally be disability-specific wherever possible, however, in case sufficient number of people for formation of disability-specific groups are not available, a group may comprise of persons with diverse disabilities or a group may comprise of both disabled and non-disabled persons below the poverty line.

Marketing

Those groups, which are engaged in the economic activities, it has been observed that marketing of their product is a big problem. The products more often than not, are not demand driven, lack of quality and sustenance and rural products do not have reached the scale to become part of the big supply chains. The rural products fail to meet the demands of quality and value for money. The problem is going to get aggravated due to the on-going processes of capitalisation, liberalisation and globalisation.

The rural livelihoods in a number of sectors are being threatened. The rural markets are going to witness major structural changes in the near future.

The SGSY guidelines[2] suggest that the key activity should be identified on the basis of market demand. Further it suggests that the choice of activity should be based on the resources of an area, the available skills and the market.

SGSY guidelines[3] also recommend at length that the marketing of goods outside the districts require an intermediary agency. This can be in the governmental, non-governmental or private sector. These agencies may market the products in the national or international markets.

Government of India presses itself into providing a facilitating agency with an exclusive focus on the marketing of the rural products of the country. Included in the expression 'Marketing', are Market intelligence, forecasting, market surveys, New Market Creations, expansion of current markets, Better Product Design, Concept Marketing etc.

Ministry of Rural Development organises Regional Saras Fairs to provide market to SHG producers. In 2003-04 six Regional Saras Fairs were organised, in 2004-05 eighteen and in 2005-06 twenty one and in 2006-07 twenty three fairs were organised. The graph below shown the cumulative sales in all the fairs and number of fairs year-wise.

Fig. 4.1: Organization of SARS and Sales in it

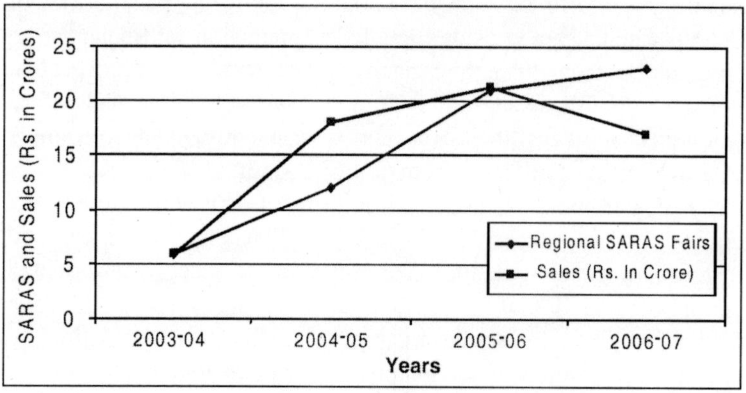

Besides Regional Saras Fairs, 8 fairs were organized at IITF Pragati Maidan since 1999[4]. About 25000 members of Self-Help Group have been benefited so far by these fairs.

The role of these melas in marketing the rural goods in the cities is gaining recognition over a period of time. These melas have also helped the rural entrepreneurs to acquire competitive strength and exposure in the urban market[5].

Linking to Local and Distant Markets

Market linkages were considered very crucial for promotion of micro enterprises. As globalisation is redefining local markets, it is important that linkages of SHG products are established to both local and distant markets. For achieving this, the groups made the following suggestions:

(i) Creation of local haats (markets) within 25 kms. radius of SHGs,
(ii) Establishing information kiosks to provide market intelligence,
(iii) Provision of ready and easy transportation facility,
(iv) Conducting market survey for exploring distant markets, and
(v) Creation of storage facilities for improving the shelf-life of products.

For any financing institution, appraisal is very important for ensuring the utility of the loan and repayment of the loan. Bankers generally appraise the project and the borrower. In case of SHG financing, most of the project appraisal norms like assessing the cost benefit and profits will not be workable due to the peculiarities of SHG financing. For considering a loan application for financing the Financer has to evaluate the capacity and character of the prospective borrower. SHG's also being customers have to be appraised before extending credit facilities. But then assessment of creditworthiness of a SHG is very different from that of an individual.

SHGs are not to be assessed in terms of their ability to provide collateral or guarantees of net worth. The SHGs have to be assessed in terms of group dynamics like cohesion, vibrancy, goal-oriented action, participation of members, democratic decision and collective leadership. The appraiser has to see whether the group is functioning, actually as a group, why the members have come together, whether it is for obtaining loan from bank or the group sees other purposes, what is the group discipline and whether it is sustainable.

Institutional Experiences

Some of the institutions such as Bharatiya Agro Industries Foundation (BAIF), Development for Humane Action (DHAN) Foundation, Shri Kshethra Dharmasthala Rural Development Project (SKDRDP) etc. shared their experiences in promotion of micro-enterprises among SHG members. The experiences, though mostly are at the pilot stage, highlighted that:

(i) It is appropriate to introduce income-generating activities based on known skills, knowledge and resources.
(ii) It is better to integrate with existing livelihood activities of group members.
(iii) More emphasis needs to be laid on developing business skills than on providing backward and forward linkages.
(iv) Micro-enterprise development is not a stand-alone activity, but requires a combination of factors to enable growth as a business entity.
(v) It is both efficient and cost effective to promote farm sector micro-enterprises because backward and forward linkages are locally available.
(vi) Promotion of non-farm sector activities, particularly those in manufacturing sector, is a challenge for providing market linkages because significant sales turnover is required by each member to earn incomes which are even equivalent of minimum wages or to cross the poverty line.

For any goods or services that are produced, existence of a suitable market is essential. Traditionally, the self-employment programmes concentrated on the inputs rather than the outputs and their marketing. The Self-Help Groups are encouraged to try out the markets on their own so that they slowly develop marketing skills. They can also start marketing the goods of the individual Swarozgaris. Infrastructure fund can be use for strengthening marketing infrastructure and related activities.

The marketing of goods outside the districts requires an intermediary agency. This can be in the governmental, non-governmental or private sector. The one aspect that requires to be taken care of is the stability of the agency, their own competence and their capacity to ensure that the rural producer is getting his/her fair share of the profits.

Some State Governments have established District Supply and Marketing Societies (DSMS) to provide non-credit inputs like procurement or purchase of raw material and also for sale of products. In States such as Orissa and Kerala, there are marketing societies at the State level. Their capacity and product range can be suitably expanded.

Organizations like Handicrafts Boards and Handloom Corporations and also KVIC/KVIB can play a prominent role in promotion of SGSY. The marketing outlets of KVIC/KVIB must be made use of for SGSY products. Keeping the market trends in view, linkages with apex bodies can ensure a stable market at remunerative prices.

Such links also result in quality improvements while reducing the market risks to the poor. There are several NGO and other independent institutions to market products from rural artisans/craftsmen across the country. DRDAs also strive to develop linkages with such groups.

A few States have organized Melas to give publicity to the range of products produced by the Swarozgaris. Organizing of Exhibitions periodically in urban centres will offer better price to the goods of SGSY Swarozgaris. The State level organizations and boards have to develop an organic link professional bodies can guide the poor in supply of designs and in quality assurance. Attempts to establish State emporia for display and sales of SGSY products in major urban cities need to be given a fair trial.

One of the serious constraints experienced in operationalising the group enterprise concept with SHGs under SGSY was disciplining the free riders *i.e.*, such members who did not adhere to the agreed enterprise norms relating to the individual. Responsibility towards the enterprise but at the same time insisted on the contribution of other members and made claims on the benefits of the organization's operations.

Skill Up-gradation/Training

It has been well recognized that for success of self-employment endeavours and also for their sustainability, the required skill to successfully run the enterprise is a pre-requisite.

SGSY proposes a number of measures for upgrading the capacity of Swarozgaries both in individual as well as group oriented activities.

Training of SHGs member is one of the important components of SGSY. In Bihar 61507 SHG member were trained during 2004-05, 79672 members in 2005-06 and 78618 during 2006-07[6] and 23.29 crore rupees were expended on training during these three years.

In the State most of the DWCRA groups disintegrated during the IRDP era and the SHG movement had been taken afresh along with the launching of SGSY. By March 31, 2004 about 60,000 SHGs including 27,710 women groups and 25,826 SHGs covering SC and ST communities were organized. The growth of SHG movement in the State was slow and steady.

Basic Orientation Programme

Where the Swarozgari possesses the required skills, he/she may be put through a basic orientation programme after the loan is sanctioned and before it is disbursed. This mandatory programme may be organized at the block headquarters, not far from the place of residence. This basic orientation programme will seek to familiarize the Swarozgaris with SGSY and its objectives, the responsibilities of the Swarozgari, as well as the behavioural aspects. This programme includes elements of book keeping, knowledge of market, identification and appraisal, acquaintance with produce costing and product pricing, familiarization with project financing by banks as well as some basic skills in the key activity identified. It is of very short duration, not normally more than two days. BDOs, Bankers and line departments can act as resource persons for this training. Training expenses like training material, honorarium to resource persons, travel and food expenses of Swarozgaris can be met by DRDA from SGSY Training Fund. No stipend will be admissible.

Skill Development Training

For the identified activities, Swarozgaries who need additional skill development/upgradation of skills appropriate training may be identified and suitable training programmes organized. Government institutions like engineering colleges, it is, Polytechnics, Universities and NGOs may be approached to imparting training. The objective of this training is to ensure that the Swarozgaris possess the Minimum

Skill Requirement (MSR). Swarozgaris will be eligible for assistance only when they possesses MSR and loans will be disbursed only when they have satisfactorily completed skill training.

For this training, Swarozgaris will be entitled for financial assistance if they require to undergo training for more than a week. The rate of assistance is fixed locally. The bank gives this money to the Swarozgaries as a soft loan.

SGSY Training Fund

Up to 10 per cent of SGSY funds will be set aside as training fund and will be utilized to provide both orientation and training programmes to the Swarozgaris, as indicated above. A separate Head of Account should be opened for this purpose.

The DRDA will be entitled to meet the expenses, incurred by the training institution for both Basic Orientation and Skill Development Training from out of the SGSY Fund. The Basic Orientation Training may include topics on concept of Self-Help, group dynamics, conflict resolution, conduct of group meetings, maintenance of records, awareness about social and family welfare programmes etc. The training for skill development may include skill up-gradation through exposure to latest tools and technology, value addition and diversification of products, entrepreneur development, marketing skills, packaging, labeling etc.

The total expenditure on Basic Orientation and skill development training will not exceed Rs. 5,000 per trainee.

Status in Bihar

Swarna Jayanti Gram Swarozgar Yojana is being implemented in all the districts of Bihar. The implementation, achievement and monitoring is not satisfactory. During the year 2006-07 number of the SHGs formed is 17977, 10843 crossed grade I stage and 6567 reached to grade II, 6540 taken the economic activities, 63563 members of the SHGs were assisted during the year[7].

Physical Impact of SGSY[8]

The Financial Progress includes credit and subsidy disbursed, total investment and per Swarozgaris investment made under the scheme during the year 2006-07. For the State of Bihar, the total credit allotment was 35461.96 lakhs, out of which 5012.42 was the share of SHGs and

5351.77 was for Individual Swarozgaris *i.e.* a total of 10,364 lakhs (29.23%) of credit was allotted to the target groups. The subsidy allotment for disbursement was 6672.82 lakhs out of which to SHGs, it was 4021.97 lakhs and to Individual Swarozgaris it was 2650.85 lakhs. In total, 17037.02 lakhs (10364.19 + 6672.82) was disbursed to the target groups in the form of credit and subsidy. Percentage-wise this investment is 53.03 per cent for SHGs and 46.97 per cent for Individual Swarozgaris. So if we see the per family investment in terms of rupees, it is coming to Rs. 25,609 and the credit subsidy ratio is coming to 1.55.

Physical Progress[9]

The physical progress includes members of SHGs and the Swarozgaris assisted under SGSY. For the State of Bihar, a total of 66,527 (35,448 are members of SHGs and 31,079 are Individual Swarozgaris) Swarozgaris were assisted during the period. Amongst the disadvantaged groups, women have been targeted in large and 23,303 (35.03 %) have been covered under the scheme. Secondly, is the SC and ST which is 21,331 and 959 members respectively. However, the proportion of handicapped persons is less as compared to others which is 203. Amongst the Minorities, no Swarozgaris is covered so far. Percentage-wise, it is 32.06 per cent SC and 1.44 per cent ST and 0.31 per cent Handicapped.

Sector-wise Physical Coverage[10]

The sector-wise coverage shows that SGSY has covered all the three sectors of the economy. In Primary Sector, it is Rs. 37,665 lakhs out of which 2243 is on Irrigation, maximum of 23,571 on Miltch cattle and 11851 is spent on others.

In the Secondary Sector Rs. 12,404 lakhs was spent which included the allocation on the following heads: 4500 on Village Industries, 7140 on others, 466 on Handicrafts and 298 on Handloom Industries. However, in Tertiary Sector, the proportionate of investment is comparatively low as compared to other sectors. The only investment of Rs. 19,614 is made under the head ‘Others’. In total, Rs. 69,683 was spend on the sector-wise growth of the SHGs and Individual Swarozgaris.

SGSY Status in Muzaffarpur[11]

For the year 2006-07, the total allocation was Rs. 902.97 lakhs out of which 677.23 was for Central and Rs. 225.74 was for State. Of these allotted funds, the release was 557.56 lakhs (338.62 from Central and 218.94 from State) i.e. as against 902.97, 557.56 only was released. Total funds available are 908 lakhs and total expenditure made is 409.82. The percentage-wise release to Central allocation is 50 per cent and percentage-wise release to State allocation is 96.99 per cent. The balancing funds at the disposal are 498.18 lakhs.

Share of SC/ST/Minorities

The percentage of SC/ST community members assisted under the programme has increased from 44 to 46 per cent and the percentage of women from 44.6 to 52 per cent. Between 1999 and March 2004, an amount of Rs. 7260 crore rupees were allocated for this programme, out of which Rs. 5011 crore (69%) were utilized. The percentage utilization of the funds available has increased from 49 per cent during 1999-2000 to 86 per cent in 2003-04 were individuals which has almost gone up by five times from 0.24 to 1.34 during this period. Similarly, the per capita investment under this programme has increased from Rs. 17,000 to Rs. 22,469.

Criteria for Allocation of Funds to the States

Swarnjayanti Gram Swarozgar Yojana is a Centrally Sponsored Scheme and the financing of the programme will be shared between the Centre and the States in the ratio of 75 : 25. The Central allocation earmarked for the States will be distributed in relation to the incidence of poverty in the States.

However, additional parameters like absorption capacity (based on past trend in utilization of SGSY funds) and special requirement will also be taken into consideration during the course of the year. Devolution of funds to the districts will be indicated by the States and approved by the Government of India. Government of India will release the funds directly to the DRDAs. Devolution to the Blocks may be decided by the Governing Body of the DRDA based on level of poverty and other local factors. Re-allocation may be made by the DRDA within a district. This can be made during January for the remained of the financial year.

SWARNJAYANTI GRAM SWAROZGAR YOJANA BANK-WISE REPORT OF MUZAFFARPUR[12].

Sl. No.	Name of the Bank	No. of Applications: Sent to Bank			Sanctioned			Disbursed			Rejected/Returned			Credit Target	Credit Disbursed (Amt s. in Lakh)		
		SHG	Individual	Total	SHG	Individual	Total	SHG	Individual	Total	SHG	Individual	Total		SHG	Individual	Total
1	*2*	*3*	*4*	*5*	*6*	*7*	*8*	*9*	*10*	*11*	*12*	*13*	*14*	*15*	*16*	*17*	*18*
1.	SBI	23	52	75	20	25	45	20	15	35	0	0	0	0	14.17	5.38	19.55
2.	CBI	24	66	90	21	46	67	21	26	47	0	0	0	0	34.21	3.25	37.46
3.	PNB	28	101	129	19	81	100	19	61	80	0	0	0	0	28.13	7.88	36.01
4.	BOI	24	57	81	24	42	66	24	37	61	0	0	0	0	35.27	3.6	38.87
5.	UBI	27	24	51	25	20	45	25	14	39	0	0	0	0	17.60	3.75	21.35
6.	BOB	20	48	68	15	28	43	14	23	37	0	0	0	0	13.95	5.76	19.71
7.	All Bank	9	30	39	8	3	11	8	3	11	0	0	0	0	23.11	1.25	24.36
8.	UCO Bank	12	32	44	9	12	21	8	12	20	0	0	0	0	7.81	1.69	9.50
9.	UBI (Union)	9	45	54	7	19	26	7	9	16	0	0	0	0	13.00	2.50	15.50
10.	Canara Bank	7	23	30	5	3	8	5	3	8	0	0	0	0	7.10	0.35	7.45
11.	Sy. Bank	11	20	31	7	0	7	5	0	5	0	0	0	0	6.00	0.00	6.00
12.	Indian Bank	15	51	66	12	5	17	10	0	10	0	0	0	0	14.64	0.00	14.64
13.	UBKGB	189	309	498	162	126	288	145	110	255	0	0	0	0	275.90	24.05	299.95
	Total	*398*	*858*	*1256*	*334*	*410*	*744*	*310*	*313*	*623*	*0*	*0*	*0*	*0*	*490.89*	*59.46*	*550.35*

Sometimes, loan to the beneficiaries of SGSY seems to be quite high in comparison to other banks. 59 per cent of the applicants sent to different banks were sanctioned and out of those which were sanctioned, funds were distributed to 84 per cent of them.

The position of receiving loan application and sanctioning of loan by some of banks is shown below:

Table 4.1: Loan Sanctioning to the Group

Bank	*Percentage of loan application sanctioned out of applications received*
State Bank of India	60
Central Bank of India	74
Punjab National Bank	77
UCO Bank	48
Canara Bank	26
Syndicate Bank	22
Indian Bank	26

PNB sanctioned the largest no. of loan applications out of the total received by it followed by CBI, Syndicate, UCO and Indian Banks. It seems they did not like to open their purses.

2. National Bank for Agriculture and Rural Development (NABARD)

National Bank for Agriculture and Rural Development came into existence on July 12, 1982. It is established for providing credit for the promotion of agriculture, small scale industries, handicrafts and other allied economic activities in rural areas with a view to promote integrated rural development. National Bank for Agriculture and Rural Development is set up as an apex Development Bank with a mandate for facilitating credit flow for promotion and development of agriculture, small-scale industries, cottage and village industries, handicrafts and other rural crafts. It also has the mandate to support all other allied economic activities in rural areas, promote integrated and sustainable rural development and secure prosperity of rural areas.

One of the major success stories of NABARD, the SHG Bank linkage programme started as a pilot project in 1992 with 500 SHGs. SHGs comprise homogeneous groups of poor people who have voluntarily come together mainly with the idea of overcoming their common problems of low social and economic status. SHGs enable the poor, especially the women from the poor households, to collectively identify, prioritize and tackle the problems they face in their socio-economic environment. By pooling their meager resources and using them for lending among themselves, they develop the habit of thrift and the skill of credit appraisal, before getting mature enough to access a loan from banks, which is called credit linkage. Starting with small loans for consumption they soon graduate to bigger loans for setting up of income generating micro-enterprises.

Today, NABARD's SHG Bank Linkage Programme boasts of over 26 lakh SHGs and 3.9 crore households influencing the lives of over 16 crore poor population. During the year 2006-07 alone, as many as 458591 groups were credit linked.

SHG-Bank Linkage Programme

Facilitating SHGs to access credits from formal banking channels. SHG-Bank Linkage Programme has proved to be the major supplementary credit delivery system with wide acceptance by banks, NGOs and various Government departments.

Region-specific Initiatives

NABARD has intensified its efforts for roping in new partners for promotion and linkage of groups in regions where the growth of groups has not been commensurate with potential.

Priority has been assigned to awareness building and for identification of NGOs and other partners in 13 priority States, which account for 70 per cent of rural poor in the country.

Identification of Mature Groups for Promotion of Micro-Enterprises

(i) Building profiles of identified groups.
(ii) Identifying groups/members who would like to work with the on-going enterprises.
(iii) Identifying groups/members who would like to set up new enterprises.
(iv) Assessing nature of facilitation required at group level.
(v) Assessing training needs of group members.
(vi) Land-holding/escort services required by the group members.

(vii) Net-working with various institutions for provision of identified facilities including trainings and backward and forward linkages.

(viii) The NGO/MEPA should aim at empowering the group members to manage their affair on their own after a reasonable period of time for ultimate sustainability. In other words, a withdrawal strategy by NGO/MEPA should work simultaneously with implementation of the project.

(ix) NABARD could assume the over all responsibility for implementing the programme in identified districts.

3. Women and Child Development Ministry

(a) Swa-Shakti Project

The Swa-Shakti Project, also known as Rural Women's Development and Empowerment Project, was sanctioned on 16 October, 1998 as a Centrally-sponsored Project for a period of 5 years with an estimated outlay of Rs. 186.21 crore. In addition, an amount of Rs. 5 crore was provided for facilitating the setting up of Revolving Funds for giving interest-bearing loans to beneficiary groups primarily during their initial formative stage. The project aims at enhancing women's access to resources for better quality of life through use of drudgery and time reduction devices, health, literacy and confidence enhancement and increasing their control over their income through their involvement in skill development and income generating activities. The specific objectives of the project are:

- Establishment of 7400 to 12000 self-reliant women's self-help-groups (SHGs) having 15-20 members each;
- Developing linkages between SHGs and lending institutions to ensure women's continued access to credit facilities for income generation activities;
- Increased control of women, particularly poor women, over income and spending, through their involvement in income generation activities, which will help in poverty alleviation;
- Enhancing women's access to resources for better quality of life, including those for drudgery reduction and time-saving devices; and

- Sensitizing and strengthening the institutional capacity of support agencies to pro-actively address women's needs.

The project originally covered parts of 7 States and 35 districts, as mentioned in the table given below:

The project is implemented through the Women's Development Corporations in the States of Bihar, Haryana and Karnataka, Gujarat Women's Economic Development Corporation Ahmedabad, Madhya Pradesh Mahila Arthik Vikas Nigam Bhopal, Uttar Pradesh Mahila Kalyan Nigam Lucknow, Uttar Pradesh Bhoomi Sudhar Nigam Lucknow and Jharkhand Women's Development Society, Ranchi. The implementing agencies actively associate NGOs to form and service the Self-Help Groups. A Project Support Unit at the Central level (CPSU) provides technical and managerial support. A Computerized Project Management Information System that includes both project and process information and a Computerized Financial Management System provide necessary information back up for effective project implementation. The MIS is designed to improve the work of the field staff to enable them to provide better services to the Self-Help Groups. Concurrent Monitoring and Evaluation is undertaken regularly throughout the Project. Four rounds of the CME have been undertaken so far and their findings have fed into mid-course corrections.

A substantial part of the outlay for the project will become available as soft-term loan/credit to the Government of India from the International Fund for Agricultural Development (IFAD) and International Development Association (IDA). Almost the entire credit needs of the beneficiaries will be met from institutional sources. Roughly, the source of project funding would be as under:

The Government of India from its own resources is providing funds needed for setting up of the Revolving Funds in States implementing various projects.

Swa-Shakti is using innovative methods to mobilize the community and create appropriate environment. Theme camps and use of traditional media are being encouraged all over the project. Conscious efforts are being made to effect convergence with various other service providers. Programmes and projects of other entities are being documented and district level orientation and sensitization workshops are used frequently.

The Project has developed strong systems for induction and contracting of NGOs and procurement and outsourcing of services. Strong focus on grassroots training of SHG members, field workers and other grassroots level implementers has been maintained. Keeping in mind the dearth of local printed material, the Project has also documented a number of success stories and other issues in the area of self-help group promotion.

After the mid-term review, the Project had focused on micro-enterprise promotion in the on-farm and non-farm sector, convergence, networking and bank-linkages. A recent assessment has zeroed down areas of focus for the next phase as micro-enterprise promotion in the on-farm and non-farm sector, convergence, improving credit absorption capacity of SHGs, community asset creation and health, hygiene and environmental sanitation.

Need-Based Interventions

Apart from the core components, the project has also sought to increase its scope in response to local needs and is addressing issues such as water harvesting techniques, agro-processing etc. Collaboration with Department of Science and Technology and National and State level institutions like Central Institute of Agricultural Engineering, IARI, National Botanical Research Institute, Avian Research Institute etc. has been established to link the SHGs with technological inputs and processes for micro-enterprise development.

- Considering adolescent girls as a section closely linked to the target category included in the SHGs, project efforts are centered on nutrition, reproductive health and confidence building of adolescent girls.
- This has been possible through convergence with adolescent girls schemes like Kishori Shakti Yojana in Madhya Pradesh. In Gujarat, adolescent girls SHGs have merged as fallout of capacity-building among women's SHGs who have effectively channelised the training inputs in forming these

SHGs. Consequently, functional literacy is being promoted in women's SHGs with the help of adolescent girls who are working as literacy volunteers, in the process giving a tremendous boost to their confidence and self-esteem.

Status of Project in Bihar and Muzaffarpur

The Swa-Shakti project in Bihar is under implementation since June-1999. Subsequent to bifurcation of the State into Bihar and Jharkhand, this is being implemented in six blocks of Muzaffarpur district.

448 groups has been formed with 19 federations which has been registered[13]. The project activities had been planned in phased manner to comply with the parameters set with regard to group nurturing and capacity-building for stakeholders and in accordance with the project objectives.

Innovative Works under Swa-Shakti Project

Musahars, extremely poor backward castes of Bihar, live on the fringes of the society and often are the first ones to be caught in case of crime as they have kleptomaniac tendency. Recognizing that the efforts required working in this area would be significantly different, an action research has been initiated along with an NGO partner to mobilize and nurture 60 Musahar women's SHGs during a period of 2 years. The process of mobilization of these SHGs would be systematically documented to allow future replication. Interventions would be need-based mainly focusing upon on health and sanitation, legal rights and income generation. All 60 SHGs have so far been formed and strategic interventions are being planned.

(b) Swawlamban

Objectives

- Establish Women SHGs.
- Sensitize and strengthen the institutional capacity of support agencies (Govt., NGOs, Banks).

❖ Increase the income of poor women by their involvement in income generating activities.
❖ Develop linkage between SHGs and lending institutions for poverty alleviation.
❖ Improve access to better healthcare, education and drudgery reduction practices.

Project Phases

(i) Identification and formation of SHGs. (0-4 months)
(ii) Group Stabilisation:

- Group training,
- Training of SHG representative,
- Training on Gender issue,
- Support to group fund of the SHG through lending institution,
- Active role of NGO and other inventors.

(iii) Growth of self-reliance (15—36 months)

- SHG takes over responsibility for managing its own affairs including payment of services,
- Promotion of interaction between the SHGs,
- Greater emphasis on economic activities,
- Linkage with other technical agencies.

Core Component

(a) *Bank Linkage*: Each and every group would be SHG through group loans to enable the members to engage in income-generating active.
(b) *Micro-Enterprise Development (MED)*: The project would focus on micro-enterprise development and hence the SHG members would be provided technical services/training private or public sector agencies to start-up MED activities.
(c) *Community Asset*: To improve quality of women's lives, the project would facilitate groups access to social services and assist in leveraging fund for the provision of community

assets. Health, Childcare, Drinking Water Supply, Sanitation and Community meeting places could be some priority areas.

(d) *Convergence*: As it is a time bound project, convergence would be the most important of all components.

Swawlamban is a Centrally Sponsored Project through Mahila Samakhya having a project period of 2004-07. It is being implemented in 20 blocks of ten districts.1011 Self Help Group were formed against the target of thousand groups in the project area, out of which 997 groups are linked to the banks and 531 groups are facilitated with the credit. These 531 groups has saved Rs. 84.33 lakh and got the credit from bank in tune of Rs. 150.51 lakh. The most important thing being seen is that it has been developed in 110 clusters and twenty federations have been formed and are registered[14].

(c) Swayamsiddha

Indira Mahila Scheme of the Central Government is redesigned and renamed as Swayam Siddha Yojana, a fully sponsored scheme of Government of India. 6300 SHGs of women belongs to Backward Caste and living below poverty line was the target in the State under this project. Against this target 6332 groups are formed in 63 blocks 19 district and for it 568 clusters are formed[15].

(d) Rashtriya Mahila Kosh (National Credit Fund for Women)

The National Commission for self-employed women in the informal sector in its report entitled "SRAMA SHAKTI" in 1988 had recommended innovations in the credit mechanism to assist poor women. This commission strongly recommended for the setting up of an exclusive credit body for poor and self-employed women, in recognition of their socio-economic realities.

On the recommendation of National Commission, the Department of Women and Child Development, Govt of India registered on 30th March 1993 a society by the name of National Credit Fund for Women or Rashtriya Mahila Kosh.

Objectives of Rashtriya Mahila Kosh

The objective behind setting up is to enable the women to achieve economic independence by extending financial support for:

- Sustenance of their existing employment,
- Generation of further employment,
- Asset creation,
- Asset redemption, and
- Tiding over consumption social and contingent needs.

Role and Responsibilities of RMK

Following roles and responsibilities are undertaken by RMK:

- Identify, select, promote and support NGO/Government Organisation/Cooperatives/Non-profit Section 25 Companies as micro-credit channelising agencies.
- Sensitizing existing Government delivery mechanism and increasing the visibility of poor women as a vital and viable clientele with the conventional institutions.
- Promote research and study to implement and replicate for the promotion of credit mechanism while enhancing livelihood issues.
- Promotion of federation and networking of women's organisation for exchange of experience, information and dissemination of knowledge, management and social mobilization.

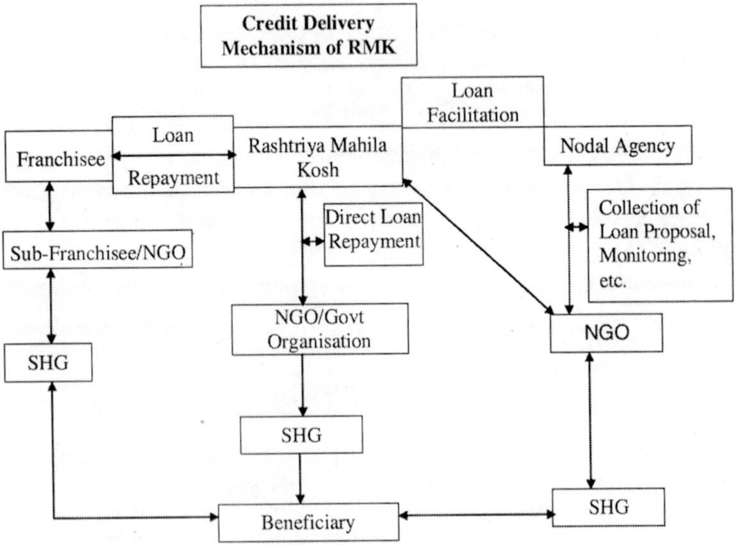

Rashtriya Mahila Kosh prefers to channelise its micro-credit programme through Non-Government organisations because

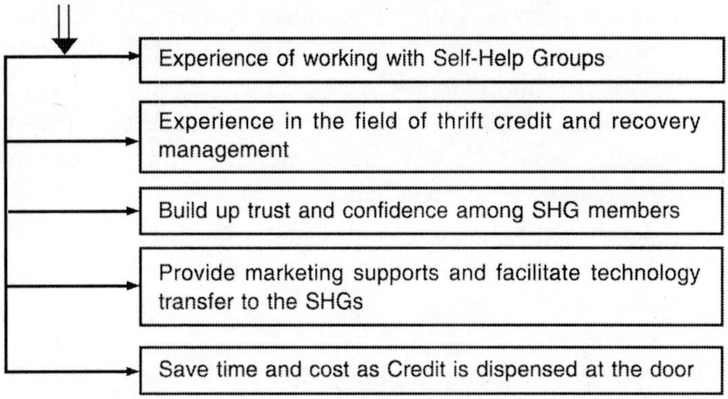

(e) National Backward Class Finance and Development Corporation (NBCFDC)

The National Backward Finance and Development Corporation was set up by the Government of India under Ministry of Welfare (now it is Ministry of Social Justice and Empowerment) on 13th January, 1992 as a company not for profit under Section 25 of the Companies Act, 1956.

Objective

NBCFDC's main objective is to promote economic and developmental activities for the benefit of Backward Classes and to assist the poorer sections of these classes in skill development and self-employment ventures.

Activities that are Financed

- *Agriculture and Allied Activities*—irrigation, purchase of agricultural machinery, animal breeding, poultry farming, horticulture, bee Keeping etc, equipments such as pesticide spray, agriculture marketing through cooperative societies/ association of farmers belonging to OBCs, setting up grading and packing houses, purchase of transport vehicles for marketing of agriculture produce etc.

- *Artisans and Traditional Occupation*—barbers, washermen, tailors, weavers, carpenters, potters, blacksmiths, masons and manufacturing of handicraft items including brass-ware, gardeners in urban areas.
- *Technical Trades*—electricians, plumbers, sheet metal, TV, radio repair, motor mechanic, tyre puncture repair, refrigeration mechanic etc.
- *Small Business*—tea shop, general provision store, books and stationery shop, newspaper and magazine shop, vendors, photocopier service, typewriting and word processing services etc.
- *Transport*—plying of bullock and other animal driven carts, cycle-rickshaw, auto-rickshaw, taxi, tempo, truck for hire etc. including cycle hiring services.

Types of Loans

NBCFDC finances mainly three types of loans under which it covers different schemes. They are as follows:

(a) General Loan Schemes

(b) Micro-Finance Schemes

(i) *Micro Credit Financing*—To implement NBCFDC schemes at grassroot level and promote and support micro- credit scheme for improvement of credit facilities for the target group specially the women beneficiary, the corporation has adopted Micro-Credit Financing through SCAs and accredited NGOs either directly or through SHGs.

(ii) *Mahila Samridhi Yojana*—To provide micro-finance to women entrepreneurs belonging to target group, the scheme is implemented through SCAs in rural and urban areas by way of financing the women beneficiaries either directly or through Self-Help Groups.

(c) *Training Grant Schemes*

The Corporation provides financial assistance to the members of the target groups belonging to Backward Class for up-gradation of their technical skill. The assistance is provided through SCAs or technical institutions for conducting training programmes for which 90 per cent of the training expenses are borne by NBCFDC and balance 10 per cent is to be contributed by SCAs.

(f) Chief Minister's Women Empowerment Schemes

It is a State Government funded Scheme for the period of 2005–08 is being implemented through Women Development Corporation, Bihar[16]. Against the target proposed under this scheme was 100 SHG in 20 blocks of ten districts 812 groups have already been formed involving 10799 individual members.

Out of 812 groups 733 has been linked with the banks[17]. Some of the groups also facilitated with bank's loan. Their own saved money is running beyond Rs. 29 lakh.

B. NON-GOVERNMENT INITIATIVES

Role of NGOs is very critical in making and sustaining the movement of Self-Help Group. NGO has to play a role of motivator and facilitator. It has been assumed that the NGOs should make the general awareness about the strength of the Self-Help Groups, selected the members to make homogeneous group, facilitate in capacity building about group dynamism and book keeping, linking with the banks. Moreover NGOs should have survey of the area about the probable activities, economic activities viable for the area, facilitate the product in branding, packaging and marketing. For these support various schemes like SGSY, NABARD, and Deep Yojna etc. have the provision for NGOs, which is not less than ten thousand per SHG for nation. Unfortunately the NGOs has taken simple role of making a forming a group and facilitating it for grading and credit linkage. Beneficiaries has a concept that if a NGOs does this mechanical job it is good enough to be accoladed as excellent NGO.

Self-Help Promoting Institutions (SHPIs)

There are many types of Self-Help Promoting Institutions (SHPIs) as follows[18]:

- NGOs or trusts or societies, which promote SHGs for bank linkage. NGOs/Micro-finance institutions, which are themselves financial intermediaries are excluded from the list. SHG promotion may be major or minor part.

- There are many Self-Help Group Promotion Institutions active in the district level self-help formation and promotion activities using various means and ways to inculcate the habits of saving and taking small economic activities.

The major agencies that are engaged in this field are DRDA, NABARD, Mahila Samakhya and Women Development Corporation.

District Rural Development Agency (DRDA), it basically implements the anti-poverty programme of Ministry of Rural Development including SGSY. DRDA has many specialized wings including women wing, self-employment wing, wage employment wing, watershed wing, and Engineering and Accounts wing with Monitoring and Evaluation.

DRDA engages NGOs for the formation, facilitation, motivation, capacity-building, linkages to bank and providing facilities for marketing etc., of Self-Help Groups.

Muzaffarpur DRDA has engaged, NGOs for this purpose. The exhaustive lists of Panchayats allotted to them are given in the table at annexure.

Non-Government Organizations

NGOs have been actively involved since the beginning in mobilizing and organizing SHGs as part of externally funded programmes. Many of these NGOs have spent considerable time and efforts in training their staff on mobilization and organization of the community. This along with the limited area of operation and the close rapport with community places the NGOs in a relatively advantageous position for mobilizing and organizing the poor.

Apart from organizing their own groups, many NGOs through their cadres of field coordinators, animators and facilitators are involved not only in social mobilization and group formation but also in implementing the Government programmes either as anchor NGOs or as resource and training NGOs. In almost all the States under the aegis of NABARD, DRDA, DWCD, WDC, NGOs are actively involved in implementation of SGSY, Streeshakti and Swashakti and Swayamsiddha programmes.

Table 4.2: Facilitator in the Formation of SHGs

Name of Block	NGO		Government Official		Total	
	No.	%	No.	%	No.	%
Kanti	104	100	0	0	104	100
Sahebganj	107	97	3	3	110	100
Madwan	63	97	2	3	65	100
Kudhni	125	94	8	6	133	100
Paru	82	92	7	8	89	100
Total	*481*	*96*	*20*	*4*	*501*	*100*

The role of Goverment Officials in the formation of self-help groups was negligible. It was the NGOs, which played the main role in their formation, 96 per cent as against 4 per cent of Government Officials.

Role of NGO as Facilitator

NGOs are treated at par with the Government in implementation and coordinating various developmental programmes. In this direction, the NGOs are given complete autonomy and SHG members have also expressed their satisfaction with regard to their involvement in the programme and also the way they conducted training programmes and coordinated with various other agencies and consultants. The details of the responses are presented below:

Table 4.3: Satisfaction with Facilitator's Services

Name of Block	Yes		No		Total	
	No.	%	No.	%	No.	%
Kanti	102	100	0	0	102	100
Sahebganj	97	93	7	7	104	100
Madwan	46	75	15	25	61	100
Kudhni	114	93	8	7	122	100
Paru	80	99	1	1	81	100
Total	*439*	*93*	*31*	*7*	*470*	*100*

93 per cent members of the Self-Help Group were satisfied with the services provided by the facilitator, which were basically the members or employees of the NGOs. The table 4.4 shows the training provided to them by the NGOs.

Training Received

Table 4.4: Respondent's taken Training for formation of Groups

Name of Block	*Yes*		*No*		*Total*	
	No.	*%*	*No.*	*%*	*No.*	*%*
Kanti	90	87	14	13	104	100
Sahebganj	64	58	46	42	110	100
Madwan	18	28	47	72	65	100
Kudhni	91	68	42	32	133	100
Paru	88	99	1	1	89	100
Total	*351*	*70*	*150*	*30*	*501*	*100*

70 per cent had received training in conducting the affairs of the SHGs. The training curriculum included identification of the income generation activities, implementation, marketing, accounting etc. However, about 30 per cent of them have not received training at all.

Table 4.5: SHGs Formation under Schemes

Name of Block	*S.G.S.Y*		*Deep Priyojna*		*D.R.D.A* .		*SHG*		*Animal Husbandry*		*Don't Know*		*Total*	
	No.	*%*	*No.*	*%*	*No.*	*%*	*No.*	*%*	*No.*	*%*	*No.*	*%*	*No.*	*%*
Kanti	42	40	49	47		0		0		0	13	13	104	100
Sahebganj	95	86	1	1		0	7	6		0	7	6	110	100
Madwan	13	20	33	51	4	6		0	13	20	2	3	65	100
Kudhni	122	92		0		0		0		0	11	8	133	100
Paru	86	97		0		0		0		0	3	3	89	100
Total	*358*	*71*	*83*	*17*	*4*	*1*	*7*	*1*	*13*	*3*	*36*	*7*	*501*	*100*

Among the various schemes implemented in Muzaffarpur district, SHGs were formed in SGSY and Deep Priyojna schemes whereas in other schemes it was nil or negligible. The role of NGOs in this area is important and their involvement ensures smooth implementation.

Mahila Samakhya

Provision of educational opportunities for women has been an important part of the national agenda for empowering women through education since Independence. Though these endeavours did resulted significant results, gender disparities still persist with uncompromising tenacity, more in rural areas and that too among disadvantaged sections and under-priviliaged groups.

Keeping this view in mind, the National Policy on Education (NPE, 1986) was revised in 1992 which became a landmark in the field of policy on women's education is that it recognized the need to redress the issues related to traditional gender imbalances in the field of educational access.

Thus, education was viewed as an agent of bringing about basic change in the status of women and to neutralize the distortions in the past occurred. This led to the initiation and launching of Mahila Samakhya (MS) programme in 1987-89 in order to translate the goals of NPE into action by educationally empowering them particularly women from socially and economically marginalized communities. The MS programme was started with the objective of joining the women community with the mainstream of development.

Objective

- To enhance the self-image and self-confidence of women and thereby enabling them to recognize their contribution to the economy as producers and workers, reinforcing their need for participating in educational programmes.
- To create an environment where women can seek knowledge and information and thereby empower them to play a positive role in their own development and development of society.
- To establish a decentralized and participative mode of management, with the decision-making powers developed to the district level and to Mahila Sangha which in turn will provide the necessary conditions for effective participation.
- To enable Mahila Sangha to actively assist and monitor educational activities in the villages—including the primary school, AE, NFE Centres and facilities for continuing education.
- To provide women and adolescent girls with the necessary support structure and in informal learning environment to create opportunities for education.
- To set in motion circumstances for larger participation of women and girls in formal and non-formal educational programmes, and to create an environment in which education can serve the objectives of women's equality.

STATUS OF MAHILA SAMAKHYA: AN OVERVIEW[19]

Name of District	Blocks Covered	Panchayat Covered	Villages Mohalla Covered	Sahyoginis	Mahila Samooh	No. of Women in Samooh	Trained Samooh	Samooh Maintaning Thrift & Credit	Trained Sakhis	No. of Women in Thrift Credit only Samooh	SGSY	NABARD	Total Enrolment Villages
Rohtas	3	40	305	18	331	11718	127	389	663	10146	31	25	120
W Champaran	5	113	435	22	528	12109	289	434	860	7534	6	149	56
Muzaffarpur	5	105	410	23	923	18976	319	904	1297	13218	365	55	54
Sitamarhi	10	95	272	18	407	7168	480	324	738	5425	36	50	12
Darbhanga	2	49	227	13	277	5309	85	248	391	4017	103	0	0
Bhojpur	2	33	200	11	250	7935	209	163	261	2173	1		20
Gaya	3	33	349	19	465	11506	275	416	746	8681		4	76
Sheohar	3	23	89	5	146	2200	63	141	201	2145	12	6	0
Kaimur	2	24	164	14	116	2325	44	54	73	873			4
Supaul	3	33	100	9									
Banka	1	16	100	10									
Kishanganj	1	16	101	10									
Jamui	1	9	100										
TOTAL	*41*	*589*	*2852*	*172*	*3443*	*79246*	*2091*	*3073*	*5230*	*54212*	*554*	*289*	*342*

STATUS OF MAHILA SAMAKHYA: AN OVERVIEW[20]

	Jagjagi Centres				Bal Jagjagi				Kishori Manch				
Name of District	Jagjagi Centres	Women Enrolled in Jagjagi	Girls Enrolled in Jagjagi	Mainstreaming to Format School	Centres	Girls Enrolled	Boys Enrolled	Mainstreaming to Format School	Kishori Manch	Kishoris in Munch	Trained Kishoris	No. of Jhola Pustakalaya	M.S.K.
Rohtas	51	664	777	1718	70	1479	1277	3998	91	2546	741	21	1
W. Champaran	119	407	3086	4377	87	1387	1299	5424	108	2639	630	22	1
Muzaffarpur	215	948	6392	3032	134	2389	2021	5336	189	3383	1233	9	1
Sitamarhi	214	499	6647	684	96	1551	1442	2668	210	2171	1224	6	1
Darbhanga	155	185	3942						156	4184	447		1
Bhojpur	190	1889	3516	3659	107	2577	1831	1811	112	3272	293	6	1
Gaya	117	403	3032	366	85	1846	1447	570	127	5376	661	7	1
Sheohar	70	187	2358	101	63	1261	1012	156	70	1905	201	2	1
Kaimur	8	132	175	125	30	498	443	53	12	360	40	5	
Supaul													
Banka													
Kishanganj													
Jamui													
TOTAL	*1139*	*5314*	*29925*	*14062*	*672*	*12988*	*10772*	*20016*	*1069*	*25836*	*5470*	*78*	*8*

Coverage of the Programme

MS was firstly launched in Karnataka, Gujarat and Uttar Pradesh in 1989. It was then extended to Andhra Pradesh at the end of 1992 and in two districts in Kerala in 1998. The programme is currently being implemented in a total of 15823 villages spread over 63 districts in 9 States.

Table 4.6: Coverage of the Programme

Sl. No	*States*	*No. of Districts*	*No. of Villages*
1.	Assam	6	1591
2.	Andhra Pradesh	9	2383
3.	Bihar	9	2098
4.	Gujarat	7	1621
5.	Jharkhand	5	2480
6.	Karnataka	9	1566
7.	Kerala	2	221
8.	Uttar Pradesh	12	2765
9.	Uttaranchal	4	1098
	Total	*63*	*15823*

The average number of villages covered in each district ranges from 150 to 250 in the 10th Plan guideline, however, no of villages to be covered in a district have been laid which is 250 villages in order to demonstrate the impact of the Mahila Samakhya strategies.

Work Area

In Bihar, Mahila Samakhya is operating in 41 blocks of 13 districts. In Muzaffarpur district, it is operating in 5 blocks namely Mushari, Bochaha, Kudhni, Gaighat and Aurai.

The programme is implemented in 5287 villages in 33 districts of Uttar Pradesh, Uttranchal, Karnataka, Gujarat, Andhra Pradesh and Kerala. During the 10th Plan, the programme will be extended to 27 new districts, which are especially identified as educationally and socially backward States of Bihar, Jharkhand, Assam, Uttar Pradesh, Uttranchal, Karnataka and Andhra Pradesh.

Mahila Samakhya programme is also implemented in 2252 villages in U.P., Bihar, Madhya Pradesh and Assam. In U.P. 6 districts are covered while in Bihar, it is implemented in 7 districts. In M.P. and Assam, it is working in 3 districts respectively.

Training

Training is an important process for building and strengthening the values and vision of the programme. Training in MS is viewed as an ongoing activity rather than one-time event. Each training programme, either for the project functionaries or Sangha women, is itself a microcosm of the philosophy of the project. The traditional line between trainer and learner is systematically broken down, both engaging in a learning process. Training is experimental and the starting point is an acknowledgement of the experiences, strengths and potential of each individual. Experiences and insights gained in the implementation process becomes part of the training curriculum, in future.

In the environment of mutual support and trust created in the training interactions, women learn to take decisions, assume leadership qualities and evolve collective strategies to change their own destinies.

Training is done at several levels; to develop a gender perspective, sharpen the conceptual understanding of the programme philosophy and strategies, develop a critical faculty to respond flexibly to Sangha needs, enhance specific skills like communication and process documentation. It is also done to develop specialised understanding in sectors like health, resource management, legal literacy, appropriate technology and non-traditional skills among many others.

Training Process

Training is imparted to the women in the following four steps:

- *What is to be Imparted*—It includes providing training on the issues such as Gender, Leadership, Education, Health, Women's Right/Responsibilities, Panchayati Raj and Savings.
- *Whom to Impart*—It decides as to training to be provided to whom like it is to be given to Mahila Samuh, Saheli, Balmitra, Teenagers (Kishori), Master/Teacher and other Mahila Samakhya workers.
- *Evaluation*—It includes monitoring and evaluation of meetings at State, District, Block and Village level and also

regional tours/visits, analysis of the programme for further continuation.

- *Documentation*—It includes recording of minutes of the meetings conducted and preparation of monthly and yearly reports, preparing different formats of folders, pamphlets, newspapers, songs to be sung, slogans, reading materials, training materials etc.

As the programme has gained in strength and experience, a pool of trainers and resource persons have emerged from within the programme. The involvement of MS personnel as trainers to other programmes has become a vehicle for dissemination of the MS perspective, strategies and resource support for other sectors.

Projects run by Mahila Samakhya

(a) Swa-Shakti Project

The Swa-Shakti Project, also known as Rural Women's Development and Empowerment Project, was sanctioned on 16 October, 1998 as a Centrally-sponsored Project for a period of 5 years with an estimated outlay of Rs. 186.21 crore. In addition, an amount of Rs. 5 crore was provided for facilitating the setting up of Revolving Funds for giving interest-bearing loans to beneficiary groups primarily during their initial formative stage. The project aims at enhancing women's access to resources for better quality of life through use of drudgery and time reduction devices, health, literacy and confidence enhancement and increasing their control over their income through their involvement in skill development and income generating activities. The specific objectives of the project are:

Swa-Shakti Project in Bihar: The Swa-Shakti Project in Bihar is under implementation since June-1999. Subsequent to bifurcation of the State into Bihar and Jharkhand, this is running in six blocks of one district named Muzaffarpur. 448 groups has been formed with 19 federations which has been registered[21]. The project activities had been planned in phased manner to comply with the parameters set with regard to group nurturing and capacity-building for stakeholders and in accordance with the project objectives.

(b) Swawlamban

Swawlamban is a Centrally Sponsored Project through Mahila Samakhya having a project period of 2004-07. It is being implemented in 20 blocks of ten districts. 1011 Self-Help Groups were formed against the target of thousand groups in the project area, out of which 997 groups are linked to the banks and 531 groups are facilitated with the credit.

These 531 groups has saved Rs. 84.33 lakh and got the credit from bank in tune of Rs. 150.51 lakh. The most important thing is that it has been developed in 110 clusters and twenty federations have been so far formed and being registered[22].

Nirdesh

Nirdesh an NGO established in 1995 is operating from Majhaulia village, Post Khabara of Muzaffarpur district working in seven districts of Bihar namely, Muzaffarpur, Vaishali, East Champaran, West Champaran, Sitamarhi, Darbhanga and Madhubani districts.

Objectives

- ❖ Creating awareness among the marginalized men, women and youth on socio-economic issues and problems and ensure change for holistic development.
- ❖ Organizing more women's Self-Help Groups and federate them for Income Generating Activity Programmes.
- ❖ Incorporating the SHGs and the Cluster Level/Federated SHGs into Micro-Finance Institutions for economic development.
- ❖ Facilitating functional literacy to the disadvantaged, drop-outs and non-school going children as well as adult women SHGs for motivating and community-building process.
- ❖ Promoting livelihood opportunities through vocational and job oriented training to the illiterate boys and girls for employment opportunities.
- ❖ Addressing the need of vulnerable communities for disaster mitigation programme.
- ❖ Conducting community-based health education programme like—HIV/AIDS, Sex Education, Gender Sensitization etc.

and creating health funds to meet the needs of the disadvantaged.

- Ensuring participation of weaker sections of the people specially of women in the Panchayati Raj Institutions.
- Liaisoning, lobbying and advocating with Government, NGOs and Funding Agencies.
- Conducting action-based research and documentation for development process.
- Organizing various community-based training programme for rural and marginalized people.

Functional Areas

- Programme Support Services.
- Community-Based Skilled Development and Technical Support Services to the underprivileged stakeholders.
- Training and capacity building programmes to Panchayati Raj Institutions (PRIs) and Government run educational units.
- Women and Child Development Programmes for promotive, preventive and curative measures.
- Consultancy Services: Networking with Govt. and like minded Institutions/Organizations and Business Development, Service-need Assessment Study, Project Formulation, Pre-project appraisal on project services and support, Concurrent Monitoring and Evaluation.
- Research and Documentation, Networking and Linkages.
- To discharge its obligation as a better functionary of Lead NGOs.
- To establish as a Micro-Finance Institutions (MFIs) for community support.

Major Programmes and Projects

Following Projects are run by the NGO

- *Swa-Shakti*—It is rural women's development and empowerment programme supported by World Bank, IFAD and Government of India. In Bihar, it is implemented by WDC based in Patna the State Capital, Bihar who entrusted NIRDESH for implementing in the selected blocks of Muzaffarpur.

- *Swawalamban*: This project is sponsored by State Govt. owned WDC, Bihar. The basic objective of this programme is to organize women and form groups which are women centered, leading to an increase in their self-confidence, regained dignity and become the unit of local self-governance. The programme enabled the women to articulate their basic rights and needs for their demands and justice.

The project is being implemented in the Motihari and Raxaul blocks of East Champaran district. Here total no of SHGs formed are 201 and the membership in these groups is 2610. The cumulative savings of these groups are 19,21,878.00 and the credit turnover from the banks is around 19,75,000.00. The percentage of women engaged in economic activities is 60 per cent.

- *Deep Project*: This project is also supported by WDC which is for the empowerment of Dalit Women through formation of SHGs especially and exclusively for the Scheduled Caste women. The operational area of the programmes are Muzaffarpur, East Champaran and Darbhanga districts covering those blocks only where the percentage of SC women are more.

  The project was started in 2004. Total SHGs formed under it are 255 and the membership of these groups is 3464 out of which 1458 are women i.e. 42 per cent women are engaged in income generating activity. The cumulative savings of these groups are 11,37,561 and the credit turnover is 2,65,000.
- *SGSY—Nirdesh* has provided opportunity to 4140 women to start Income Generation Programme in order to ensure an increase in the economic and social bargain power of the poor families living below poverty line under Swarn Jayanti Swarozgar Yojana. The objective is being achieved by organizing rural women under one umbrella.

Hanuman Prasad Grameen Vikas Seva Samiti

Hanuman Prasad Grameen Vikas Seva Samiti was set up with the objective of breaking the hindrances like poverty, illiteracy, ignorance and hesitation existing among the women today. For this, it was felt necessary that the women community should be organized which was possible through SHGs. Through the group formation, the women were made aware of their rights. So for bringing about financial and social development amongst the women community, Hanuman Prasad Grameen Vikas Seva Samiti was set up in the year 1995 in Sakari Saraiya, Kudhni Block of Muzaffarpur. From 1999 onwards, the organization is working under the SGSY in Kudhni Block and is actively involved in strengthening and making successful the groups. The organization is working in different districts of Bihar; however the major work area is in Vaishali and Muzaffarpur.

Objectives

The main objective of the organization is to bring about self confidence among the women and girls and make them self independent. The organization also aims at creating awareness/ imparting information about the different schemes that are running by the Government.

Training Programme

With the objective of making the groups more empowered, training programmes at Block Level are organized by the organization. Under this training programme, information regarding formation of SHGs, participation in Panchayati Raj Institutions, preparation of time-table and minutes of the meetings conducted, and other related information required to strengthen the capacity of the group is imparted to them in these training programmes.

As a result of this training programme, the capacity-building of the groups already formed, took pace. As a result of this, the coordination between the Block Level Offiers (BDO), representatives of NGOs and SHGs increased resulting which, the opening of account in banks became easier. The North Region's Regional Rural Bank in Turki Branch is live example wherein the branch, more than 100 accounts of SHGs have been opened and all the groups are functioning smoothly.

Skill Up-gradation Training

Apart from laying emphasis on the capacity-building programme of the group, the skill up-gradation training programme is also in venture. For this, training workshop on Skill Up-gradation is also organized in the Training Centre at Sakari Saraiya where SHG Swarozgaries at block level are benefited. Through this training programme, useful information required to enhance the skills in order to improve the quality of their work is imparted which helps these groups in better functioning.

State Bank of India and SHG Bank Linkage Programme

State Bank of India is the first Commercial Bank to which NABARD has recently given SHPI status.

SBI has taken up SHG movement as a mission, a noble mission to reach those families who have no access to the credit by any formal or financial institution so they were depending on some informal sources and money-lenders.

Microfinance is not new to SBI. Bank's association with the NGOs in extending financial help can be traced far back as 1976, well before NABARD introduced SHG-Bank Credit Linkage Programme as a pilot project in 1992.

SBI is maintaining its position as a leader among Commercial Banks in credit linking of SHGs. At the end of March 2006, SBI's share was approx. 47 per cent of total SHGs financed by Commercial Banks which is far ahead of others.

Initiatives Undertaken by SBI

Bank has successfully initiated the following measures in widening SHG network:

- Sensitization of staff.
- Special training programmes in SHGs.
- Close liaison with NGOs.
- SHG cells.
- Lending to NGOs/Federations of SHGs.
- Sahayog Niwas.

- SBI Life-Shakti.
- Rural Training Institutes.
- SBI staff as SHPI.

Future Plans

SBI has set for itself an ambitious target of credit linking 1 million SHGs up to March 2008. Apart from that, the bank has also started to leverage out vast SHG network for various services.

Conclusion

Since independence, several welfare and developmental schemes and programmes have been put into action for the benefit of various sections of the society. Other then focusing on marginalized communities, Government of India's initiative in empowering women is a major programme. Some of the prominent programmes for women were in education, economic activities, health and social sectors. Schemes like girl child's education, Reproductive and child health, Self-Help Groups in economic fronts etc. has gradually changed the outlook of the women. Women have become socially and economically independent and decision-makers in the family as well as in the society.

Similar changes can also be observed among marginalized communities. Economic programmes/schemes have helped them in raising their social standard in the society.

Notes

1. www.rural.nic.in
2. SGSY Guidelines, Ministry of Rural Development, *Para 7.1*—For any goods or services that are produced, existence of a suitable market is essential. Traditionally, the self-employment programmes concentrated on the inputs rather than the outputs and their marketing. It was not uncommon to find production strategies in place of overlooking the market aspects. One often finds that the recommendation of an activity is not proceeded by the much needed market survey. There is a false notion that market surveys are not required in case of the self-employment opportunities for the rural

poor. In fact, it is as critical, if not more, for the poor. For, he/she cannot sustain the loss arising out of a lack of market even for short period. It is, therefore, necessary that the project profile of every key activity identify the market availability. The forecast of the incomes to be earned by the Swarozgari must take into account this factor and forecast the incomes only on the basis of an assured market. This would be a critical factor in the choice of the key activity itself.

- *Para 7.2*: It is possible that this might appear to be formidable proposition and that the field functionaries might feel that they are unequal to the task. Happily, this is not so. While to most of us, market mechanism may appear unintelligible and a complex task, in reality it means checking out what sells and what does not. Goods and services are traded every day in all parts of the country. What is needed is to see what sells in the local markets. A study conducted some years ago for the Ministry of Rural Development indicated that the Rural Haats (markets) play a significant role. An analysis of these markets therefore reveals the opportunities. Secondly, an analysis of the daily requirements, either for personal use or in agriculture and exploring ways of meeting the demand locally; can leads to some useful results. At times, the product concerned might require some promotional activity in order to raise demand.
- *Para 7.3*: A study of the local markets might reveal that what the villagers purchase can as well be produced locally. The opportunities must be fully explored. At the same time, it must be remembered that it is neither feasible nor desirable to produce all goods in all places. The choice of activity therefore must be governed by the possibilities that exist on account of the resources of an area, the available skills and the market. It is always possible to develop the skills or even the markets but this must be weighed against the fact that it would require time and effort.
- *Para 7.4:* Next in the importance are the markets in urban areas. There is an increasing trend towards urbanization in the country alongwith a change of consumer tastes and demands. The goods in demand could be in the primary sector or otherwise. An analysis of these urban markets would reveal the consumer preferences and the potential for the rural entrepreneurs. There can be a good potential for value added items, such as cleaned and packaged

food items, processed fruit and vegetables etc. The emerging urban markets can be a good area for developing clientele for the rural products. Provision of marketing infrastructure in these areas can go a long way in enabling the rural poor to market their goods and at the same time building an identity for the products. The Self-Help Groups can be encouraged to try out these markets on their own so that they slowly develop marketing skills. They can also start marketing the goods of the individual Swarozgaris. Infrastructure fund can be use for strengthening marketing infrastructure and related activities.

3. SGSY Guidelines, Ministry of Rural Development, *Para 7.5*: The marketing of goods outside the districts requires an intermediary agency. This can be in the governmental, non-governmental or private sector. The one aspect that requires to be taken care of is the stability of the agency, their own competence and their capacity to ensure that the rural producer is getting his/her fair share of the profits. Care should be taken to see that only such agencies that do not exploit the rural producers and are well established in the business are chosen for the purpose. These agencies may market the products in the national or international markets.

   - *Para 7.6:* Some State Governments have established District Supply and Marketing Societies (DSMS) to provide non-credit inputs like procurement or purchase of raw-material and also for sale of products. Wherever these societies are doing good work, they can be suitably strengthened. Similarly, in States such as Orissa and Kerala, there are marketing societies at the State level. Their capacity and product range can be suitably expanded. However, it is not always necessary to establish new agencies. It should be a felt need after a careful analysis of the existing infrastructure, and should be part of a strategy for promotion of marketing support to products under SGSY.
   - *Para 7.7*: Organisations like Handicrafts Boards and Handloom Corporations and also KVI C/KVIB can play a prominent role in promotion of SGSY. The marketing outlets of KVIC/KVIB must be made use of for SGSY products. Keeping the market trends in view, linkages with apex bodies can ensure a stable market at remunerative prices. Such a link will also result in quality improvements while reducing the market risks to the poor, Bankers can also encourage such initiatives through liberal credit

delivery since the loan recovery can be built into the project. There are several NGO and other independent institutions to market product from rural artisans/craftsmen across the country. DRDAs should strive to develop linkages with such groups.

- *Para 7.8*: A few States have organized Melas to give publicity to the range of products produced by the Swarozgaris. Such efforts need further encouragement so that SGSY Swarozgaris will be integrated with the regional markets. Organizing of exhibitions periodically in urban centres will offer better price to the goods of SGSY Swarozgaris. This also serves as forum for sensitizing the SGSY group to the demand patterns of the market. The State level organizations and boards have to develop an organic link with the SGSY Groups and provide virtual linkage. Thus, professional bodies can guide the poor in supply of designs and in quality assurance. Attempts to establish State emporia for display and sales of SGSY Products in major urban cities need to be given a fair trial.
- *Para 7.9*: Quality of products is vital not only for the development of entrepreneurs but also for the nation as a whole. It must be the responsiblity of the marketing agencies to ensure that the Swarozgaris are trained in quality control. The goods marketed must conform to a minimum and uniform quality so as to be able to develop a brand image. This is important even in respect of the goods that are produced for local consumption. The DRDAs must organize periodic meets of the Swarozgaris and ensure that they are given the necessary guidance in quality control. There must also be a system of the experts in the relevant fields visiting the work places and guiding the Swarozgaris.

4. Press Release of Ministry of Rural Development dated 17th April, 2007 at the occasion of Basant Saras at Dilli Hat.
5. Y. Gangi Reddy, Role of Melas in Marketing of Rurals Industries Products, *Animpact Study of Grams Shree Melas*, 2006.
6. Report of SGSY division, Ministry of Rural Development, Governmnt of India.
7. Performance of Programmes of Rural Development, Ministry of Rural Development, as on 20 April, 2007.
8. *Swarnjayanti Gram SwarozgarYojana* (SGSY), Agenda for the 10th Meeting of the Central Level Co-ordination Committee (CLCC), Ministry of Rural Development.

9. *Swarnjayanti Gram SwarozgarYojana* (SGSY), Agenda for the 10th Meeting of the Central Level Co-ordination Committee (CLCC), Ministry of Rural Development.
10. *Swarnjayanti Gram SwarozgarYojana* (SGSY), Agenda for the 10th Meeting of the Central Level Co-ordination Committee (CLCC), Ministry of Rural Development.
11. Performance of Programmes of Department of Rural Development, Department of Land Resources, Department of Drinking Water Supply, Ministry of Rural Development.
12. Monthly Report of Feb, 2007 submitted by Muzaffapur District.
13. Report of Women Development Corporation, Bihar, 2007.
14. Report of Women Development Corporation, Bihar, 2007.
15. *ibid*
16. Women Development Corporation is an autonomous society established under the umbrella of Bihar State Government.
17. Report of Women Development Corporation, Bihar, 2007.
18. Malcolm Harper, "Promotion of Self-Help Groups under the SHG Bank Linkage Programme in India", New Delhi, Nov., 2002.
19. Monthly Report of January, 2007 submitted by Bihar Government.
20. Monthly Report of January, 2007 submitted by Bihar Government.
21. Report of Women Development Corporation, Bihar, 2007.
22. Report of Women Development Corporation, Bihar, 2007.

Chapter Five

Social Impact of SHGs on Marginalised Communities

The Government's policies and plans are made with a view to benefit all sections of the society but it has been found that due to various reasons like low educational status, poor socio-economic conditions and lack of information has left a sizeable section of the society in the process of development. Scheduled Castes, Scheduled Tribes and other minorities are the excluded communities of the society who are devoid of all the facilities and benefits provided by the Government. Representatives of these groups were very elusive in their responses towards the Government's policies and programmes basically due to the fact that such benefits do not reach them. It was strongly felt during discussions with them that a strong and cohesive group would be a better option in putting forth the problems and in some cases the solutions, thereof. In this case it was felt necessary that the backward and marginalized community member are trained to accept the challenges and always find solutions despite the fact that they have been subjugated for many years.

The 1960's decade saw strong women's liberation movement all over the world which has helped the women to empower themselves in various facets of life. But these have not helped women of rural areas and also other backward and marginal communities in uplifting themselves and lead decent life. But over the years this movement has gained momentum and women were respected and their views were seriously taken into consideration.

In the 1990's, Self-Help Group became an effective tool for economic development, social change, change in attitude and an organisation for building of self-confidence. It is a medium of learning, educating, communicating and capacity-building.

Moreover, the groups motivate and mobilise people to fight against the social evils. A nation cannot think of attaining a position amongst the developed nations when a large section of society remains socially and economically backward.

Social Composition of the Respondents

The present section has dealt in great details the social situation of the marginalized communities. Thus, these groups were minutely scrutinized and the following responses have emerged. Some of the responses are spontaneous, sometimes probing too was done.

However, it needs to be mentioned here that each Table has been presented in capsule form instead of lengthy discussions as it would be repetitive and would not yield fruitful summarization. Wherever, necessary the essence has been included in the text.

Religion[1]

India is a multi-religious nation. All religions are respected though the number of persons in each religion following may vary from State to State.

As the study focuses on marginalized groups, scheduled castes and tribes, it was felt necessary to include Hindus (largest religious group) and Muslims (second largest group) as both the religions have rigid vertical hierarchy (not allowing upward mobility) and those who are in the lower rung of the hierarchy are devoid of all benefits of the Government.

Table 5.1 gives the details of the respondents by religious break-up.

Table 5.1: Respondents by Religion

Name of Block	*Hindus*		*Muslims*		*Total*	
	No.	*%*	*No.*	*%*	*No.*	*%*
Kanti	70	67	34	33	104	100
Sahebganj	76	69	34	31	110	100
Madwan	59	91	6	9	65	100
Kudhni	109	82	24	18	133	100
Paru	85	96	4	4	89	100
Total	*399*	*80*	*102*	*20*	*501*	*100*

80 per cent of the respondents belonged to Hindu religion and block-wise distribution shows that Hindus have outnumbered Muslims among all the five blocks.

Social Groups

The study focused on respondents belonging to Scheduled Castes, Scheduled Tribes, Backward Castes and Muslims. But respondents from general category too were included in the study. The following **Table 5.2** gives social composition of the respondents:

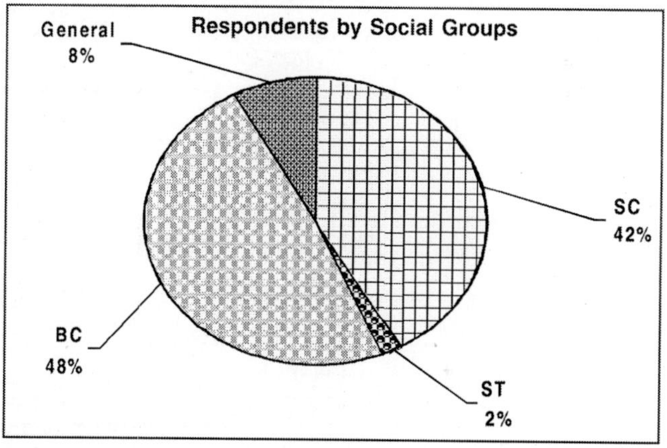

Table 5.2: Respondents by Social Groups

Name of Block	SC		ST		BC		General		Total	
	No.	%	No.	%	No.	%	No.	%	No.	%
1. Kanti	65	63	1	1	38	37		0	104	100
2. Sahebganj	42	38	2	2	50	45	16	15	110	100
3. Madwan	35	54	2	3	28	43		0	65	100
4. Kudhni	38	29	3	2	72	54	20	15	133	100
5. Paru	31	35		0	56	63	2	2	89	100
Total	*211*	*42*	*8*	*2*	*244*	*49*	*38*	*8*	*501*	*100*

Majority of Muslims belonged to Backward Caste and among Hindus it is the Scheduled Caste. The percentage is almost negligible in case of tribal. The benefits and programmes are equally chalked out for such deprived groups by the Government. The same analysis is presented in diagrammatic form also.

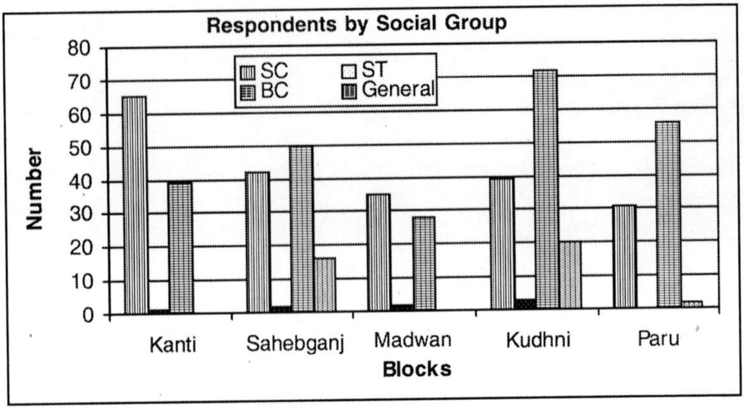

Age of the Respondents

Age is an important demographic indicator. The following two **Tables 5.3 and 5.4** are related to age and their explanation has been given below:

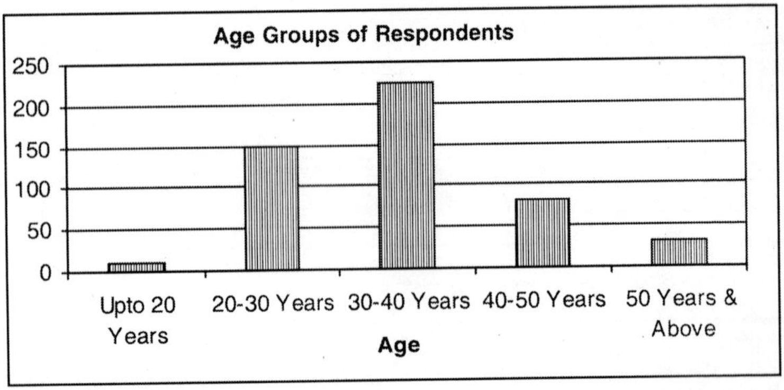

Table 5.3: Respondents by Age: Religion-wise

Age/Category	*Hindus*		*Muslims*		*Total*	
	No.	*%*	*No.*	*%*	*No.*	*%*
Upto 20	9	2	1	1	10	2
20-30 Years	122	31	28	27	150	30
30-40 Years	184	46	42	41	226	45
40-50 Years	63	16	24	24	87	17
50 Years and Above	21	5	7	7	28	6
Total	*399*	*100*	*102*	*100*	*501*	*100*

Table 5.4: Respondents by Age: Social Group-wise

Age / Category	*SC*		*ST*		*BC*		*General*		*Total*	
	No.	*%*	*No.*	*%*	*No.*	*%*	*No.*	*%*	*No.*	*%*
Upto 20	6	3		0	3	1	1	3	10	2
20-30 Years	70	33	2	25	63	26	15	39	150	30
30-40 Years	90	43	5	63	111	45	20	53	226	45
40-50 Years	38	18		0	47	19	2	5	87	17
50 Years and Above	7	3	1	13	20	8		0	28	6
Total	*211*	*100*	*8*	*100*	*244*	*100*	*38*	*100*	*501*	*100*

Majority of the respondents (about 75%) belonging to both religious and social groups were in the age groups of 20-30 years and 30-40 years. This age is considered to be prime age to undertake risks and accept challenges in life. As a matter of fact, most of the Government programmes are directed towards the population belonging to this age group.

The learning capacity compounded by physical energy leads to initiation of new enterprises. Age group of the respondents is shown in the following graph.

Educational Status

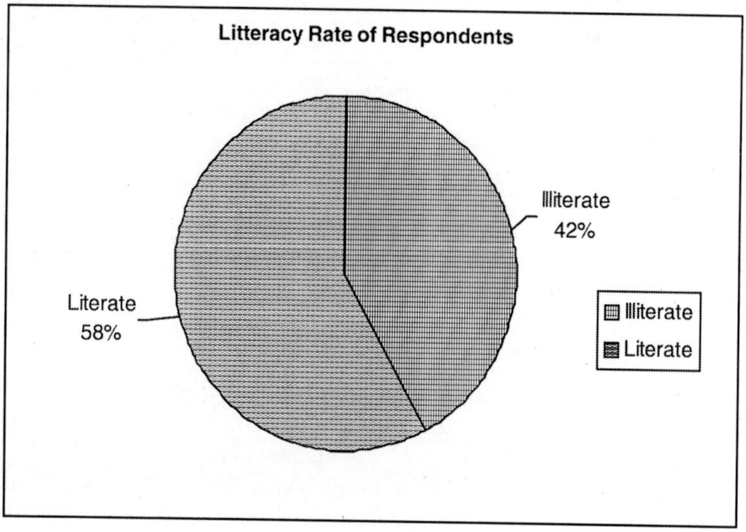

Table 5.5: Respondents by Education: Social Group-wise

Education Level	SC		ST		BC		General		Total	
	No.	%	No.	%	No.	%	No.	%	No.	%
Illiterate	95	45	5	63	97	40	12	32	209	42
Literate	60	28	1	13	86	35	4	11	151	30
Primary	17	8		0	17	7	1	3	35	7
Middle	18	9	1	13	23	9	5	13	47	9
High School	13	6		0	14	6	7	18	34	7
Intermediate	3	1	1	13	7	3	6	16	17	3
Graduate and Above	5	2		0		0	3	8	8	2
Total	*211*	*100*	*8*	*100*	*244*	*100*	*38*	*100*	*501*	*100*

42 per cent of the respondents are illiterate, the rate of illiteracy is highest amongst ST community (63%) followed by SC community (45%) and BC community (40%). The percentage is very low for matriculates, it is just 7 per cent, it is 6 per cent for SC and BC community. College education seems to be a dream.

Table 5.6: Respondents by Education: Religion-wise

Education Level	Hindus		Muslims		Total	
	No.	%	No.	%	No.	%
Illiterate	166	42	43	42	209	42
Just Literate	106	27	45	44	151	30
Primary	31	8	4	4	35	7
Middle	42	11	5	5	47	9
High School	30	8	4	4	34	7
Intermediate	16	4	1	1	17	3
Graduate and Above	8	2		0	8	2
Total	*399*	*100*	*102*	*100*	*501*	*100*

The percentage of illiterates among both the social groups is the same. As the level of education is increasing, the percentage of respondents receiving education decreases. The percentage of just literates amongst Muslim community is very high (44%) mainly due to their interest in small entrepreneur or self-employment.

Table 5.7: Enrolled in Adult Education Centres: Social Group-wise

Yes/No	SC		ST		BC		General		Total	
	No.	%	No.	%	No.	%	No.	%	No.	%
Yes	88	42	4	50	98	40	23	61	213	43
No	123	58	4	50	146	60	15	39	288	57
Total	*211*	*100*	*8*	*100*	*244*	*100*	*38*	*100*	*501*	*100*

The response to enrolment in adult education centers among the illiterate respondents is satisfactory, a gift of Self-Help Group to its members. The awareness and motivation are the bye-product of Self Help Groups. The enrolment percentage is higher for the group in which there are more illiterate. Out of 45 per cent illiterate SC community 42 per cent enrolled for Adult Education, and almost all the illiterate of BC community enrolled for it.

Table 5.8: Enrolled in Adult Education Centres: Religion-wise

Yes/No	Hindus		Muslims		Total	
	No.	%	No.	%	No.	%
Yes	160	40	53	52	213	43
No	239	60	49	48	288	57
Total	*399*	*100*	*102*	*100*	*501*	*100*

Not only the illiterates but a sizeable portion of just literates also joined the adult education centers.

42 per cent of Muslims are illiterate and 44 per cent are just literate, out of that 52 per cent joined the adult education. Out of 42 per cent illiterate Hindu community 40 per cent joined the Adult Education Centres.

Table 5.9: Enrolled in Adult Education Centres: Age-wise

Age/Group	Yes		No		Total	
	No.	%	No.	%	No.	%
Upto 20	7	3	3	1	10	2
20-30 Years	69	32	81	28	150	30
30-40 Years	83	39	143	50	226	45
40-50 Years	38	18	49	17	87	17
50 Years and Above	16	8	12	4	28	6
Total	*213*	*100*	*288*	*100*	*501*	*100*

The age-wise response for enrolment in adult education is directly proportional to the age-wise proportion of the respondents.

Marital Status[2] and Size of Family

Marriage and family are two stable and recognized institutions. India has rich traditional family values and respect for elders and women can be seen in urban as well as in rural areas.

Marriage is considered to be important and its percentage is very high in rural areas. The following Tables give details of marital status and family size of the respondents.

Table 5.10: Respondents by Marital Status

Name of Block	Married		Un-Married		Total	
	No.	%	No.	%	No.	%
Kanti	104	100		0	104	100
Sahebganj	106	96	4	4	110	100
Madwan	64	98	1	2	65	100
Kudhni	120	90	13	10	133	100
Paru	88	99	1	1	89	100
Total	*482*	*96*	*19*	*4*	*501*	*100*

It is important to note that 96 per cent of the people interviewed were mature and married.

Table 5.11: Size of the Family

Name of Block	No. of Members						Total	
	Upto 2		3 to 5		6 to 10			
	No.	%	No.	%	No.	%	No.	%
Kanti	3	3	52	50	49	47	104	100
Sahebganj	6	5	65	59	39	35	110	100
Madwan	5	8	33	51	27	42	65	100
Kudhni	12	9	79	59	42	32	133	100
Paru	9	10	43	48	37	42	89	100
Total	*35*	*7*	*272*	*54*	*194*	*39*	*501*	*100*

The respondents had one to six children, but most of them had just one to three children. Fifty per cent of them said that they were using family planning methods. Inspite of this, 93 per cent had more than 2 children. It means that either the family planning methods used were ineffective or not used regularly.

Table 5.12: Size of the Family: Religion-wise

No. of Members	Hindus		Muslims		Total	
	No.	%	No.	%	No.	%
Upto 2	25	6	10	10	35	7
3-5	222	56	50	49	272	54
6-10	151	38	42	41	193	39
11 and Above	1	0		0	1	0
Total	*399*	*100*	*102*	*100*	*501*	*100*

Table 5.13: Size of the Family: Social Group-wise

No. of Members	SC		ST		BC		General		Total	
	No.	%	No.	%	No.	%	No.	%	No.	%
Upto 2	16	8		0	18	7	1	3	35	7
3-5	117	55	5	63	125	51	25	66	272	54
6-10	77	36	3	38	101	41	12	32	193	39
11 and Above	1	0		0		0		0	1	0
Total	*211*	*100*	*8*	*100*	*244*	*100*	*38*	*100*	*501*	*100*

An interesting trend can be seen from the above Tables showing the family size among religious groups and social groups. Quite a high percentage of the respondents had children between 3-5. This figure is almost equal to Hindus as well as to Muslims. The respondents have disproved the tall claims made by the Government in curbing the population as each family had more than two children (which is the norm of the Government's Family Welfare Programme).

It needs to be mentioned here that the developmental planning in such areas have been failure due to excessive population and also the disbursement of funds are based on factors like unemployment ratio, feasibility and willingness of the people, availability of resources etc.

Keeping in view the above-mentioned factors, any amount that is put into the district does not reach all sections of the society and thus a vast majority remains deprived of the benefits.

Family

Family[3] is most respected and dependable institution. The institution of family has existed since time immemorial and the values attached to it still exist. However, there is change in the pattern of family but the respect and status of elders is still maintained. This is more so in rural areas rather than in urban areas. The joint family is gradually disintegrating in urban areas due to several reasons like space constraint, high cost of living, emotional adjustment problems etc. Family ties are strong in rural areas and all members jointly stay together. Family values and emotional attachment among each other are presented in the following Tables:

Table 5.14: Respondents' Family by Type: Religion-wise

Family Type	*Hindus*		*Muslims*		*Total*	
	No.	*%*	*No.*	*%*	*No.*	*%*
Nuclear	86	22	28	27	114	23
Joint	313	78	74	73	387	77
Total	*399*	*100*	*102*	*100*	*501*	*100*

Table 5.15: Respondents' Family by Type: Social Group-wise

Family Type	*SC*		*ST*		*BC*		*General*		*Total*	
	No.	*%*	*No.*	*%*	*No.*	*%*	*No.*	*%*	*No.*	*%*
Nuclear	50	24	2	25	54	22	8	21	114	23
Joint	161	76	6	75	190	78	30	79	387	77
Total	*211*	*100*	*8*	*100*	*244*	*100*	*38*	*100*	*501*	*100*

Table 5.16: Type of Family

Name of Block	*Nuclear*		*Joint*		*Total*	
	No.	*%*	*No.*	*%*	*No.*	*%*
Kanti	21	20	83	80	104	100
Sahebganj	33	30	77	70	110	100
Madwan	18	28	47	72	65	100
Kudhni	18	14	115	86	133	100
Paru	24	27	65	73	89	100
Total	*114*	*23*	*387*	*77*	*501*	*100*

As per the study 77 per cent of the respondents belongs to rural areas of the Muzaffarpur, it can be seen that lived in joint family system. The size of the family varies from 5 to 10 persons. Quite a high percentage of Muslims too preferred joint family to nuclear family.

Establishment of Self Help-Groups

The SHG movement started in 1990s. The rate of adoption of SHG scheme was rather slow in most of the places. This was due to various factors like low literacy level, apathy towards Government schemes, no initiative and enthusiasm from the people and above all tardiness at district level government officials. Despite all the factors, the SHG scheme was implemented in all the blocks of Muzaffarpur from the year 2001. The details are presented below:

Table 5.17: Year of SHGs Establishment

Name of Block	*2001*		*2002*		*2003*		*2004*		*2005*		*2006*		*Total*	
	No.	*%*	*No.*	*%*	*No.*	*%*	*No.*	*%*	*No.*	*%*	*No.*	*%*	*No.*	*%*
Kanti	5	5	13	13	9	9	54	52	23	22		0	104	100
Sahebganj		0	3	3	7	6	33	30	56	51	11	10	110	100
Madwan	16	25	10	15		0	4	6	35	54		0	65	100
Kudhni	1	1	36	27	2	2		0	60	45	34	26	133	100
Paru		0	47	53	20	22	13	15		0	9	10	89	100
Total	*22*	*4*	*109*	*22*	*38*	*8*	*104*	*21*	*174*	*35*	*54*	*11*	*501*	*100*

All the respondents selected for the study are members of SHGs. They became members since 2001 and those who joined recently belonged to 2006 batch. 22 of them were members from as early as 2001. Only 54 (11%) were new members (joined in 2006).

Group Composition and Status

Group dynamism plays an important role in the rural situation. There are certain groups, which do not have compatibility with others. But the SHG scheme has brought together people from all groups/religions together. Members of religious and social groups who have opted SHG scheme are presented in the following Tables 5.18 and 5.19:

More and more women have started taking interest and opted to join for learning and earning from this scheme. All the respondents are women.

Table 5.18: Respondents/SHG Members: Religion-wise

Name of Block	Hindus		Muslims		Total	
	No.	%	No.	%	No.	%
Kanti	70	18	34	33	104	21
Sahebganj	76	19	34	33	110	22
Madwan	59	15	6	6	65	13
Kudhni	109	27	24	24	133	27
Paru	85	21	4	4	89	18
Total	*399*	*100*	*102*	*100*	*501*	*100*

Table 5.19: Respondents/SHG Members: Social Group-wise

Name of Block	SC		ST		BC		General		Total	
	No.	%	No.	%	No.	%	No.	%	No.	%
Kanti	65	31	1	13	38	16		0	104	21
Sahebganj	42	20	2	25	50	20	16	42	110	22
Madwan	35	17	2	25	28	11		0	65	13
Kudhni	38	18	3	38	72	30	20	53	133	27
Paru	31	15		0	56	23	2	5	89	18
Total	*211*	*100*	*8*	*100*	*244*	*100*	*38*	*100*	*501*	*100*

Involvement and Participation of Respondents in SHG Activities

The aim of SHG is to mobilize women from different groups to plan future activities and create more income generation activities. Meetings are regularly held and participation in it is mandatory. A majority of women despite their commitments at home attend the meetings.

The **Tables 5.20 and 5.21** give details of participation of the members (both religion and group-wise) in the meetings held:

Table 5.20: Frequency of Participation in SHG Meetings: Religion-wise

Frequency of Participation	Hindus		Muslims		Total	
	No.	%	No.	%	No.	%
Regular	368	92	92	90	460	92
Sometimes	31	8	10	10	41	8
Total	*399*	*100*	*102*	*100*	*501*	*100*

Almost equal number of Hindu and Muslim members attended the SHG meetings.

Table 5.21: Frequency of Participation in SHG Meetings: Social Group-wise

Frequency of Participation	*SC*		*ST*		*BC*		*General*		*Total*	
	No.	*%*	*No.*	*%*	*No.*	*%*	*No.*	*%*	*No.*	*%*
Regular	186	88	7	88	230	94	37	97	460	92
Sometimes	25	12	1	13	14	6	1	3	41	8
Total	*211*	*100*	*8*	*100*	*244*	*100*	*38*	*100*	*501*	*100*

The participation of the BC group was significantly higher. But the general group's participation has been highest.

Membership in SHG

On an average the total number of members in SHG is 10-15 but there is flexibility in the number of persons who can join the Group. The membership count goes up to 18. **Table 5.22** gives total number of members from different blocks of Muzaffarpur.

Table 5.22: No. of Members Per SHG

Name of Block	*Average Members*	*Upto 10*		*11 to 15*		*16 & Above*		*Total*	
		No.	*%*	*No.*	*%*	*No.*	*%*	*No.*	*%*
Kanti	13	5	5	99	95		0	104	100
Sahebganj	11	56	51	54	49		0	110	100
Madwan	11	30	46	29	45	6	9	65	100
Kudhni	10	124	93	9	7		0	133	100
Paru	10	65	73	24	27		0	89	100
Total	*11*	*280*	*56*	*215*	*43*	*6*	*1*	*501*	*100*

As can be see from the above Table, the SHGs from all the blocks had about 10 to 13 members. This is the average norm in Muzaffarpur.

Grading of the SHGs

Based upon the membership strength, activities, money collected, disbursement of loan etc. the SHGs are given grades. The best are those, which fulfil all the criteria. The grading of SHGs is done for the blocks, religion and group composition and it is presented in **Table 5.23**

Table 5.23: Grading of SHGs

Name of Block	*Not Graded Yet*		*Grade I*		*Grade II*		*Total*	
	No.	*%*	*No.*	*%*	*No.*	*%*	*No.*	*%*
Kanti	74	71	18	17	12	12	104	100
Sahebganj	65	59	22	20	23	21	110	100
Madwan	41	63	7	11	17	26	65	100
Kudhni	99	74	16	12	18	14	133	100
Paru	10	11	25	28	54	61	89	100
Total	*289*	*58*	*88*	*18*	*124*	*25*	*501*	*100*

As the concept of SHG is new, the members were not aware about the criteria on which they were graded. The SHG were placed in three grades. 58 per cent were not graded whereas only 54 (11%) were new established SHGs, during 2006. A group can attain grade I in six months but it is a matter of concern that there are SHGs of two to three years standing having grade I only. Similarly, for grade II further six months should be enough but unfortunately, there are delays. The grading process delayed mainly due to apathetic approach from bank and block officials and their non-availability for grading. This led to de-motivation and dysfunction of the group.

Table 5.24: Grading of Groups: Religion-wise

Grade of Groups	*Hindus*		*Muslims*		*Total*	
	No.	*%*	*No.*	*%*	*No.*	*%*
Grade I	55	14	33	32	88	18
Grade II	96	24	28	27	124	25
Not Graded	248	62	41	40	289	58
Total	*399*	*100*	*102*	*100*	*501*	*100*

Table 5.25: Grading of Groups: Social Group-wise

Grade of Groups	SC		ST		BC		General		Total	
	No.	%	No.	%	No.	%	No.	%	No.	%
Grade I	20	9		0	59	24	9	24	88	18
Grade II	39	18		0	82	34	3	8	124	25
Not Graded	152	72	8	100	103	42	26	68	289	58
Total	*211*	*100*	*8*	*100*	*244*	*100*	*38*	*100*	*501*	*100*

The data shows that the group having Muslims and BC and general category members attain grade I and grade II relatively higher, may be because they were relatively better aware of the norms and having better accessibility to the officials. SCs, STs and weaker castes amongst the Muslims and BCs were left out of the periodic evaluation and consequently they did not get financial and technical support from the Government, Banks and NGOs.

Selection of Office Bearers

For effective and smooth management of the programme, it is necessary to have elected office-bearers. The designations may be as per the choice of the committee and accordingly the following designations have been decided for the office bearers at Muzaffarpur. The details can be seen in the **Table 5.26**.

Table 5.26: Designation of Respondents in the Group: Religion-wise

Designation	Hindu		Muslims		Total	
	No.	%	No.	%	No.	%
President	93	23	22	22	115	23
Secretary	55	14	11	11	66	13
Treasurer	22	6	3	3	25	5
Member	239	57	66	65	295	59
Total	*399*	*100*	*102*	*100*	*501*	*100*

There appears to be no discrimination in the selection to the posts of President, Secretary and Treasurer, as religion did not play an important role. The selection appears to be fair and almost equal percentage of Presidents belonged to Hindus and Muslims and some variations found in case of other positions.

Table 5.27: Office Holders in the Group: Social Group-wise

Designation	SC		ST		BC		General		Total	
	No.	%	No.	%	No.	%	No.	%	No.	%
President	54	26	2	25	45	18	14	37	115	23
Secretary	21	10		0	40	16	5	13	66	13
Treasurer	11	5	1	13	10	4	3	8	25	5
Member	125	59	5	63	149	61	16	42	295	59
Total	*211*	*100*	*8*	*100*	*244*	*100*	*38*	*100*	*501*	*100*

Similarly, variations found in the office positions for various social groups. The higher percentage of office positions were held by general groups followed by other groups.

Views of Government and Non-Government Officials Regarding SHG Scheme

Other stakeholders like Bank Officials, Government Officials and Representatives of NGOs were contacted to get their opinion about the scheme. The officials who were interviewed were Karamcharies and Panchayat Sewaks at grass root level, Lady Extension Officer and Industries Extension Officer involved in the process at supervisory level, Block Development Officer and Deputy Development Commissioner (Project Director) at district level. Twenty officers from the banks recorded their views on the scheme. Amongst them sixteen were at Manager level and three are from field officer level.

Three Officers belonged to Sahebganj, seven from Saraiyya seven from Paru and three from Kurhani block.

Awareness about Various Governmental Schemes

The impact of Self-Help Groups on the level of their awareness, attitude towards education, health, marriage and family welfare etc. have been dealt with detail. The changes in their social status, living standard and response towards social issues and decision taking capacities have also been studied.

The level of awareness about different development schemes, differed between Hindu and Muslim members. A large percentage of Hindu members were aware of the SGSY (88%) and Pradhan Mantri Rojgar Yojana. The least known schemes among them were NREGA followed by BMDFC/BSIFDC.

Table 5.28: Awareness about Schemes after becoming a SHG Member: Religion-wise

Awareness about Scheme	Hindus		Muslims		Total	
	Aware	%	Aware	%	No.	%
SGSY	352	88	78	76	430	86
NREGA	127	32	23	23	150	30
Old Age Pension	305	76	82	80	387	77
National Family Benefit Yojana	223	56	52	51	275	55
National Maternity Benefit Yojana	249	62	54	53	303	60
Widow Pension Yojana	277	69	66	65	343	68
Assistance to Handicapped and Orphan Scheme	223	56	48	47	271	54
Annapurna Scheme	275	69	63	62	338	67
Indira Aawas Yojana	258	65	65	64	323	64
Pradhan Mantri Rojgar Yojana	279	70	65	64	344	69
BMDFC/BSIFDC	185	46	43	42	228	46
Total Respondents	*399*	*100*	*102*	*100*	*501*	*100*

The trend was different among the Muslim members. Largest number was aware of Old Age Pension followed by SGSY. The least popular of the schemes were the same between both the groups.

It seems extra efforts have to be made for the awareness about NREGA and BMDFC schemes by the District and field officers.

Similar level of awareness of the respondents could be seen belonging to different social groups with regard to awareness about various schemes. The most aware group belonged to the General Category but they were not covered by many of the schemes. In some case, it is the girl child belonging to General Category who is benefited by mid-day meal/scholarship/free books and uniforms etc. Respondents belonging to Scheduled Castes and Backward Caste were also aware of most of the schemes.

Table 5.29: Awareness about Scheme after becoming a SHG Member: Social Group-wise

Awareness about Scheme	*SC*		*ST*		*BC*		*General*		*Total*	
	Aware	*%*	*Aware*	*%*	*Aware*	*%*	*Aware*	*%*	*Aware*	*%*
SGSY	185	88	7	88	204	84	34	89	430	86
NREGA	161	76	6	75	180	74	31	82	378	75
Old Age Pension	163	77	6	75	189	77	29	76	387	77
National Family Benefit Yojana	109	52	4	50	136	56	26	68	275	55
National Maternity Benefit Yojana	126	60	3	38	145	59	29	76	303	60
Widow Pension Yojana	137	65	8	100	171	70	27	71	343	68
Assistance to Handicapped and Orphan Scheme	114	54	5	63	131	54	21	55	271	54
Annapurna Scheme	139	66	4	50	168	69	27	71	338	67
Indira Aawas Yojana	133	63	6	75	158	65	26	68	323	64
Pradhan Mantri Rojgar Yojana	142	67	6	75	168	69	28	74	344	69
BMDFC/BSIFDC	100	47	3	38	105	43	20	53	228	46

Improvement in Personal Habits and Hygiene

Personal Hygiene[4]: Practices Followed after Using Toilet

It has been found that personal hygiene is very poor among majority of population residing either in urban or rural areas. This is more so in people residing in rural areas. Lack of awareness, health education and basic facilities like availability of safe drinking water are the reasons. All these factors lead to unhygienic environment not only for the individual but also for the family and in larger context to the society itself. Medical Sociologists and Community Health Educators have conducted several studies in the area of personal hygiene and the overall results pointed out that lack of health education and associated basic facilities are the root causes for lack of personal hygiene in Muzaffarpur District. The study focused on personal hygiene in the areas of proper washing of hand after toilet and before and after meals. The following Tables give details of personal hygiene of the respondents.

Table 5.30: Wash Hands after Toilet with Soap/Detergents, before and after becoming a Group Member: Religion-wise

Community	*Before*		*After*		*Shift*	
	No.	*%*	*No.*	*%*	*No.*	*%*
Hindu	325	81	382	96	57	15
Muslim	85	83	102	100	17	17
Total	*410*	*82*	*484*	*97*	*74*	*15*

There appears to be slight variation in personal hygiene among Hindus and Muslims with respect to washing of hands after using the toilet before becoming the Member of SHG. However, after becoming Member there is vast change in the personal habits of the respondents and their family members. Jairam Ramesh has reiterated the new role of SHGs in the area of health.[5]

Similar habits could be seen in the Social Groups with respect to washing of hands after using toilet. After joining SHG, respondents and their family members have initiated a campaign in the village and insisted to adopt clean and hygienic health practices. This had great impact on the villagers and almost all of them started adopting such habits for the betterment of their family's health. Children too were benefited from this campaign.

Table 5.31: Wash Hand After Toilet with soap/detergent before and after becoming a Group Member: Social Group-wise

Community	Before		After		Shift	
	No.	%	No.	%	No.	%
SC	183	87	199	94	16	7
ST	6	75	6	75	0	0
BC	189	77	241	99	52	22
General	32	84	38	100	6	16
Total	*410*	*82*	*484*	*97*	*74*	*15*

Personal Hygiene: Cleaning of Hands Before and After Meals

The practice of washing hands as a practice before meals is almost negligible all over the country. This is more due to casual approach rather than practicing hygiene. This was seen among the respondents in the study area and religion-wise and social group-wise details about the above habits are given in **Table 5.32**:

Table 5.32: Washing Hands before taking Meal: Before and After becoming a Group Member; Religion-wise

Community	Before		After		Shift	
	No.	%	No.	%	No.	%
Hindu	334	84	377	94	43	10
Muslim	86	84	99	97	13	13
Total	*420*	*84*	*476*	*95*	*56*	*11*

Table 5.33: Washing Hands before taking Meal: Before and After Becoming a Group Member: Social Group-wise

Community	Before		After		Shift	
	No.	%	No.	%	No.	%
SC	184	87	195	92	11	5
ST	7	88	7	88	0	0
BC	198	81	236	97	38	16
General	31	82	38	100	7	18
Total	*420*	*83*	*476*	*95*	*56*	*11*

82 per cent washed their hands before taking meal, even before they joined the SHG and 98 per cent began washing their hands after joining the SHG. This means that 14 per cent more washed their hands after joining the SHGs. Similarly, there was a 15 per cent positive shift in the habit of washing hands after using the toilet. These positive shifts in behaviour indicate that the membership of SHG did have a healthy effect in changing old age habits. The shift was slightly more among the BC group as compared to the SC group.

In a nutshell, it can be said that SHGs approach in many aspects other than collection of money and disbursement of loan such as hygiene consciousness, etc. have been positively taken up by the members of SHGs.

Change in Drug Addiction

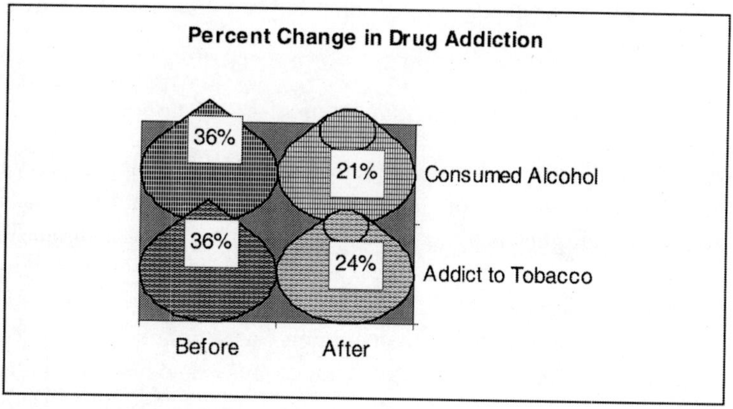

Table 5.34: Alcohol Addiction before and after Becoming Member of SHG

Name of Block	*After*				*Before*				*Shift*	
	Yes		*No*		*Yes*		*No*			
	No.	*%*	*No.*	*%*	*No.*	*%*	*No.*	*%*	*No.*	*%*
1. Kanti	34	33	70	67	53	51	51	49	19	18
2. Sahebganj	28	25	82	75	33	30	77	70	5	5
3. Madwan	18	28	47	72	18	28	47	72	0	0
4. Kudhni	15	11	118	89	50	38	83	62	35	26
5. Paru	10	11	79	89	26	29	63	71	16	18
Total	*105*	*21*	*396*	*79*	*180*	*36*	*321*	*64*	*75*	*15*

Table 5.35: Addicted to Tobacco: After and Before Becoming a Group Member

Name of Block	*After*				*Before*				*Shift*	
	Yes		*No*		*Yes*		*No*			
	No.	*%*	*No.*	*%*	*No.*	*%*	*No.*	*%*	*No.*	*%*
1. Kanti	34	33	70	67	41	39	63	61	7	7
2. Sahebganj	26	24	84	76	39	35	71	65	13	12
3. Madwan	18	28	47	72	22	34	43	66	4	6
4. Kudhni	15	11	118	89	55	41	78	59	40	30
5. Paru	26	29	63	71	23	26	66	74	-3	-3
Total	*119*	*24*	*382*	*76*	*180*	*36*	*321*	*64*	*61*	*12*

There is a very positive change in de-addiction of alcoholic and tobacco takers. Respondents of Kudhni showed a remarkable recovery from addiction.

Opinion on Socio-economic and Political-Based Issues

Almost all the respondents were females, and it was felt necessary to get their views on the role and involvement of women in the social gamut, which goes beyond social aspects alone. This encompasses economic empowerment, political sensitiveness, health and family-based issues etc.

Most of the issues on which opinion was sought have been dealt with in a brief form in Yes or No. They expressed no broad definition or individual views on the issues raised during discussion/interview. However, all the issues have been dealt as per situation-based.

Custodian of Finances

One of the key factors to remain in power and hold supremacy is to control the finances.

Women have never been given the power to spend the money due to prevalence of male dominated society. But gradually women have felt that real empowerment comes from handling money, though less than fifty per cent only have responded that they themselves should keep the money, even then it is an encouraging figure. The responses of women are given in **Tables 5.36 and 5.37**:

Table 5.36: Opinion in Response to 'Who should Keep Money in the Family?': Religion-wise

Family Member	*Hindus*		*Muslims*		*Total*	
	No.	*%*	*No.*	*%*	*No.*	*%*
Self	181	45	59	58	240	48
Husband	182	46	39	38	221	44
Guardian	21	5	1	1	22	4
In-Laws	15	4	3	3	18	4
Total	*399*	*100*	*102*	*100*	*501*	*100*

Table 5.37: Opinion in response to 'Who should Keep Money in the Family?': Caste-wise

Member of the Family	*SC*		*ST*		*BC*		*General*		*Total*	
	No.	*%*	*No.*	*%*	*No.*	*%*	*No.*	*%*	*No.*	*%*
Self	88	42	3	38	122	50	27	71	240	48
Husband	98	46	5	63	111	45	7	18	221	44
Guardian	17	8		0	3	1	2	5	22	4
In-Laws	8	4		0	8	3	2	5	18	4
Total	*211*	*100*	*8*	*100*	*244*	*100*	*38*	*100*	*501*	*100*

Religion-wise and Social Group opinion with regards to handling money is tilting towards Muslims and those belonging to Backward Cates (again majority belonging to Muslims).

Women have strongly said that they are capable and responsible to handle money. It is a reflection that economic freedom is more in Muslim society than its counterpart community.

Girl's Education

Government of India has launched several schemes to promote school education particularly for girls. Most of them have benefited from provision of free uniforms, books, stationary, meals, exemption of fees etc.

Gradual realization about importance of girl's education has increased the attendance in schools. The following *Tables* show religion-based and social-group-based responses:

Table 5.38: Respondents' Opinion 'Education is Necessary for Girls' Religion-wise

Yes/No	Hindus		Muslims		Total	
	No.	%	No.	%	No.	%
Necessary	352	88	86	84	438	87
Not Necessary	47	12	16	16	63	13
Total	*399*	*100*	*102*	*100*	*501*	*100*

A total of 87 per cent women belonging to Hindus and Muslims were of the opinion that girls' education was very necessary and they also opined that girls should receive higher education. The reaction varied from group to group, but the overall percentage is in favour of girl's education.

Table 5.39: Respondents Opinion 'Education is Necessary for Girls': Caste-wise

Yes/No	SC		ST		BC		General		Total	
	No.	%	No.	%	No.	%	No.	%	No.	%
Necessary	177	84	7	88	220	90	34	89	438	87
Not Necessary	34	16	1	12	24	10	4	11	63	13
Total	*211*	*100*	*8*	*100*	*244*	*100*	*38*	*100*	*501*	*100*

A positive trend is being observed in the opinion of the respondents belonging to backward caste. More and more of them are sending their daughters to school for mastering.

Political Sensitivity and Participation

A majority of the women in both urban and rural areas are not politically sensitive and this is higher in rural areas. The primary reason is low literacy rate and awareness level amongst women. However, SHG movement gave a great fillip in motivating women to participate in all social and political activities along with their male counterpart. Their initiation started with participating in Gram Sabha Meeting followed by becoming members and also contesting Panchayat elections etc. The following *Tables* give opinion of women with regards to participation in the political activities.

Table 5.40: Respondents Opinion 'Should Women Participate in Political Activities'; Religion-wise

Yes/No	*Hindus*		*Muslims*		*Total*	
	No.	*%*	*No.*	*%*	*No.*	*%*
Yes	368	92	94	92	462	92
No	31	8	8	8	39	8
Total	*399*	*100*	*102*	*100*	*501*	*100*

Table 5.41: Respondents Opinion 'Should Women Participate in Political Activities': Caste-wise

Yes/No	*SC*		*ST*		*BC*		*General*		*Total*	
	No.	*%*	*No.*	*%*	*No.*	*%*	*No.*	*%*	*No.*	*%*
Yes	190	90	7	88	228	93	37	97	462	92
No	21	10	1	13	16	7	1	3	39	8
Total	*211*	*100*	*8*	*100*	*244*	*100*	*38*	*100*	*501*	*100*

A very high percentage of respondents are in favour of women's participation in political activities and they have started participating in Panchayat meetings and contesting the elections.

This can be seen from the respondents of both the community and also belonging to different social groups.

Kanti Block has proximity to the town and this has definitely a plus point for their exposure and empowerment implicit in the above mention table which shows that 30 per cent of the SHG members were involved in politics. Paru which is distant place from the district town headquarter and it has least impact on the member, only 8 per cent are involved in the active politics.

Table 5.42: Designation of Members

Name of Block	*Panchayat Member*		*President of SHG*		*Mahila Mandal*		*Total*	
	No.	*%*	*No.*	*%*	*No.*	*%*	*No.*	*%*
1. Kanti	5	16	3	10	23	74	31	100
2. Sahebganj	2	13	1	7	12	80	15	100
3. Madwan	1	14		0	6	86	7	100
4. Kudhni	1	7	5	36	8	57	14	100
5. Paru		0	1	14	6	86	7	100
Total	*9*	*12*	*10*	*14*	*55*	*74*	*74*	*100*

Nine respondents of the member SHG joined Panchayat system to contribute in local area development and politics, rest are providing leadership in SHG Federation and Mahila Mandal.

In nutshell, it can be stated women's participation in political activities is real empowerment and they can understand the problems better and find solutions. Also, their involvement is an example for other women to come forward and participate in social, economic and political activities for making their lives totally independent.

Table 5.43: Member of Panchayat/Mahila Mandalor SHG Federation: Before and After becaming Group Members

Name of Block	*Before*		*After*		*Total*	
	No.	*%*	*No.*	*%*	*No.*	*%*
1. Kanti	14	45	17	55	31	100
2. Sahebganj	7	47	8	53	15	100
3. Madwan	2	29	5	71	7	100
4. Kudhni	4	29	10	71	14	100
5. Paru	1	14	6	86	7	100
Total	*28*	*38*	*46*	*62*	*74*	*100*

Out of seventy four who were engaged in active local politics before becoming member of SHG, 46 *i.e.* 62 per cent got involved in it after joining SHG. This is a very good phenomenon or sign that Self Help Group empowers and motivate them enough to actively participate in political and social activity.

Table 5.44: Elected Panchayat Member among SHGs

Sl. No.	*Block*	*Total No. of SHGs Formed*	*Total Membership*	*No. of Women elected in Panchayat Election from SHGs*
1.	Kanti	705	8953	141
2.	Madwan	456	5654	115

141 Panchayat members elected in Kanti who were members of Self Help Groups, likewise 115 Panchayat members were elected in Madwan Block who were members of an SHG. It is a good number that shows how the SHG helps in empowering the poor rural women of different caste politically and socially with economically.

Noorjahan of Pakri Pakohi of Madwan block belongs to a socio-economically deprived Muslim Ansari Family. Against all odds she passed matric from Assam at the age of 16 years. She belonged to a very conservative and rigid family, where Purda was strictly observed. She became a member of SHG in 2005. Thereafter she got "Capacity Building" training sponsored by Hunger Project. She was elected as a Ward Member in 2006 and later on she was elected as an Up-Mukhia of her Panchayat.

Dowry[6]: A Social Curse or Financial Gain

Dowry was started with the purpose of establishing the girls' family by providing token household items but it has taken an ugly turn over the years. Dowry has now become prestige-issue rather than remaining as a custom.

Several incidences of bride burning and family break-up have been reported and this has lead to mass awakening among the parents and they have strongly responded against this practice. The view of the respondents with regards to the practice has been given below:

Table 5.45: Respondents Opinion 'Should Dowry be Demanded': Religion-wise

Yes/No	Hindus		Muslims		Total	
	No.	%	No.	%	No.	%
No	276	69	88	86	364	73
Yes	123	31	14	14	137	27
Total	*399*	*100*	*102*	*100*	*501*	*100*

Table 5.46: R's Opinion 'Should Dowry be Demanded': Social Group-wise

Yes/No	SC		ST		BC		General		Total	
	No.	%	No.	%	No.	%	No.	%	No.	%
No	168	80	6	75	164	67	26	68	364	73
Yes	43	20	2	25	80	33	12	32	137	27
Total	*211*	*100*	*8*	*100*	*244*	*100*	*38*	*100*	*501*	*100*

As can be seen there has been strong negative feelings for the practice of dowry. This is applicable for both religious and social groups. But, it is surprising to note that quite a sizeable section of Hindus belonging to various castes still believed that some form of give and take between both the families should continue as a matter of tradition. The percentages of those not approving is much lower among Muslims.

Age of Marriage

The National Health Policy and the Population Policy has strongly emphasized that the age of marriage for boys should be 21 years and 18 years for the girls. This age has been fixed with a view that girls will be able to finish their schooling and physically they will be mature enough to endure childbearing.

It has been generally found that in rural areas and that too among socio-economically backward sections of the society, the trend of getting off the girls is rampantly followed. With the formation of SHGs and women's involvement in political and social activities there has been a gradual change in marriageable age.

Table 5.47: R's Opinion Girls Marriage Age should be 18 Years and above: Religion-wise

Yes/No	*Hindus*		*Muslims*		*Total*	
	No.	*%*	*No.*	*%*	*No.*	*%*
Yes	351	88	98	96	449	90
No	48	12	4	4	52	10
Total	*399*	*100*	*102*	*100*	*501*	*100*

Table 5.48: R's Opinion Girls Marriage age should be 18 Years and Above: Social Group-wise

Yes/No	*SC*		*ST*		*BC*		*General*		*Total*	
	No.	*%*	*No.*	*%*	*No.*	*%*	*No.*	*%*	*No.*	*%*
Yes	201	95	7	88	204	84	37	97	449	90
No	10	5	1	13	40	16	1	3	52	10
Total	*211*	*100*	*8*	*101*	*244*	*100*	*38*	*100*	*501*	*100*

90 per cent were strongly against child marriage. This was a surprising response as they belonged to marginalised community where early marriage is prevalent; they believed that girls' marriage should take place when they are above eighteen years of age.

Health and Welfare Components

Health and family welfare issues now covered in Reproductive and Child Health (RCH) is looking at women and child's health from wider angle. A new programme on RCH was launched at National Level. For the success and welfare of mother and child programme, Government of India has involved several agencies like State Governments, Non-Government Agencies, Self-help Groups, Panchayat, and School Teachers etc. The RCH related programmes emphasized on immunization, nutrition, family planning, pre and post delivery care etc.

In this study also, the components of immunization and practice of family planning methods have been dealt in length. The overall trend from the study shows very interesting findings particularly among the marginal communities, who are now showing positive trend towards adopting healthy practices for their family's betterment.

The behaviour of respondents on health issues like immunizing their children and pregnant women and practice of family planning methods, before and after becoming a member of SHG was enquired.

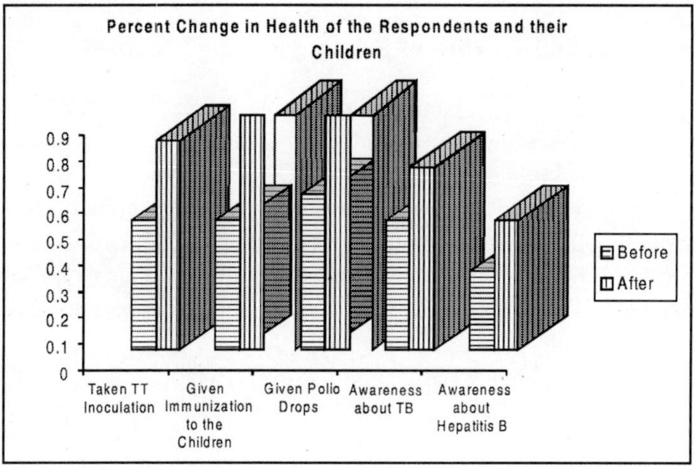

An overwhelming number of members of the marginalized group began to immunize[8] their children and use family planning methods after becoming the member of SHG. It shows that in the meetings of the group discussion does not limited to economic activities only rather it goes beyond that to social and daily activities.

Slightly lower percentages of Muslims were getting their children and pregnant women immunized (41%) as compared to Hindu Members (50%). The interactions in the groups motivates the members of SHGs in creating positive attitude on issues like immunizing children from six dreadful [9]diseases and women in protecting them from tetanus and anemia. A very high percentage of both the community members began to immunize their children. Among Muslims, the overall rate of change has been 37 per cent in providing immunization to their children and pregnant women. Similarly, the other social groups have also changed their habit.

As far as General Category of respondents were concerned, there has been marginal increase in immunization rates. This group was already aware of the benefits and it was getting pregnant women and children immunized as per schedule, whereas among Scheduled Caste and Backward Caste there was substantial increase in the overall rate of change of immunization. The change among these group was to the tune of 86 per cent and 85 per cent from 55 per cent and 37 per cent respectively.

Awareness and Practice of Family Planning[10] Methods

The National Family Planning Programme was launched in the year 1951 with the objective to reduce the family size and increase longevity of both mother and child. This has lead to increase in population, wide disparity among males and females, higher maternal mortality, poor health of mother and children etc. Due to the partial success of the family planning programme, Government of India has renamed the programme to Family Welfare Programme, increase in age of marriage, literacy, immunization etc.

This programme was successful. Several agencies were involved in its implementation. The details of increased family planning practices are given in **Table 5.49**.

Table 5.49: Response Towards Immunisation of Children

Social Groups	*Before*	*After*	*Shift*
Hindus	50	88	38
Muslims	41	78	37
General	71	83	12
BC	37	85	48
SC	55	86	31
Total	*254*	*420*	*166*

(*All Data are in Percentage*)

Muslims who are regarded culturally conservative and sensitive to several issues particularly related to family planning were at par with Hindu members as far as adoption of Family Planning methods was concerned. The shift was 28 per cent in both the social groups prior and after becoming members of SHG.

Inter-personal Communication and its Impact on Personality Development

Inter-personal skills are developed in individuals rather than inherited. This can be developed by constant learning process and regular interaction. For this, several schools are there which emphasis on developing the personality of an individual. Such institutions are not there in rural areas but an alternative to this is Gram Sabha and other Panchayat Institutions gives them opportunity to interact with Government Officials and Local Level Leaders. Self-help Groups have come in a way for providing the women to participate in various social activities.

Visit to Town

The SHG Movement, which started in 1990s, has helped women in various ways particularly in handle cash, tackle and suggest solutions to social problems, interacting with Government officials etc. Some of the parameters on which the level of confidence has been judged are given in the following **Tables 5.50 and 5.51**.

The above two Tables show women's visit to the market. As mentioned earlier, the Indian social system is so rigid that it leaves no scope for them to go out the homes. Particularly except in case of agricultural work, women hardly step out of homes.

Table 5.50: Response towards using Family Planning Method

Social Groups	*Before*	*After*	*Shift*
Hindus	39	67	28
Muslims	37	66	29
General	63	66	3
BC	36	73	37
SC	38	60	22
Total	*213*	*332*	*119*

Table 5.51: Visited Nearby Town in Last 3 Months: Religion-wise

Yes/No	*Hindus*		*Muslims*		*Total*	
	No.	*%*	*No.*	*%*	*No.*	*%*
Yes	213	53	69	68	282	56
No	186	47	33	32	219	44
Total	*399*	*100*	*102*	*100*	*501*	*100*

Table 5.52: Visited Nearby Town in Last 3 Months: Social Group-wise

Yes/No	*SC*		*ST*		*BC*		*General*		*Total*	
	No.	*%*	*No.*	*%*	*No.*	*%*	*No.*	*%*	*No.*	*%*
Yes	118	56	5	62	128	52	31	82	282	56
No	93	44	3	38	116	48	7	18	219	44
Total	*211*	*100*	*8*	*100*	*244*	*100*	*38*	*100*	*501*	*100*

But with the formation of SHG and the need for financial transactions, SHG members have to visit financial institutions frequently and also interact with marketing agents for selling various products developed by them as part of income generation activities.

The group meeting leads to a paradigm shift in their outlook and these women wants more exposure and economic freedom. Now they used to go to the markets for daily business.

Meeting with Government Functionaries

Women seldom meet Government functionaries due to various social and personal reasons. Individual and collective problems are discussed with Government functionaries and are sorted out amicably by men. Women seldom get out of their homes to discuss problems of the village with strangers and the same is presented in the following Tables. Meeting three different but important persons like Block Development Officer (BDO), Auxiliary Nurse Midwife (ANM) and

School Headmaster by women in the past three months are given for both religious and social groups.

Table 5.53: Met B.D.O. in the Last 3 Months: Religion-wise

Yes/No	Hindus		Muslims		Total	
	No.	%	No.	%	No.	%
Yes	120	30	50	49	170	34
No	279	70	52	51	331	66
Total	*399*	*100*	*102*	*100*	*501*	*100*

Table 5.54: Met B.D.O in the Last 3 Months: Social Group-wise

Yes/No	SC		ST		BC		General		Total	
	No.	%	No.	%	No.	%	No.	%	No.	%
Yes	68	32	3	38	77	32	22	58	170	34
No	143	68	5	62	167	68	16	42	331	66
Total	*211*	*100*	*8*	*100*	*244*	*100*	*38*	*100*	*501*	*100*

Table 5.55: Met A.N.M. in Last 3 Months: Religion-wise

Yes/No	Hindus		Muslims		Total	
	No.	%	No.	%	No.	%
Yes	183	46	38	37	221	44
No	216	54	64	63	280	56
Total	*399*	*100*	*102*	*100*	*501*	*100*

Table 5.56: Met A.N.M. in Last 3 Months: Social Group-wise

Yes/No	SC		ST		BC		General		Total	
	No.	%	No.	%	No.	%	No.	%	No.	%
Yes	92	44	3	38	104	43	22	58	221	44
No	119	56	5	62	140	57	16	42	280	56
Total	*211*	*100*	*8*	*100*	*244*	*100*	*38*	*100*	*501*	*100*

Table 5.57: Met Headmaster in the Last 3 Months: Religion-wise

Yes/No	Hindus		Muslims		Total	
	No.	%	No.	%	No.	%
Yes	159	40	46	45	205	41
No	240	60	56	55	296	59
Total	*399*	*100*	*102*	*100*	*501*	*100*

Table 5.58: Met Headmaster in the Last 3 Months: Social Group-wise

Yes/No	SC		ST		BC		General		Total	
	No.	%	No.	%	No.	%	No.	%	No.	%
Yes	75	36	3	38	98	40	29	76	205	41
No	136	64	5	62	146	60	9	24	296	59
Total	*211*	*100*	*8*	*100*	*244*	*100*	*38*	*100*	*501*	*100*

The above Tables show very poor interaction of women with the Government functionaries. The overall percentage of women's meeting the functionaries is only 34 per cent. The percentages are varying for different blocks. More and more women are joining SHG and various other village level bodies and thus there is variation in block level responses with regard to interaction with Government functionaries. When enquired about their meeting the Block Development Officers during the last three months only 34 per cent responded in affirmat. It is important that Kanti (58%), Sahebgunj (40%), Madwan and Kudhni have a higher percentage. Likewise, it has been asked whether they have met any local elected representatives like Sarpanch/Panch/Ward Member about the issues of development of village during the last three months, 43 per cent respondents had met to discuss local problems. The trend is quite encouraging for the empowerment of women.

Blocks near the town like Kudhni (71%) and Kanti (52%) have a higher percentage of those meeting Government functionaries. 59 per cent of the respondent also attended the Gram Sabha meetings during the last six months. These encouraging and increased percentages in terms of women's attendance are an indication of confidence and awareness about rights, which they are getting from various forums.

Women as Decision-Makers

Decision-making in Family Affairs

Women have always been denied as decision-makers in the family affairs and their participation and suggestions were rarely accepted in matters outside family affairs. There are several reasons like, low or no outside exposure, no interaction with males other than family members, low educational attainment and above all strict social customs.

India saw many drastic changes in the outlook of women. Women no longer are confined to homes. Their participation in socio-cultural, political, science and technology and many other activities have brought about a tremendous revolution in their position. The change has effected of women of towns and rural areas and all social groups.

The SHG movement has also helped rural women to actively take part in decision-making not only in the family but in community affairs as well. The following Tables give the religion and social group wise decision-making taken by women.

Table 5.59: Decision-Making in Family Matters: Religion-wise

Family Members	*Hindus*		*Muslims*		*Total*	
	No.	*%*	*No.*	*%*	*No.*	*%*
Self	164	41	57	56	221	44
Husband	197	49	44	43	241	48
Guardian	25	6		0	25	5
In-Laws	13	3	1	1	14	3
Total	*399*	*100*	*102*	*100*	*501*	*100*

Table 5.60: Decision-Making in Family Matters: Social Group-wise

Family Members	*SC*		*ST*		*BC*		*General*		*Total*	
	No.	*%*	*No.*	*%*	*No.*	*%*	*No.*	*%*	*No.*	*%*
Self	76	36	3	38	115	47	27	71	221	44
Husband	110	52	4	50	119	49	8	21	241	48
Guardian	21	10		0	2	1	2	5	25	5
In-Laws	4	2	1	13	8	3	1	3	14	3
Total	*211*	*100*	*8*	*100*	*244*	*100*	*38*	*100*	*501*	*100*

The percentage of decision taken by self among Muslims is much higher than those belonging to Hindus and this trend can be seen in social group also (backward caste mainly comprising Muslims). Muslims in this case have disproved the myth that they are very conservative. It is observed that Muslim Women have more social and economic freedom in the family and society compare to their counter part.

They were in favour of the husband shouldering this responsibility.

Decision-Making in Admissions to School

Schooling is an important stepping-stone in a child's life and due to mushrooming of educational institutions selection of a reasonably standard and affordable institution has become very difficult. The respondents belonging to religious and social groups felt that joint decision is much better than an individual's decision. But the results show that majority of women wanted to take self-decision. The following Tables show the decision taken in matters of admission to schools.

Table 5.61: Decision-Making about Children's Schools Admission: Religion-wise

Family Members	Hindus		Muslims		Total	
	No.	%	No.	%	No.	%
Self	190	48	53	52	243	48
Husband	200	50	48	47	248	50
Guardian	8	2	1	1	9	2
In-Laws	1	0		0	1	0
Total	*399*	*100*	*102*	*100*	*501*	*100*

Table 5.62: Decision-Making about Children's Schools Admission: Social Group-wise

Family Members	SC		ST		BC		General		Total	
	No.	%	No.	%	No.	%	No.	%	No.	%
Self	92	43	5	62	115	48	31	82	243	48
Husband	115	55	3	38	125	51	5	13	248	50
Guardian	4	2		0	3	1	2	5	9	2
In-Laws		0		0	1	0		0	1	0
Total	*211*	*100*	*8*	*100*	*244*	*100*	*38*	*100*	*501*	*100*

Backward Caste and General Members were in favour of taking decision themselves as compared to SC members, 52 per cent of whom were in favour of the husband making decisions in family matters. This was the situation about children's admission in school. More Muslim members (52%) wanted that they themselves should make this decision, on the other hand only 48 per cent Hindu members wanted to share this responsibility.

Sources of Information

Traditionally, the rural areas witnessed an iron curtain before the information flow for the deprived section especially for the fair sex. There is a *baithaka* (a place where male members resides) and an *Angon* (courtyard) where the life of women burnt without the air of freedom and in deprivation of every source of information. Now the thing is cracking in favour of the deprived section in the era of knowledge and communication. Communication revolution has connected the whole world. People have wide range of choices to access the information. Among the choices, radio and newspaper are still considered to be the best medium particularly in rural areas where power is a problem. The respondents were enquired about their main sources of information and the results are summarized in the following Tables.

Table 5.63: Listen Radio: Religion-wise

Yes/No	*Before*				*After*			
	Hindu		*Muslim*		*Hindu*		*Muslim*	
	No.	*%*	*No.*	*%*	*No.*	*%*	*No.*	*%*
Yes	173	43	38	37	235	59	53	52
No	226	57	64	63	164	41	49	48
Total	*399*	*100*	*102*	*100*	*399*	*100*	*102*	*100*

It is seen that after becoming the group member, the awareness among the members have increased.

Earlier where only 43 per cent of Hindu respondents use to listen to radio, and after they became members, the percentage has risen to 59 per cent. This proportion has also increased among Muslim too (53 per cent increase as compared to 37 per cent prior to becoming SHG Members).

Table 5.64: Listen Radio: Social Group-wise

Social Group	*Before*		*After*		*Shift*	
	No.	*%*	*No.*	*%*	*No.*	*%*
SC	83	39	114	54	31	15
ST	3	38	6	75	3	37
BC	97	40	138	57	41	17
General	28	74	30	79	2	5
Total	*211*	*42.12*	*288*	*57.49*	*77*	*15*

Social group-wise classification also reveals the same picture. Hindu respondents were among the highest percentage of respondents who listen to radio, but after joining the group, the percentage of SC and BC both showed a steep rise while general category showed a marginal rise.

Table 5.65: Read Newspaper: Religion-wise

Community	*Before*		*After*		*Shift*	
	No.	*%*	*No.*	*%*	*No.*	*%*
Hindu	111	28	135	34	24	6
Muslim	14	14	31	30	17	16
Total	*125*	*25*	*166*	*33.10*	*41*	*8.10*

Similar was the case with newspaper reading. Earlier while only 14 per cent of the Muslim respondents use to read newspapers, now 30 per cent of them were reading them.

Inter-Community Dialogue

Self-Help Groups are becoming a major instrument in breaking the inter caste and communal antagonizing attitude. People, especially women who were thought to be more orthodox, are now sits with men and women of other caste and community and discuss the issues including local social and political ones. This is creating an environment of peace and harmony in rural areas.

Table 5.66: Composition of SC/ST Members in SHGs

S. No.	*Block*	*Total No. of SHGs formed*	*Total Membership*	*No. of SHGs having all members (100%) of SC/ST community*		*No. of SHGs having more than 50% members of SC/ST community*		*No. of SHGs having less than 50% members of SC/ST community*		*No. of SHGs having no members of SC/ST community*	
1.	Kanti	705	8953	127	18%	108	15%	286	41%	184	26%
2.	Marwan	456	5654	116	25%	133	29%	135	30%	72	16%

There are total 705 Self-Help Groups in Kanti Block in which 127 (18%) have only SC/ST members, 108 (15%) groups have more than 50 per cent SC/ST members means less than 50 per cent members are of different other cast and communities. 286 (41%) groups have more than 50 per cent members of other than SC/ST members and rest are SC/ST members. Only 26 per cent in Kanti 16 per cent groups in Madwan blocks have no members from SC/ST communities. 268 (59%) of the groups in Madwan Block is mixed in nature having SC/ST and other community members.

Table 5.67: Composition of Muslims Members in SHGs

S. No.	Block	Total No. of SHGs formed	Total Membership	No. of SHGs having all members (100%) of Muslim community		No. of SHGs having more than 50% members of Muslim community		No. of SHGs having less than 50% members of Muslim community		No. of SHGs having no members of Muslim community	
1.	Kanti	705	8953	23	3%	26	4%	105	15%	551	78%
2.	Marwan	456	5654	12	3%	19	4%	88	19%	337	74%

131 (19%) of the groups in Kanti Block 107 (33%) groups in Madwan Block have the members from Muslim communities with Hindu communities and provides a platform for inter communal dialogue and discussion on various secular issues brings the two communities closer to each other.

Case of a Helpless Scheduled Caste SHG Woman Member to Become a District Councillor

The Chamarua village of Madwan block at Muzaffarpur District is a subject of discussion nowadays. The reason behind this is that a woman Neera Devi who belongs to a poor Scheduled Caste family at Madwan block (Region No. 22) has won the election for the seat of District Councillor. This constituency was made for the general woman category and winning this seat by Smt. Devi a Scheduled Caste Woman was really a challenge where money was being used and wine flowed.

The childhood of Neera Devi was spent in Chanmari village of Motihari block. She was the youngest amongst four brothers/sisters. She was fearless since the very beginning. Once dacoits intruded her house, all the members of her family fled but Neera stood her ground and fought with them.

At the age of 19, Neera married Ardhesh Kumar of a different caste. After marriage, she moved to her in-laws in Madwan block of Muzaffarpur District. The economic condition of the family was not good. She was not allowed to go out of her house because the family was very orthodox. She had studied upto matriculation before her marriage and inspite of having interest in further study, she could not continue. But Swa Shakti project opened the door of unlimited expectation for her.

In 2001, she got in touch with a World Bank funded Swa Shakti Project, through an NGO Nirdesh. She formed 75 Self-Help Groups (SHGs) in Madwan block. She played an important role in forming Swa Shakti Chetna Group. The members of the group elected her the head of the federation of the group. By her skilful leadership, she strengthened the federation. The groups got bank loan for micro-enterprises to improve their economic position.

She became Director of Balika Kishori Chetna Kendra, and made many girls and women literate. She used to have

(Contd).

every social event take place in her village and Panchayat. She raised her voice against atrocities against women and she organized her group members to oppose excesses on them. Gradually she became very popular especially amongst the women of deprived section of the area.

Later on she developed her federation of groups as women cooperative. She was elected head of the Jeevan Dhara Swa Shakti Mahila Cooperative Society of Kodariya Panchayat (Madwan block). She performed the duties of the Cooperative head honestly and efficiently.

She got various trainings under Swa Shakti Project which increased her leadership capacity. She travelled to many places in the country which provided her a new exposer and raised her knowledge. She got training in Panchayati Raj and leadership capacity from the Hunger Project 'Didi' through Nirdesh Sanstha and prepared her to fight the election in Panchayat. The women of the group encouraged her and as a result of this, she filled up her nomination for District Councillor from Madwan block.

She formed and nurtured 105 Self-Help Groups which was put under grading system and got revolving fund. The strength and motivating factor for Neera Devi was women members of these 105 Self-Help Groups. The support of 400 groups of Madwan block was also rallied behind her. Women members of the groups supported her and by the endless efforts of groups of women, Neera Devi won the election with thumping majority by 1695 votes.

Case of Anita Devi

Anita Devi of Dadar, Dadar Kolhua (Kanti block) was born in a socially and economically backward Mallah family. She was the eldest among her four sisters. Anita was married after she had cleared intermediate. After marriage she couldn't continue her study.

(*Contd*).

In Dadar Kolhua Panchayat, an informal education centre was being run by Nirdesh Sanstha with which Anita Devi was associated. When the Sanstha extended its scope to form women's organization under Swa Shakti Project, she was elected as the head of Swa Shakti Nari Kalyan Group. Being associated with the group she got various types of training which developed her leadership ability. After getting loan from the bank the women of the group started their own business. Anita started a poultry farm which increased her income. This strengthened her economic condition. Now there is a bank account and some land in her name. To purchase land, she gave Rs. 20,000/- to her husband from her own income. Her family and husband began to respect her.

With her strong will-power, she succeeded step by step and became popular. In 2003, with the cooperation of the Hunger Project, Nirdesh Sanstha organized Panchayati Raj and leadership development workshop. Anita participated in the workshop. In 2005-06, she participated in the training and workshop under pre-poll awareness campaign organized by the Hunger Project. She participated in the meeting of Gram Sabha. After getting information about the Government schemes she tried to give those poor women the benefits of Government schemes. In important matters of the family such as marriage, election, education of children the family takes her advice. Now, she has become an important member of the family.

Women of the 16 groups, the family members *i.e.* husband, father-in-law, mother-in-law and sisters supported Anita Devi. The pamphlets, handbills etc. were also distributed. Women of the group and the community propagated. Proposers were Smt. Gita Devi and Shri Om Prakash Chowdhary. She is associated with the organizations for the last 10 years. She associated with the election process after her election in the meeting held before the nomination.

(*Contd*).

Training by Sanstha, time to time information, posters, handbills, books related to election etc. were provided by information centre.

She won the election for the post of Sarpanch in her Panchayat Election in 2006.

The future course of her strategy is to do away atrocity on women in the society and provide them equal rights. So it is said where there is a will, there is a way.

Notes

1. According to Wikipedia—A religion is a set of common beliefs and practices generally held by a group of people, often codified as prayer, ritual, and religious low, Religion also encompasses ancestral or cultural tradition, writings history, and mythology, as well as personal faith and mystic experience the term religion refer to both the personal practices related to communal faith and group ritualised and communication stemming from shared conviction.
2. According to Census 2000 Brief: Marital Status was reported for each person as either "now married", "widowed", "divorced", "separated" or "never married".
3. According to The Wordsworth Encyclopedia, family is defined as—'group of people' related to each other by blood or by marriage, families are usually described as either 'extended' (a large group of relations living together or in close contact with each other) or 'nuclear' (a family consisting of two parents and their children), Volume 2, p. 778.
4. Hygiene is derived from Hygienia, the Greek Goddess of Health, cleanliness and sanitation. It refers to the maintenance of health and healthy living (as per Wikipedia).
5. Self-Help Groups Revolution: What Next? Economic and Political Weekly Sep. 8-14, 2007 Vol XLII No. 36.
6. As per the definition of The Wordsworth Encyclopedia, dowry is defined as 'property or money given by the bride's family to the groom or his family as part of the marriage agreement; the opposite of bride wealth', Volume 2, p. 677.
7. According to World Health Organisation (WHO) health is defined as 'a state of complete physical, mental and social well-being and

not merely the absence of disease or infirmity.' (http://en.wikipedia.org/wiki/Health).

8. WHO defines immunization as—'the process whereby a person is made immune or resistant to an infectious disease, typically by the administration of a vaccine. Vaccines stimulate the body's own immune system to protect the person against subsequent infection or disease. (http://www.who.int/topics/immunization/en/).
9. The Wordsworth Encyclopedia defines disease in the following way—'any condition that impairs the normal state of an organism, and usually alters the functioning of one or more of its organs or systems. A disease is usually characterized by a set of characteristic symptoms and signs, although these may not always be apparent to the sufferer. Disease may be inborn or acquired through infection, injury or other cause. Many diseases have unknown causes'. Vol. 2, p. 656.
10. As per the definition of The Wordsworth Encyclopedia, 'family planning is spacing or preventing the birth of children'. Volume 2, p. 778.

Chapter Six

Economic Impact on Marginalized Communities

Planning and development are continuous process and are closely linked to the growth and prosperity of the area and its inhabitants. It is generally found that the felt-needs of the people are responsible for bringing changes in the lives of the inhabitants. Thus, the process of development and planning emanate from within the society itself. Economic development is now one of the most important parameters for any community or section of the society to assess the pace of upward movement. There are a number of objective and subjective criteria for judging the growth of the communities or sections of the society. Broadly speaking there is a growing trend and at times necessity of shifting occupations which affect the overall growth pattern, increased per capita income, growth in saving tendencies, growth in consumption pattern and change in living standards of the inhabitants.

A. ECONOMIC PROFILE OF THE RESPONDENTS

Land Holding Size

Land is still considered as an asset in the rural areas but the evils of the new family system has disintegrated the families and fragmented the agricultural/pastures land. The unit of land has drastically reduced and number of claimants has increased leading low yield from the crops. Details gathered during the investigations are presented in the **Tables 6.1 and 6.2**, which reveal individual as well as religion-wise land holding status:

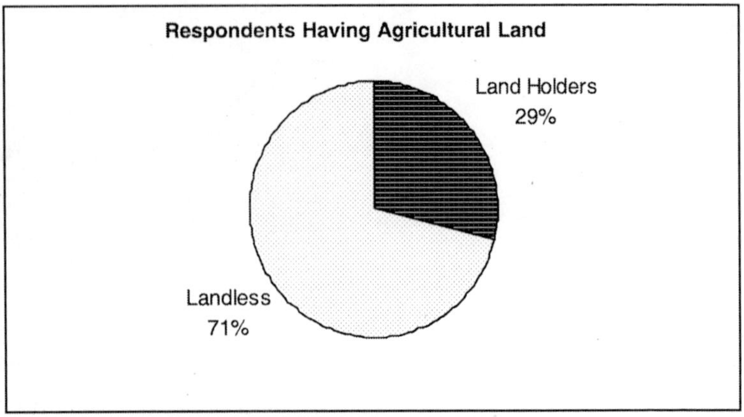

Table 6.1: Respondents Havimg Land

Name of Block	*Yes*		*No*		*Total*	
	Number	*%*	*Number*	*%*	*Number*	*%*
Kanti	24	23	80	77	104	100
Sahebgunj	23	21	87	79	110	100
Madwan	28	43	37	57	65	100
Kudhni	53	40	80	60	133	100
Paru	17	19	72	81	89	100
Total	145	29	356	71	501	100

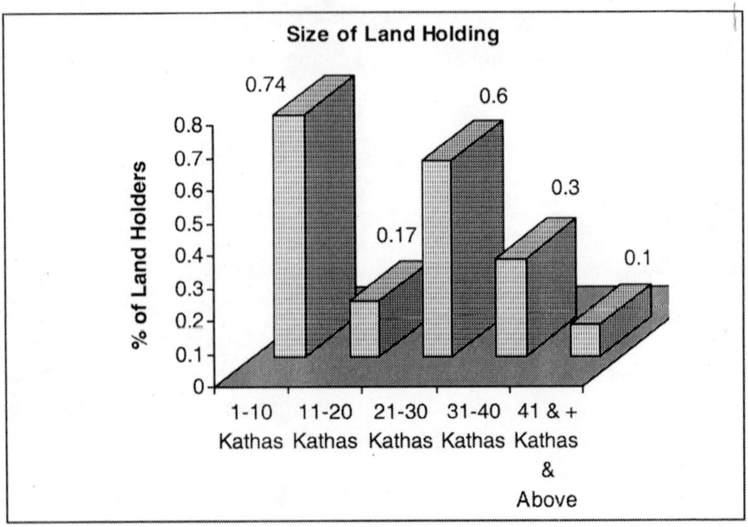

Table 6.2: Land Holding Size: Religion-wise

Land Size	*Hindus*		*Muslims*		*Total*	
	Number	*%*	*Number*	*%*	*Number*	*%*
1-10 Kathas	90	73	17	77	107	74
11-20 Kathas	21	17	3	14	24	17
21-30 Kathas	6	5	2	9	8	6
31-40 Kathas	4	3	0	0	4	3
41 Kathas and Above	2	2	0	0	2	1
Total	*123*	*100*	*22*	*100*	*145*	*100*

The overall percentage of the land available among the respondents is just 29 per cent from all the five blocks. This is an indication that majority of the respondents belonged to socio-economically backward section of the society and were devoid of any property in terms of land and cash etc. The affects of modernization can be seen in this area where the land has already started shrinking and very few families possessed land for their personal usage. The overall scenario of the land distribution shows that there is unequal percentage of land holding by individual persons of the village.

Religion-wise both Hindus and Muslims had equal land holding in terms of size, however, the General Group has the largest size of land, as can be seen from the below given **Table 6.3** on Land Holding Size with respect to Social Groups. Traditionally the respondents of BC category were artisans and earn their livelihood through semi-skilled small or cottage level self-employment activities.

Table 6.3: Land Holding Size: Social Group-wise

Land Size	*SC*		*ST*		*BC*		*Genral*		*Total*	
	No.	*%*	*No.*	*%*	*No.*	*%*	*No.*	*%*	*No.*	*%*
1-10 Kathas	41	72	1	100	54	76	11	69	107	74
11-20 Kathas	9	16	0	0	12	17	3	19	24	17
21-30 Kathas	4	7	0	0	3	4	1	6	8	6
31-40 Kathas	2	4	0	0	2	3	0	0	4	3
41 Kathas and Above	1	2	0	0	0	0	1	6	2	1
Total	*57*	*100*	*1*	*100*	*71*	*100*	*16*	*100*	*145*	*100*

Land is gradually disappearing from the hands of families belonging to lower middle class and lower classes due to heavy out-migration place from villages to towns to cities. Most of them are selling the land to local moneylender or to big farmers. The General Group has the largest size of land. 12 per cent of them had land over 21 kathas, whereas only 13 per cent of SC and 7 per cent BC group had this area of land *i.e.* the BC group own the least chunk of the land.

Occupational Structure

There are varied rural occupations and most of the people get their choice of work. Both men and women contribute equally for running the family. Needless to add here that women's contribution is much more than males. Their contribution is much more in kind which include gathering firewood, working in the fields, taking care of family business etc. or working for others in return for wages or income. Women's contribution in the entire economic process is treated as secondary earning rather than co-contributor. However, the results from the following **Table 6.4** point towards women as housewives rather than bread-winners.

Table 6.4: Resspondents' Occupation: Religion-wise

Name of Occupation	*Hindus*		*Muslims*		*Total*	
	No.	*%*	*No.*	*%*	*No.*	*%*
House Wife	297	74	76	75	373	74
Agriculture	40	10	11	11	51	10
Labour	47	12	13	13	60	12
Business	14	4	2	2	16	3
Govt.Service	1	0	0	0	1	0
Total	*399*	*100*	*102*	*101*	*501*	*100*

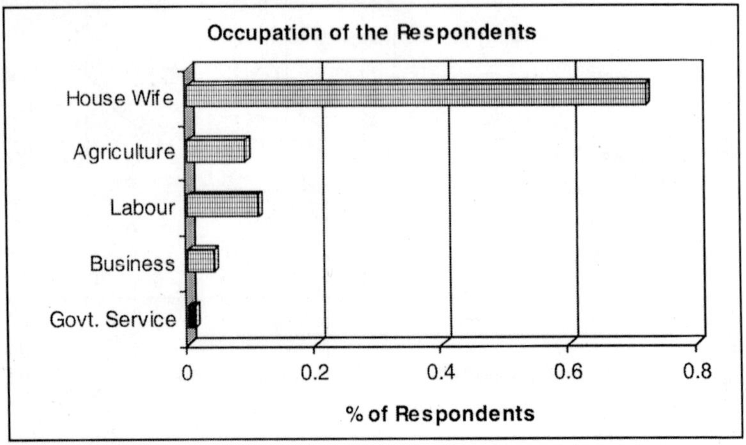

Of the total 501 respondents interviewed for the study, which includes various groups of the society, 74 per cent have stated that they are housewives and are not involved in any earning activities. This statement of the respondents is incorrect as their contribution in varied activities like agriculture, labour, business etc. are totally ignored and not counted as productive earning.

It can be seen that there is change-taking place in the rural areas in terms of economic independence among women. Women are no longer tied to the threshold of the house. A new world is waiting for them with the beginning of SHGs Movement.

Similar trend has been observed in other occupations to particularly among Social Groups. The details are presented in **Table 6.5.** As can be seen that almost similar trend which was observed in the religious groups is emerging here to.

Table 6.5: Respondents' Occupation: Social Group-wise

Name of Occupation	*SC*		*ST*		*BC*		*Genral*		*Total*	
	No.	*%*	*No.*	*%*	*No.*	*%*	*No.*	*%*	*No.*	*%*
House Wife	163	77	5	63	184	75	21	55	373	74
Agriculture	18	9	1	13	28	11	4	11	51	10
Labour	21	10	0	0	28	11	11	29	60	12
Business	8	4	2	25	4	2	2	5	16	3
Govt.Service	1	0	0	0	0	0	0	0	1	0
Total	*211*	*100*	*8*	*100*	*244*	*100*	*38*	*100*	*501*	*100*

Family Occupation

Table 6.6: Family Occupation of Respondents

Name of Block	*Agriculture*		*Labour*		*Business*		*Pvt. Service*		*Govt. Service*		*Total*	
	No.	*%*	*No.*	*%*	*No.*	*%*	*No.*	*%*	*No.*	*%*	*No.*	*%*
Kanti	3	3	84	81	12	12	3	3	2	2	104	100
Sahebgang	25	23	71	65	12	11		0	2	2	110	100
Madwan	1	2	59	91	3	5	1	2	1	2	65	100
Kudhni	24	18	79	59	19	14	11	8		0	133	100
Paru	17	19	67	75	4	4	1	1		0	89	100
Total	*70*	*14*	*360*	*72*	*50*	*10*	*16*	*3*	*5*	*1*	*501*	*100*

Table 6.6 presents occupational pattern among various Social Groups. The most surprising element is that majority of the respondents were involved in agricultural activities, whether it directly or indirectly.

The Table also highlight various other occupations that interested the respondents. After agriculture it is labour (both agriculture as well as construction), which has maximum percentage of respondents. Some of the women are also involved in family business like shop keeping, tailoring etc.

Table 6.7: Family Occupation of the Respondents: Religion-wise

Name of Occupation	*Hindus*		*Muslims*		*Total*	
	No.	%	No.	%	No.	%
Agriculture	54	14	16	16	70	14
Labour	286	72	74	73	360	72
Business	43	11	7	7	50	10
Pvt. Service	13	3	3	3	16	3
Govt. Service	3	1	2	2	5	1
Total	*399*	*100*	*102*	*101*	*501*	*100*

In rural areas, family occupations are continued very sincerely. Other occupations also become part of the family earning. Details of family occupation are shown in Table 6.7.

Tables 6.7 and 6.8 show importance of religion and caste in choosing occupations. The trend emerging from both the Tables indicate that the rural areas are still governed by the religious and social laws. Thus, occupations involving constant interaction with strangers are left out for males and females are put into jobs, which are less laborious and earn them little monetary benefits.

Table 6.8: Family Occupation of the Respondents: Caste-wise.

Name of Occupation	*SC*		*ST*		*BC*		*Genral*		*Total*	
	No.	%	No.	%	No.	%	No.	%	No.	%
Agriculture	17	8	3	38	39	16	11	29	70	14
Labour	159	75	3	38	180	74	18	47	360	72
Business	28	13	2	25	17	7	3	8	50	10
Pvt.Service	4	2	0	0	8	3	4	11	16	3
Govt.Service	3	1	0	0	0	0	2	5	5	1
Total	*211*	*100*	*8*	*100*	*244*	*100*	*38*	*100*	*501*	*100*

In the new world order, tremendous changes are taking place in the occupational ventures. There is scope for all in this new and innovative structure.

Various subsidiary units support the primary occupation, for instance, ready-made shirts and pants making unit which is supported by those who sell buttons and threads, sell zips, prepare packaging material, involve in transportation and marketing etc. These entire chains of persons who are involved in shirt making are complementary to each other. With the success of the primary unit, the subsidiary units also flourish and achieve self-reliance in their own area of specialization. Several new ventures are being explored in primary, secondary or tertiary sectors and prominent among them are animal husbandry, poultry, manufacturing of bangles, tailoring shops, grocery shops etc. It needs to be emphasized that the scope for creating employment opportunities are more and contributing GDP to the nation.

BPL and Non-BPL Families

Disparity in Incomes: There is widespread disparity in income of the respondents, who were surveyed for study. A majority of them fall in the Below Poverty Line (BPL) category. This is true of most places in the country. By definition, 'A family with an annual income of Rs. 20,000 and below per annum is considered to be below the poverty line based on the 1998 below Poverty Line Census'.

Religion-wise details of BPL Respondents are presented in **Table 6.9** below.

Table 6.9: BPL Families of Respondents: Religion-wise

APL/BPL	*Hindus*		*Muslims*		*Total*	
	No.	*%*	*No.*	*%*	*No.*	*%*
BPL Families	375	94	96	94	471	94
APL Families	24	6	6	6	30	6
Total	*399*	*100*	*102*	*100*	*501*	*100*

It can be seen that equal number of Hindu and Muslim families belonged to the status of BPL, as per the directive of Government of India.

Similar, results can be seen for the Social Groups also and the same are presented in **Table 6.10.**

Table 6.10: BPL Families of Respondents: Social Group-wise

APL/BPL	SC		ST		BC		Genral		Total	
	No.	%	No.	%	No.	%	No.	%	No.	%
BPL Families	202	96	8	100	227	93	34	89	471	94
APL Families	9	4		0	17	7	4	11	30	6
Total	*211*	*100*	*8*	*100*	*244*	*100*	*38*	*100*	*501*	*100*

3 per cent more BC families as compared to BC families were BPL. Almost equal number of General families was BPL.

The present study focused on BPL families; and those who were interviewed for the study have already been surveyed in 1997 by the District Rural Development Team in identifying BPL families. Thus, 47 per cent of the respondents belong to below poverty line and rest of them had more than Rs. 12,000 p.a.

The present study gathered information on the total family earnings from all sources on monthly basis. Information has been gathered for various occupations and also how different social groups fared in the earning from all sources.

Respondents' Monthly Income

The figures of monthly income earned by the respondents are presented in **Table 6.11.**

Table 6.11: Monthly Income of the Respondents: Occupation-wise

Occupation Type	Average Income (Rs.)	Income Category							
		Upto Rs.1000		Rs.1001 to 2000		Rs.2001 & Above		Total	
		No.	%	No.	%	No.	%	No.	%
Agriculture	852	41	80	9	18	1	2	51	100
Labour	1090	35	58	24	40	1	2	60	100
Business	1403	7	44	7	44	2	13	16	100
Govt.Service	1500	0	0	1	100	0	0	1	100
Total	*976*	*83*	*65*	*41*	*32*	*4*	*3*	*128*	*100*

Note: Excluding House Wives.

The results from the Table indicate that majority of the respondents fall in the category of income up to Rs. 1000/-. However, the overall average income from various occupations is between Rs. 1500/- to Rs. 852. Respondents who were doing business of any nature were high earners followed by persons in service where income is steady but not very high. Those engaged in any form of primary sector were least paid and also had very flexible earning.

Tables 6.12 and 6.13 give the details of monthly income of the respondents both religion and social group. A big majority of the respondents are in the BPL category. Details are given just after both the Tables.

Table 6.12: Monthly Income of the Respondents: Religion-wise

Religion of Respondents	*Average Income (Rs.)*	*Income Category*							
		Upto Rs.1000		*Rs.1001 to Rs. 2000*		*Rs.2001 & Above*		*Total*	
		No.	*%*	*No.*	*%*	*No.*	*%*	*No.*	*%*
Hindus	961	63	63	35	35	2	2	100	100
Muslims	1032	20	71	6	21	2	7	28	100
Total	*976*	*83*	*65*	*41*	*32*	*4*	*3*	*128*	*100*

Note: Excluding House Wives.

Table 6.13: Monthly Income of the Respondents: Social Group-wise

Social Group of Respondents	*Average Income (Rs.)*	*Income Category*							
		Upto Rs.1000		*Rs.1001 to Rs. 2000*		*Rs.2001 & Above*		*Total*	
		No.	*%*	*No.*	*%*	*No.*	*%*	*No.*	*%*
SC	965	32	65	14	29	3	6	49	100
ST	883	3	75	1	25	0	0	4	100
BC	940	39	68	17	30	1	2	57	100
General	1150	9	50	9	50	0	0	18	100
Total	*976*	*83*	*65*	*41*	*32*	*4*	*3*	*128*	*100*

Note: Excluding House Wives.

It can be seen from above two tables, there is hardly any major difference in the earning per month of either Muslims or Hindus. With slightly higher average income Muslims are better off than

Hindus. This difference can be seen in the highest category of the income group whereas in the lower groups both the groups are at par.

Similar trend can be seen among Backward Castes, Scheduled Castes and Scheduled Tribes respondents. Their average monthly income is between Rs. 883/- to Rs. 965/-.

Family Monthly Income

The study also focused on several areas and in the case of income, total family also has been considered as an independent research topic. As described in the previous section, this section also concentrates on family income vis-à-vis with religion, occupation, and social group and also by family system.

Table 6.14: Respondents' Family Monthly Income: Occupation-wise

Occupation Type	Average Income (Rs.)	Income Category: Upto Rs. 2000		Rs. 2001 to Rs. 4000		Rs. 4001 & Above		Total	
		No.	%	No.	%	No.	%	No.	%
Agriculture	1537	65	93	4	6	1	1	70	100
Labour	1640	307	85	41	11	12	3	360	100
Business	2301	34	68	11	22	5	10	50	100
Pvt. Service	3656	7	44	3	19	6	38	16	100
Govt. Service	4600	1	20	2	40	2	40	5	100
Total	*1785*	*414*	*83*	*61*	*12*	*26*	*5*	*501*	*100*

Table 6.15: Respondents' Family Monthly Income: Religion-wise

Religion of Respondents	Average Income (Rs.)	Income Category: Upto Rs. 2000		Rs. 2001 to Rs. 4000		Rs. 4001 & Above		Total	
		No.	%	No.	%	No.	%	No.	%
Hindus	1770	333	83	47	12	19	5	399	100
Muslims	1847	81	79	14	14	7	7	102	100
Total	*1785*	*414*	*83*	*61*	*12*	*26*	*5*	*501*	*100*

Tables 6.14 and 6.15 show religion-wise and occupation-wise incomes of the entire family. The above Table (6.14) shows the earning

from the point of religion. As can be seen there is very slight margin, which could probably because of bigger families or their involvement in various business activities.

A wide disparity in the earnings, as can be seen in Table 6.14, has been observed in the organized sectors and unorganized sectors. There could be several reasons but the primary ones are availability of abundant unskilled labour, women workers (rates vary among sexes), necessity to earn for the survival etc. It is more so in rural areas than in urban areas where the workers are rightfully protected by Trade Unions and Labour Laws. It is very essential that a Uniform Code be implemented for both urban as well as rural areas.

Table 6.16: Respondents' Family Monthly Income: Social Group-wise

Social Groups	*Average Income (Rs.)*	*Income Category*							
		Upto Rs. 2000		*Rs. 2001 to Rs. 4000*		*Rs. 4001 and Above*		*Total*	
		No.	*%*	*No.*	*%*	*No.*	*%*	*No.*	*%*
SC	1902	166	79	35	17	10	5	211	100
ST	1906	5	63	3	38		0	8	100
BC	1567	215	88	21	9	8	3	244	100
General	2516	28	74	2	5	8	21	38	100
Total	*1785*	*414*	*83*	*61*	*12*	*26*	*5*	*501*	*100*

Table 6.17: Respondents' Family Monthly Income: Family Type

Family Type	*Average Income (Rs.)*	*Income Category*							
		Upto Rs. 2000		*Rs. 2001 to Rs. 4000*		*Rs. 4001 and Above*		*Total*	
		No.	*%*	*No.*	*%*	*No.*	*%*	*No.*	*%*
Nuclear	1610	98	86	13	11	3	3	114	100
Joint	1837	316	82	48	12	23	6	387	100
Total	*1785*	*414*	*83*	*61*	*12*	*26*	*5*	*501*	*100*

Tables 6.16 and 6.17 describe the incomes of the social groups and also of respondents residing in either nuclear or joint families. A surprising trend that can be seen from Table 6.17 is that backward castes are way of than rest of the social groups in terms of income.

This shows that backward castes have been selective in choosing the job and not showing inclination in undertaking menial tasks, which could fetch more incomes.

In this direction, SHGs and other local bodies have to be involved in this mission and raise the standard of living of the rural families. It is also required that local NGOs are involved in this task and they be assigned the responsibility of introducing new and innovative income generation programmes.

Satisfaction with the Growth in Income

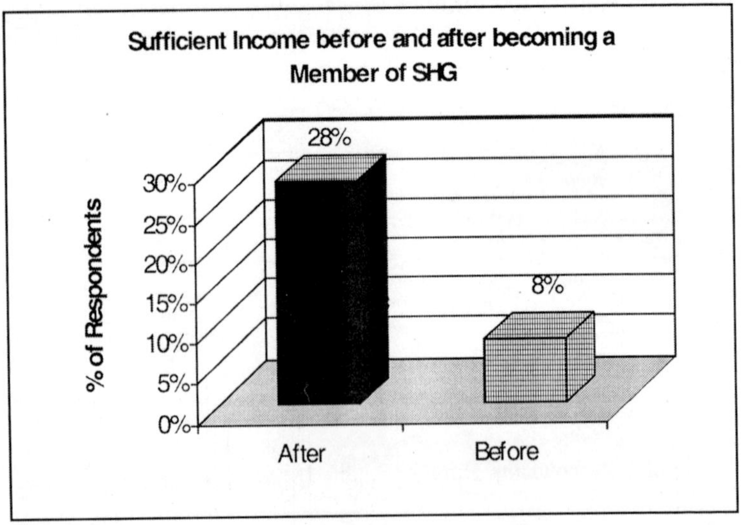

Table 6.18: Sufficient Income after and before becoming a Group Member

Name of Block	After				Before				Total	
	Yes		No		Yes		No			
	No.	%	No.	%	No.	%	No.	%	No.	%
1. Kanti	23	22	81	78	9	9	95	91	104	100
2. Sahebganj	35	32	75	68	10	9	100	91	110	100
3. Madwan	18	28	47	72	5	8	60	92	65	100
4. Kudhni	36	27	97	73	18	14	115	86	133	100
5. Paru	26	29	63	71	0	0	89	100	89	100
Total	*138*	*28*	*363*	*72*	*42*	*8*	*459*	*92*	*501*	*100*

B. ECONOMIC ACTIVITY OF SHGs

Loan Taken from Banks by SHGs

As per the guidelines of SGSY and NABARD the revolving fund can only be released when the group qualifies the grade I step. The amount of revolving fund may vary from on the basis of amount of the savings of the group; normally it is ten thousand rupees. 68 per cent of grade I respondents got up to Rs. 10000 and 32 per cent got more than Rs. 10000 up to Rs. 50000. With better utilization of revolving fund grade I SHGs qualifies for grade II. The grade II groups may apply for loans based on the project and amount of saving of the group. 40 per cent of grade II got Rupees one lakh to two lakh and seventeen per cent got more than two lakh rupees; seventeen per cent got less than fifty thousand and eleven per cent just the revolving fund.

Table 6.19: Loan Taken from Banks by SHGs

Name of Block	*Yes*		*No*		*Total*	
	No.	*%*	*No.*	*%*	*No.*	*%*
Kanti	27	26	77	74	104	100
Sahebgunj	19	17	91	83	110	100
Madwan	14	22	51	78	65	100
Kudhni	41	31	92	69	133	100
Paru	75	84	14	16	89	100
Total	*176*	*35*	*325*	*65*	*501*	*100*

Table 6.20: Amount of Loan Taken from Banks by SHGs: Grade-wise

Grade of Group	*Average Income (Rs.)*	*Amount Category*							
		Upto Rs. 50000		*Rs. 50000 – Rs. 100000*		*Rs. 100000 and Above*		*Total*	
		No.	*%*	*No.*	*%*	*No.*	*%*	*No.*	*%*
Grade A	12,995	41	100	0	0	0	0	41	100
Grade B	134,950	25	28	13	15	50	57	88	100
Not Graded	22,523	43	91	3	6	1	2	47	100
Total	*76,527*	*109*	*62*	*16*	*9*	*51*	*29*	*176*	*100*

Loan Taken from Groups by Group Members/Respondents

Table 6.21: Loan Taken from Group by Respondents

Name of Block	Yes		No	
	No.	%	No.	%
Kanti	51	49	53	51
Sahebgunj	39	35	71	65
Madwan	32	49	33	51
Kudhni	89	67	44	33
Paru	71	80	18	20
Total	*282*	*56*	*219*	*44*

Table 6.22: Amount of Loan Taken from Group by Respondents: Religion-wise

Grade of Group	Average Income (Rs.)	Amount Category							
		Upto Rs.1000		Rs.1000 — Rs. 5000		Rs.5000 and Above		Total	
		No.	%	No.	%	No.	%	No.	%
Hindus	5,887	92	42	62	28	67	30	221	100
Muslims	10,792	13	21	21	34	27	44	61	100
Total	*6,948*	*105*	*37*	*83*	*29*	*94*	*33*	*282*	*100*

Table 6.23: Amount of Loan Taken from Group by Respondents: Social Group-wise

Grade of Group	Average Income (Rs.)	Amount Category							
		Upto Rs. 1000		Rs. 1000 — Rs. 5000		Rs. 5000 and Above		Total	
		No.	%	No.	%	No.	%	No.	%
SC	3,522	58	55	27	25	21	20	106	100
ST	1,120	3	60	2	40	0	0	5	100
BC	9,828	39	25	46	29	73	16	158	100
General	2123	5	38	8	62	0	0	13	100
Total	*6948*	*105*	*37*	*83*	*29*	*94*	*33*	*282*	*100*

The SHGs Movement was initiated with the primary aim of providing loans at nominal interest rate to fulfil their needs. This movement has eliminated the money-lender from the scenario. The SHGs have their own corpus money for lending purposes. However, the loan amounts have to be moderately low. In case of higher amount, Gramin Banks and other nationalized banks are there for granting loans.

The banks have started playing important role in lending money on individual basis also, since their nationalization and also due to excesses meted out by money-lenders on the borrowers. There are so many financial institutions in the towns, which offer loans on nominal interest rates under various schemes.

SHGs have linkages with the financial institutions for deposits as well as for taking loan of bigger amount.

Monthly Saving done by Group Members/Respondents

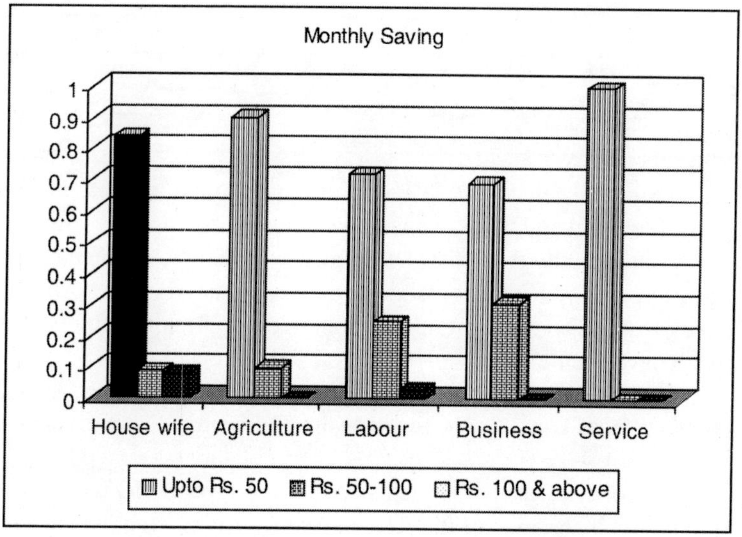

Table 6.24: Monthly Saving done by Respondents: Religion-wise

Occupation Type	*Average Income (Rs.)*	*Saving Amount Category*							
		Upto Rs.50		*Rs.50 to 100*		*Rs.100 and Above*		*Total*	
		No.	*%*	*No.*	*%*	*No.*	*%*	*No.*	*%*
House Wife	68	313	84	32	9	28	8	373	100
Agriculture	45	46	90	5	10	0	0	51	100
Labour	68	43	72	15	25	2	3	60	100
Business	49	11	69	5	31	0	0	16	100
Service	30	1	100	0	0	0	0	1	100
Total	*65*	*414*	*83*	*57*	*11*	*30*	*6*	*501*	*100*

The above Table shows that there is lot of saving (up to Rs. 100/-) done by most respondents in different occupations. However, it is amazing to note that nearly 76 per cent of women who are housewives are able to save money up to Rs. 50/- per month.

Table 6.25: Monthly Saving done by Respondents: Religion-wise

Religion	Average Income (Rs.)	Saving Amount Category							
		Upto Rs.50		Rs.50 - 100		Rs.100 and Above		Total	
		No.	%	No.	%	No.	%	No.	%
Hindus	65	337	84	38	10	24	6	399	100
Muslims	66	77	75	19	19	6	6	102	100
Total	*65*	*414*	*83*	*57*	*11*	*30*	*6*	*501*	*100*

Women are considered as better managers and homemakers and this is true in several cases. The habit of savings comes from women. Savings are usually done either at home (by putting it a container) or deposited with SHGs. The detail of the saving trends by amount of money that is saved per month is given in the following Tables. The Tables have been categorized on several parameters like social group-wise, religion-wise, age-wise etc. The Tables are self-explanatory but a detailed note is presented towards the end in the Discussions and Comments.

A majority of the respondents could only save Rs. 50 per month from the total earnings of the family. As majority of respondents are only housewives and others mostly are engaged in various small level activities, which does not leave with big range of savings.

Table 6.26: Monthly Saving done by Respondents: Social Group-wise

Social Group	Average Income (Rs.)	Saving Amount Category							
		Upto Rs.50		Rs.50 - 100		Rs.100 and Above		Total	
		No.	%	No.	%	No.	%	No.	%
SC	67	179	85	17	8	15	7	211	100
ST	41	7	88	1	13		0	8	100
BC	63	203	83	28	11	13	5	244	100
General	73	25	66	11	29	2	5	38	100
Total	*65*	*414*	*83*	*57*	*11*	*30*	*6*	*501*	*100*

Savings done by Hindus is much higher than Muslims in lower and higher amounts whereas Muslims appear to be saving moderately (upto Rs. 100).

Table 6.27: Monthly Saving done by Respondents to the Group: Age-wise

Social Group	*Average Income (Rs.)*	*Saving Amount Category*							
		Upto Rs.50		*Rs.50 - 100*		*Rs.100 & Above*		*Total*	
		No.	*%*	*No.*	*%*	*No.*	*%*	*No.*	*%*
Upto	37	9	90	1	10	0	0	10	100
20-30 Years	49	130	87	18	12	2	1	150	100
30-40 Years	60	186	82	29	13	11	5	226	100
40-50 Years	95	69	79	7	8	11	13	87	100
50 Years & Above	115	20	71	2	7	6	21	28	100
Total	*65*	*414*	*83*	*57*	*11*	*30*	*6*	*501*	*100*

Age plays an important role in the savings. Lower the age, higher is the saving habit. It can only be analyzed from the findings that with the advancement of age, there is decrease in saving amount due to low energy levels.

The nature of saving comes more from women than males particularly in rural areas. "Savings for women is more a psychological phenomena rather than a futuristic planning". Women save petty amount on daily basis. In such cases religion and social groups hardly plays any role.

Motivation, bank and block officials, Panchayat member support the groups morally, technically and financially time to time. These SHGs may become a reckoning force in the future and as assets for the area also.

As far as saving habits are concerned it is the women who have been saving for the family and it is of no concern whether they belong to any religious or social affiliations. Age also plays an important role in inculcating saving habits. There is tendency to save money among the younger age group rather than those in advancing age. The young are more energetic and enthusiastic in earning as well as in saving.

They tend to find out various schemes, which will accrue more interest and also provide long-term benefits.

The present day economic scenario is very competitive and there is plenty of scope for investments. Added to this, the SHGs movement played an important role in inculcating saving habits and also in initiating income generation activities, added to the family income.

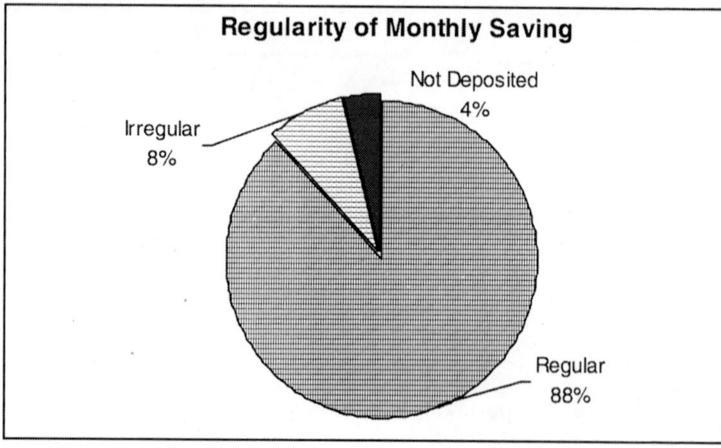

Table 6.28: Regularity of Monthly Saving: Religion-wise

Regular/Not Regular	*Hindus*		*Muslims*		*Total*	
	No.	*%*	*No.*	*%*	*No.*	*%*
Regular	352	88	90	88	442	88
Irregular	34	9	7	7	41	8
Not Deposited	13	3	5	5	18	4
Total	*399*	*100*	*102*	*100*	*501*	*100*

There is regularity in the saving habits of the people belonging to both the religious groups. This is done with the view to meet any emergency situation.

Table 6.29: Regularity of Monthly Saving: Social Group-wise

Regular/Not Regular	*SC*		*ST*		*BC*		*Genral*		*Total*	
	No.	*%*	*No.*	*%*	*No.*	*%*	*No.*	*%*	*No.*	*%*
Regular	194	92	6	75	205	84	37	97	442	88
Irregular	10	5	1	13	30	12		0	41	8
Not Deposited	7	7	1	13	9	4	1	3	18	4
Total	*211*	*104*	*8*	*101*	*244*	*100*	*38*	*100*	*501*	*100*

As can be seen the saving habits among Scheduled Castes and General Category is much higher than all other castes.

Group Savings

The concept of saving is very old and several forms of saving mechanism are followed. Saving is done individually at home or by Nationalized Banks or Cooperative or Rural Banks. The SHGs Movement has raised awareness among rural women to save for future and also for other occasions like marriage, treatment of sick, house repairs etc. The following Table gives details of year in which the SHGs were established and saving details.

Table 6.30: Group Saving: Year of Establishment

Year of Establishment	Saving Amount Category							
	Upto Rs. 10000		Rs.10000—20000		Rs. 20000 & Above		Total	
	No.	%	No.	%	No.	%	No.	%
2001	11	69	2	13	3	19	16	100
2002	21	19	73	68	14	13	108	100
2003	3	8	23	61	12	32	38	100
2004	66	65	32	31	4	4	102	100
2005	55	89	19	11	0	0	174	100
2006	49	96	2	4	0	0	51	100
Total	*305*	*62*	*151*	*31*	*33*	*7*	*489*	*100*

The groups who have been formed in last two years have motivational force and enthusiasm it has been seen that negligence of bank and block officials leads to slow down in the saving nature and saving tendency. It can be sustained if the facilitators

The above Table gives details of savings done since 2001. There is declining trend in the amount saved by the groups. The higher the amount, less is the saving by the Groups.

One of the outstanding activities of SHGs is inculcating saving habits among its members. This has helped the women to practice the same at household level also. Rural women are encouraged to take up several incomes generation activities for earning more and also diversifying in various other sectors. This is one way to increase the saving amount of the groups.

Financial institution could not successfully replace the system of money-lender. A gap remains for a longer period in the several area. SHGs now playing a major role in fulfilling the gaps. SHGs are now being considered as a relief for the poor rural folk.

Diversification and Initiation in New Economic Activities

The earlier section has dealt in detail the easy availability of loans from various sources. The loans are granted along with guidance to set up new business enterprises. Joint decisions in the family have helped in venturing into various other activities.

Table 6.31: Interested to start Income Generating Activities: Block-wise

Grade of Groups	*Yes*		*No*		*Total*	
	No.	*%*	*No.*	*%*	*No.*	*%*
Kanti	95	91	9	9	104	100
Sahebgunj	63	57	47	43	110	100
Madwan	51	78	14	22	65	100
Kudhni	98	74	35	26	133	100
Paru	82	92	7	8	89	100
Total	*389*	*78*	*112*	*22*	*501*	*100*

The following Tables give details on list of new activities are religion as well as caste-based.

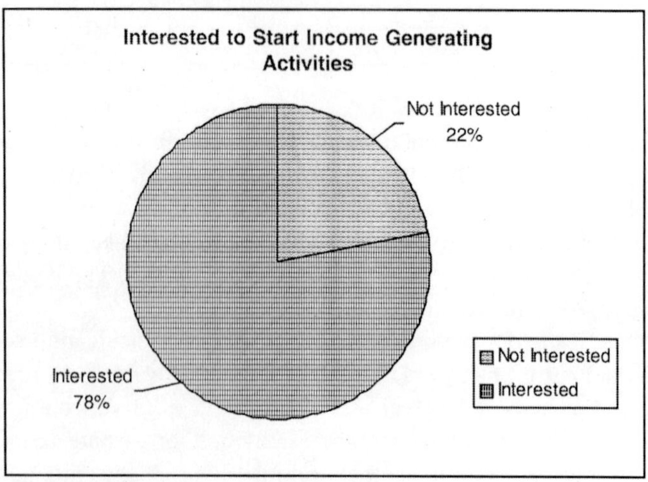

Table 6.32: Interested to Start New Business: Religion-wise

Name of Business	*Hindus*		*Muslims*		*Total*	
	No.	*%*	*No.*	*%*	*No.*	*%*
Dairy	149	47	38	51	187	48
Tailoring	18	6	6	8	24	6
Papad Making	29	9	11	15	40	10
For Tari Tree	8	3		0	8	2
Poultry Farm	14	4	3	4	17	4
General Store	23	7	1	1	24	6
Agricultrue	2	1	6	8	8	2
Vegetable Business	15	5	1	1	16	4
Goat Rearing	2	1	1	1	3	1
Agarbatti Making	21	7		0	21	5
Bidi Making		0	1	1	1	0
Other Business	3	1	3	4	6	2
Small Scale Industries	10	3	2	3	12	3
Cloth Shop	2	1	1	1	3	1
Fishery	7	2		0	7	2
Furniture Making	12	4		0	12	3
Total	*315*	*100*	*74*	*100*	*389*	*100*

The most preferred business in which both Hindus and Muslims expressed interest was dairy keeping, tailoring and papad making. A few Muslim members also thought agriculture is highly paying, when new inputs (like improved seeds, organic manure etc.) are added. Only 5 per cent Hindu members were interested in selling fruits and vegetables.

Table 6.33: Interested to Start New Business: Social Group-wise

Name of Business	SC		ST		BC	
	No.	%	No.	%	No.	%
Dairy	92	5600	1	17	81	43
Tailoring	7	4		0	17	9
Papad Making	13	8	1	17	21	11
For Tari Tree	6	4		0	2	1
Poultry Farm	6	4	1	17	8	4
General Store	11	7	1	17	11	6
Agricultrue	2	1		0	6	3
Vegetable Businesss	8	5	2	33	6	3
Goat Rearing	1	1		0	2	1
Agarbatti making	11	7		0	1	1
Bidi Making		0		0	1	1
Other Business	3	2		0	3	2
Small Scale Industries	3	2		0	9	5
Cloth Shop		0		0	3	2
Fishery		0		0	6	3
Furniture making	2	1		0	10	5
Total	*165*	*100*	*6*	*100*	*187*	*100*

Similar trend in choosing the occupations could be seen among respondents belonging to various social groups. The preferences are basically subject to factors like availability of location (shop), family unison, profitable venture etc.

Tirhut Milk Producers Union Limited (TIMUL), is very famous dairy in Muzaffarpur district, which provides the producers a market for milk at their door-step and the remuneration or prices being paid on tome with other welfare schemes and facilities out of the profit to the TIMUL. This motivates the people of Muzaffarpur to opt for dairy and that is reflected in the above table. 48 per cent of the respondents have shown their willingness to start dairy as their new business. The next favourite sector is tailoring and papad making. These are the traditional occupation of the area.

A wide range of occupations has been identified by the respondents (16 in number) as initiation to new ventures or diversifying from the existing ones. Most of the occupations can be undertaken by the entire family except in some of them where skills are required like tailoring, furniture making and fishery. There is a change in the occupational trends due to easy availability of loans and facilities like marketing and training.

Table 6.34: Interested in Getting Training of Income Generating Activities

Name of Block	*Yes*		*No*		*Total*	
	No.	*%*	*No.*	*%*	*No.*	*%*
Kanti	87	84	17	1600	104	100
Sahebgunj	92	84	18	16	110	100
Madwan	63	97	2	3	65	100
Kudhni	114	86	19	14	133	100
Paru	81	91	8	9	89	100
Total	*437*	*87*	*64*	*13*	*501*	*100*

The Missionary zeal among the respondents for getting the training of income generating activities was seen as more than three fourth of the respondents in each block have shown their interest in getting this training. This percentage was very high in Madwan block where 97 per cent respondents were in favour.

For the purpose of starting income generating activity, different types of training was organized in which large percentage of respondents took the training of starting business, followed by it was the training for Animal Husbandry. In Kanti block, the percentage of respondents showing interest for training was high compared to others.

Table 6.35: Training Required in Income Generating Activities

Name of Activities	*Kanti*		*Sahebganj*		*Madwan*		*Kudhni*		*Paru*		*Total*	
	No.	*%*	*No.*	*%*	*No.*	*%*	*No.*	*%*	*No.*	*%*	*No.*	*%*
Business	43	49	22	24	12	19	10	900	12	15	99	23
Animal Husbandry	16	18	11	12	11	17	10	9	40	49	88	20
Runing of SHGs	7	8	4	4	4	6	6	5	1	1	22	5
Making of Lahti Bangles	2	2	12	13	5	8	10	9	8	10	37	8
Cultivation Training	3	3	12	13	10	16	10	9	4	5	39	9
Cutting and Tailoring	3	3	5	5	8	13	8	7	2	2	26	6
Dari Making	1	1	4	4	3	5	3	3	2	2	13	3
Personality Devlopment	3	3	17	18	2	3	8	7	2	2	33	8
Papad and Agarbatti Making	9	10	5	5	8	13	10	9	2	2	35	8
Small Scale Industry		0		0		0	36	32	8	10	46	11
Candle Making		0		0		0	3	3		0	3	1
Total	*87*	*100*	*92*	*100*	*63*	*100*	*100*	*100*	*81*	*100*	*437*	*100*

Table 6.36: Average Amount Required to Start Income Generating Activities

Name of Activities	*Average Amount (Rs.)*	*No.of Respondents*	
		No.	*%*
Dairy	41848	187	47
Cutting and Tailoring	25795	24	6
Papad Making	30973	40	10
Dari Making	19286	8	2
Poultry Farm	33333	17	4
General Store	39417	24	6
Agricultrue	9571	8	2
Vegetable Business	8714	19	5
Goat Rearing	11333	3	1
Agarbatti Making	68381	21	5
Bidi Making	5000	3	1
Candle Making	82500	5	1
Lahti Bangles Making	50000	1	0
Small Scale Industries	48750	12	3
Cloth Shop	150000	3	1
Fishery	126429	7	2
Furniture Making	108333	12	3
Average Amount (Total)	*42495*	*394*	*100*

For starting different activities selected by the members, different amount of money was required. The minimum fund requirement was in the business of Bidi Making, where an investment of Rs. 5000 only was needed, while in opening a cloth shop, it requires an investment of around a lakh or more. Cattling was the main occupation found where in which most of the members were interested possible because of the availability of local market. As regards investment is concerned, it required an investment of 41,848, which though was a large amount, yet it would have been possible for them to get it funded through banks.

Capacity-Building of the SHGs

In all the five blocks where the study was conducted, the respondents hold the view that for strengthening of groups, training is essential. In Paru block, a high percentage of respondents (88%) agreed to it that training is necessary for effective group performance as it creates awareness among the stakeholders.

Table 6.37: Need of Training to Strengthen Group

Name of Block	*Yes*		*No*		*Total*	
	No.	*%*	*No.*	*%*	*No.*	*%*
Kanti	79	76	25	24	104	100
Sahebgunj	52	47	58	53	110	100
Madwan	36	55	29	45	65	100
Kudhni	104	78	29	22	133	100
Paru	78	88	11	12	89	100
Total	*349*	*70*	*152*	*30*	*501*	*100*

Table 6.38: Type of Training Required

Name of Block	*Total R*	*Organise SHG*		*Total R*	*Capacity-Building*	
		No	*% of Total R*		*No.*	*% of Total R*
Kanti	104	21	20	104	85	82
Sahebgunj	110	42	38	110	54	49
Madwan	65	13	20	65	41	63
Kudhni	133	28	21	133	105	79
Paru	89	21	24	89	75	84
Total	*501*	*125*	*25*	*501*	*360*	*72*

It was felt that most of the stakeholders who became the member of group, joined group keeping in mind the economic view point, meaning in order to start any new business and earn their livelihood, so when asked the question as to what type of training is needed, more than 50 per cent of the respondents in all the blocks showed their interest for the training related to business except for Paru block where very less number of respondents were interviewed.

Opinion about Benefits of SHGs

Table 6.39: Whether SHGs Beneficial

Name of Block	*Yes*		*No*		*Total*	
	No.	*%*	*No.*	*%*	*No.*	*%*
Kanti	95	91	9	9	104	100
Sahebgunj	95	86	15	14	110	100
Madwan	57	88	8	12	65	100
Kudhni	125	94	8	6	133	100
Paru	86	97	3	3	89	100
Total	*458*	*91*	*43*	*9*	*501*	*100*

Table 6.40: Respondents' Opinion about Benefits of SHGs

Name of Block	*Away from Money Landers*		*Co-operations*		*Easily Fulfilment of Needs*		*Income Generation*		*Knowledge Enhanced*		*Saving Money*		*Total*	
	No.	*%*	*No.*	*%*	*No.*	*%*	*No.*	*%*	*No.*	*%*	*No.*	*%*	*No.*	*%*
Kanti	14	15	67	71	3	3	9	9	2	2		0	95	100
Sahebgunj	27	28	43	45	7	7	6	6	4	4	8	8	95	100
Madwan	12	21	35	61	8	14	2	4		0		0	57	100
Kudhni	47	38	45	36	9	7	8	6	15	12	1	1	125	100
Paru	27	31	19	22	7	8	14	16	19	22		0	86	100
Total	*127*	*28*	*209*	*46*	*34*	*7*	*39*	*9*	*40*	*9*	*9*	*2*	*458*	*100*

SHGs were successful in improving the social and economic life of the respondents. On being asked of the benefits of SHGs, various types of responses came. Majority of the respondents stated that the prime benefit of SHGs is that it leads to cooperation among the members.

Followed by it, the second benefit of SHGs as recorded by the respondents was that it keeps the stakeholders/members away from the money-lenders. But it was surprising thing to note that very low percentage of them hold the view that SHGs have lead to creation and expansion of knowledge base in terms of many social, political and economic aspects.

Bank and SHGs: According to the Bank Officials

Table 6.41: Grading Status of SHGs Bank-wise 2005 and 2006

Name of Block	*Not Graded*		*Grade I*		*Grade II*		*Total*	
	No.	*%*	*No.*	*%*	*No.*	*%*	*No.*	*%*
			2005					
Punja National Bank	8	24	22	67	3	9	33	100
Regional Rural Bank	16	24	45	66	7	10	68	100
State Bank of India	1	5	11	55	8	40	20	100
U.B.K.G.B	6	10	32	55	20	34	58	100
United Bank of India	25	45	24	43	7	13	56	100
Total	*56*	*24*	*134*	*57*	*45*	*19*	*235*	*100*
			2006					
Central Bank of India	18	32	28	50	10	18	56	100
Punjab National Bank	10	45	4	18	8	36	22	100
Bank of Baroda	12	32	19	50	7	18	38	100
Regional Rural Bank	22	32	28	41	18	26	68	100
State Bank of India	3	9	26	79	4	12	33	100
U.B.K.G.B	2	13	13	81	1	6	16	100
United Bank of India	0	0	2	33	4	67	6	100
Canara Bank	30	48	31	49	2	3	63	100
Total	*97*	*32*	*151*	*50*	*54*	*18*	*302*	*100*

For the study, total eight banks were taken for study. In this, the percentage of groups who have received their first grading is more than those who are either not graded or have received second grading. Central Bank of India has given first grading to nearly

50 per cent groups while U.B.K.G.B and State Bank of India have given first grading to 81 and 79 per cent groups respectively. However, it is disappointing that very less number of groups have been graded through Regional Rural Banks. A high of 67 per cent of groups have received their second grading through United Bank of India.

During the year 2005, five banks were selected for grading the groups. Regional Rural Banks (RRBs) funded 55 per cent of the groups including first and second grading while 24 per cent of the groups were not graded. State Bank of India graded highest of 95 per cent of the groups during the year in which 55 per cent groups received their first grading and slightly lower 40 per cent groups received second grading.

For the study, total eight banks were taken for study. In this, the percentage of groups who have received their first grading is more than those who are either not graded or have received second grading. Central Bank of India has given first grading to nearly 50 per cent groups while U.B.K.G.B and State Bank of India have given first grading to 81 and 79 per cent groups respectively. However, it is disappointing that very less number of groups have been graded through Regional Rural Banks. A high of 67 per cent of groups have received their second grading through United Bank of India.

Table 6.42: Revolving Fund Released to SHGs in 2005 and 2006

Name of Bank	*Revolving Fund Released to SHGs*								
	2005			*2006*			*Overall*		
	Total	*No.*	*%*	*Total*	*No.*	*%*	*Total*	*No.*	*%*
Central Bank of India	0	0	0	56	28	50	56	28	50
Punjab National Bank	33	22	67	22	4	18	55	26	47
Bank of Baroda	0	0	0	38	19	50	38	19	50
Regional Rural Bank	68	45	66	68	28	41	136	73	54
State Bank of India	20	11	55	33	9	27	53	20	38
U.B.K.G.B	58	32	55	16	6	38	74	38	51
United Bank of India	56	24	43	6	2	33	62	26	42
Canara Bank	0	0	0	63	31	49	63	31	49
Total	*235*	*134*	*57*	*302*	*127*	*42*	*537*	*261*	*49*

Year 2005 has been quite better in terms of release of funds as all the banks released three fourth of the funds to the groups, and the remaining in the next year, except for some banks where the release of entire amount was made in the next year *i.e.* in the year 2006.

Table 6.43: Revolving Fund Released to SHGs in 2005 and 2006

Name of Bank	Economic Activities Started by SHGs								
	2005			2006			Overall		
	Total	No.	%	Total	No.	%	Total	No.	%
Central Bank of India	0	0	0	56	4	7	56	4	7
Punjab National Bank	33	27	82	22	8	36	55	35	64
Bank of Baroda	0		0	38	4	11	38	4	11
Regional Rural Bank	68	16	24	68	11	16	136	27	20
State Bank of India	20	7	35	33	25	76	53	32	60
U.B.K.G.B	58	35	60	16	13	81	74	48	65
United Bank of India	56	24	43	6	2	33	62	26	42
Canara Bank	0		0	63	2	3	63	2	3
Total	*235*	*109*	*46*	*302*	*69*	*23*	*537*	*178*	*33*

Similarly, for starting the economic activity, the banks released considerable proportion of funds during 2005 and the remaining in the next year.

Table 6.44: Account opened in Banks by SHGs—2005 and 2006

Name of Bank	Account opened in Banks by SHGs								
	2005			2006			Overall		
	Total	No.	%	Total	No.	%	Total	No.	%
Central Bank of India	0		0	56	40	71	56	40	71
Punjab National Bank	33	16	48	22	10	45	55	26	47
Bank of Baroda	0		0	38	38	100	38	38	100
Regional Rural Bank	68	36	53	68	10	15	136	46	34
State Bank of India	20	15	75	33	7	21	53	22	42
U.B.K.G.B	58	19	33	16	7	44	74	26	35
United Bank of India	56	6	11	6	2	33	62	8	13
Canara Bank	0		0	63	43	68	63	43	68
Total	*235*	*92*	*39*	*302*	*275*	*91*	*537*	*367*	*68*

As regards opening of account in the bank was concerned.

Table 6.45: Loan Release by Banks - 2005 and 2006

Name of Banks	*Loan 2005*			*Loan 2006*			*Overall*		
	Total	*No.*	*%*	*Total*	*No.*	*%*	*Total*	*No.*	*%*
Central Bank of India	0	0	0	56	4	7	56	4	7
Punjab National Bank	33	27	82	22	8	36	55	35	64
Bank of Bdoda	0	0	0	38	4	11	38	4	11
Regional Rural Bank	68	16	24	68	11	16	136	27	20
State Bank of India	20	7	35	33	25	76	53	32	60
U.B.K.G.B	58	35	60	16	13	81	74	48	65
United Bank of India	56	24	43	6	2	33	62	26	42
Canara Bank	0		0	63	2	3	63	2	3
Total	235	109	46	302	69	23	537	178	33

Of the total amount of loan issued to the banks for loaning.

Table 6.46: Release of Subsidy by Banks—2005 and 2006

Name of Banks	*Subsidy 2005*			*Subsidy 2006*			*Overall*		
	Total	*No.*	*%*	*Total*	*No.*	*%*	*Total*	*No.*	*%*
Central Bank of India	0	0	0	56	4	7	56	4	7
Punjab National Bank	33	27	82	22	8	36	55	35	64
Bank of Bdoda	0	0	0	38	4	11	38	4	11
Regional Rural Bank	68	16	24	68	11	16	136	27	20
State Bank of India	20	7	35	33	25	76	53	32	60
U.B.K.G.B	58	35	60	16	13	81	74	48	65
United Bank of India	56	24	43	6	2	33	62	26	42
Canara Bank	0	0	0	63	2	3	63	2	3
Total	235	109	46	302	69	23	537	178	33

During the year 2005, considerably high *i.e.* more than fifty per cent of the subsidy by all the banks was released except for some banks where either one third of the amount of subsidy or full amount of subsidy was released in next year (2006).

Views of Bank and Block Officials about the Processing of Loan

Table 6.47: Cause of Delays in Application Process According to Officials

Basis of Grading	*No.*	*%*
Invest more time in scrutiny	4	5
Not maintain register	3	4
Lack of staff in bank	4	5
Fullfilment of formalities	11	15
Lack of subsidy amount	4	5
Lack of unity between SHG member	6	8
Member's signature not matched	43	57
Total	*75*	*100*

When inquired about the causes of delay in loaning procedure and processing of application forms with the bank officials, it came out that more than fifty per cent of delay happens due to mismatch of signatures of the members. Then there are the formalities, which do not speed up the processing of the forms. Least delay was reported to be caused because of unmentioned registers by the members.

Table 6.48: Awareness level of SHG's Members about Loan Procedure

Name of Bank	*Yes*		*No*		*Total*	
	No.	*%*	*No.*	*%*	*No.*	*%*
Central Bank of India	0	0	1		1	100
Punjab National Bank	5	100	0		5	100
Bank of Baroda	0	0	1	100	1	100
Regional Rural Bank	4	100	0	0	4	100
State Bank of India	3	100	0	100	3	100
U.B.K.G.B	4	100	0	0	4	100
United Bank of India	1	100	0	0	1	100
Canara Bank	1	100	0	0	1	100
Total	*18*	*90*	*2*	*10*	*20*	*100*

CASE OF PHOOLAN DEVI

Phoolan Devi of village Makdumpur Kodariya, Madwan Block; District Muzaffarpur belongs to a very ordinary backward caste 'Nooniya' family. She was youngest among three sisters and two brothers, brought up in a very distress

(Contd).

conditions due to economical hardships. She got married in the age of 10 years with the person of three times of her age. There also, she faced the same problem of poverty; even two times meal was not available. She had to beg to fulfil family's requirements. Her husband fell ill and hence could not do his labour job, in addition, expenditure on his treatment worsen the situation. At this moment, she took to strife and started doing labour job. Unluckily, being a lady she was given less wages than male workers and also, she had to face the sexual harassment by fellow workers. Meanwhile an NGO become active in the area and facilitated formation of Women Self-Help Groups in Madwan Prakhand under Swashakti Project. Phoolan along with ten other women formed the group and used to participate in the meetings regularly under the guidance of a facilitator of the organization called Didi and started saving money regularly. The organization imparted training in group empowerment and leadership development, which helped her in realizing her leadership ability. By virtue of that, she strengthened her group and motivated the other members to start self employment by means of bank loan and own saving. She herself also started selling of churi (bangles), biscuits which gradually improved her economic condition. Since their group was very active and all were members of the BPL families, they got a loan of Rs. 2,50,000/- under the Government Scheme SGSY. She started new business and bought cattle for dairy. In due course, she got social recognition in the community along with economic empowerment. The people supported her as a candidate in 2006 Panchayat elections of ward No. 9. Though her husband made propaganda against her in the election campaign, she was elected unanimously. Today Phoolan Devi is a symbol of a strong and empowered woman who has proved herself by her dedication and honesty. Today, she has her own land, money for the future and respect in the society.

CASE STUDY OF SURRAIYYA PARWEEN

Surraiyya Parween a resident of Lukkinand Lalarpur, P.O. Sakri Sariyya, Block was an ordinary semi literate woman, belonging to a poor backward Muslim community. She was matric pass. She was hardly about thirty years of age. She was married twelve years ago when she was 18 with Abdul Kalam and settled down in his village with him. The total members in the family were 10 and the main source of income was only a small shop of scrap products. The bread earner and decision-makers in the family were her husband and her father-in-law. She was just a housewife and they had 2 children. Her husband Kalam was a socially active person in his village but do not have adequate source of livelihood. The financial status of the family was poor. To get loan they use to go to money-lender because the bank would not advance loan to them.

Kalam started a small betel shop but it failed. Meanwhile Parween met one Usha Devi who was an animator of Hanuman Prasad Grameen Vikas Seva Samiti, and a member of SHGs. She gave her detailed and complete information regarding formation of groups under SGSY and its benefits.

Thereafter Surraiyya Parween held a meeting with unemployed women in her community and thus decided to form a SHGs.

She started the group with 10 members (all were women) and took a loan of Rs. 1,00,000 from the bank to improve their financial condition and start a business of their own. She started bangle making initially then opened a poultry farm having 500 birds. She also bought a sewing machine and started dress making and tailoring. All the women after joining the group became employed. At present, the financial status of the members of the group is very good. The group is now paying back the loan also which they had taken from the bank. However, the group feels realizes that they need a loan of Rs. 5,00,000 more for expanding their work and improving their financial condition.

After joining the group, her status in terms of finance and decision-making power has changed. Earlier, she was simply a matriculate but now she has pass Inter and is pursuing graduation. She has four children; two are studying in a Government school and two in a private school. She has acquired the decision-making power in the family. She became Panchayat representative and attends meetings of Gram Sabha very punctually and actively and contributes to the improvement of the condition of her village.

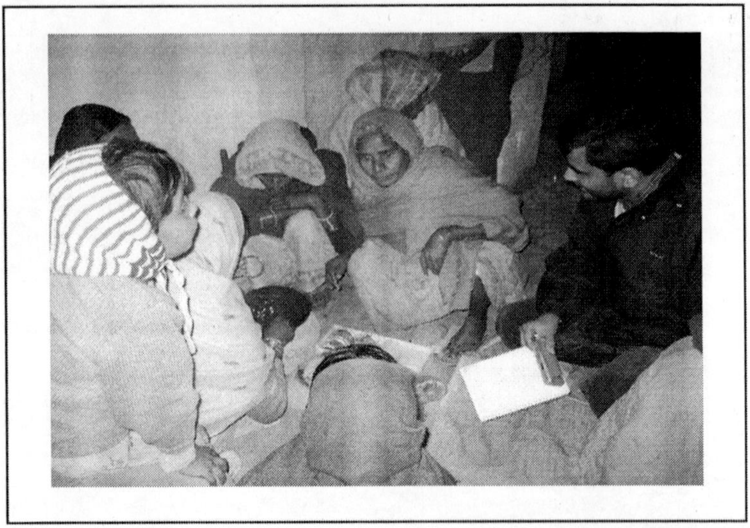

Chapter Seven

Conclusion

India even after attaining sixty years of freedom from British, have not been able to provide the physical, mental, social and political development to its citizens. The plight of poverty is still the same. Poverty years ago had been a social curse for the country. Today, though the ratio has declined a little, yet it is still an issue of concern. There have been several changes in both the Central as well as State level Governments in terms of leadership but none have been able to make any dent in the developmental process. Over the years there have been constitutional commitments, amendments, long-term and short-term planning, processes and various other minor beneficial schemes, plans and projects by the successive Governments for poverty alleviation with major issue of reaching the un-reached, yet the plight of poverty remained same. It is still a major task before all Governments for presenting a shining India before the world. In this direction the Central and State Governments and others who expressed their concern for developing the nation made several efforts. These are discussed in the following sections and also the shortcomings are highlighted as part of the initiation processes.

One of the most important programmes initiated by the Government of India in the last one decade's time is the Self-Help Groups run by women as credit giving agency and also to take up small activities which can be linked to micro-enterprises, for promoting small and medium level entrepreneurs in raising their socio-economic status. The SHG programme has support from various levels and it is perhaps the best conceived programme of the Government of India which provides empowerment to women from all sections of the society.

However, there are certain lacunae's in the formulation of the scheme. It needs to be borne in mind that any scheme that is being implemented in the rural areas should have the sanctions from the local Panchayats. It is extremely important that Panchayats are intrinsically linked with the SHGs. In fact they should be involved in periodical checks, support and guidance to SHGs within their orbit of operation. In most of the cases, this has been ignored and the SHG at its formation stage itself faced problem.

Another major limitation of SHGs as found during the investigations was that this programme has not reached the poorest of the poor. The reasons for the same appears to be threefold—lack of awareness, lack of confidence and lack of full efforts on the part of block and bank officials and in addition, lack of patience on the part of traditionally non-skilled wage earners to receive the benefit from them.

The major limitation of SHGs as found by us that this programme has not reached the poorest of the poor. The reason for the same appears to be threefold—lack of awareness, lack of confidence and lack of sufficient efforts on the part of block and bank officials and in addition lack of patience on the part of traditionally non-skilled wage earners to receive the benefit from them.

The second important limitation appears to be the methodology and approach towards the formation of SHGs. What would have been a catalystic effect is developing awareness and motivating the people to come forward to farm and participate in the SHG as a movement. The formation of SHG based on Programme Approach[1] rather than motivated and mobilized voluntary action on part of the participants or NGOs or Government bodies. There was definite lack of intensive sensitization, which would have taken mission approach or orientation. Together with this, there was not enough initiative for developing leadership among the communities as well as building capacities for group dynamism and record and account keeping.

In addition there was also of linking social issues with economic efforts/aspects. Element of cooperation and coordination among the group members were also not seen to the desirable extent. Furthermore, emphasis has been placed on expansion rather than on consolidation and then further expansion. Creating an environment for the success of a programme is extremely vital which has not been emphasized and pursued adequately.

The SHG movement initiated by the Government is facing serious teething problem and these needs to be solved immediately to avoid any serious and long-term difficulties in achieving desired results from the scheme. Some of the suggestions which can be incorporated in the scheme are given below:

(1) To achieve desirable level of success, it is imperative to shed undue bureaucratic and mechanical approach and fix accountability of actions on the part of bank and block officials and other Government or non-government official. It has been found that most of them do not undertake any responsibility and thus lead for a long-term bingo of the programme. This particular situation has to be avoided and involvement with motivation is quite essential for making this scheme a success.

(2) Grading system with regards to the evaluation of SHGs is not only important but needs to be done for reaction of the people and various Government agencies. Therefore, it is essential to form monitoring mechanism to do the needful to avoid any controversies in this area.

(3) In our federal structure Panchayati Raj Institutions has an important role to play, especially in releasing the dreams of Directive Principles of state policy enshrined in our Constitution. Overlooking the involvement of PRI in regard to formation and functioning of SHG would be counter productive. So far the involvement of Panchayati Raj Institutions is conspicuous by their absence. It is therefore felt extremely important that Panchayats should be linked with the SHG. With this, there will be periodical checks, support and guidance to SHGs within their orbit of functioning/operation.

(4) Adequate infrastructure for the success of SHG was also not available. This infrastructural support would include communication system, credit and marketing facilities, availability of raw materials, provision of training and training apparatus storage and transportation etc. Even there are no surveys to support in the selection of activities for SHGs in a particular area. The lack of adequate infrastructure

has been an important factor arresting the marketing and development of SHGs.

(5) Cohesive action on the part of SHGs could be a major factor to boost the functioning of SHGs. For this purpose, the SHGs need to be integrated more so through a federation of SHGs. But presently not much effort is being made in this connection, neither through Government initiative nor through leadership emerging out of SHGs. Such integration and cohesiveness helps sharing of experiences, problems and gains. This would also help develop better infrastructure with regard to marketing, collection of raw materials, transportation, packaging and storage.

(6) Social taboos, customs and beliefs often create hindrance in the formation and functioning of SHGs. Caste congregation, segregation, exclusion of certain communities and women folk, non-availability of space in the market to the poorest of the poor due to rigid caste structure etc. are some of the examples that come in the way of its efficient functioning. As regards the Muslim community, bank loans are profane and are not appreciated in the community. Most importantly, the interest that is paid to the lender is most sinful act under the tenets of Muslim Religion. Such beliefs are considered as most sinful activities and are not encouraged in the Muslim Law.

(7) It is felt that a large number of poor, who are not under the preview of micro finance, the institution of SHGs and micro finance programmes did not have any major impact on poverty alleviation in all the status of country. Only in some well developed States, SHGs and micro finance have gained popularity. Lot of groundwork is required to spread micro finance activities throughout the country.

The present study has intrinsically gone into various issues, its approach and solutions and for making the Self-Help Group scheme a phenomenal success. This will help the women think positive and empower themselves. Keeping this broad framework, the present research study was undertaken to assess Self-Help Groups and their socio-economic status of marginalized communities particularly in Muzaffarpur District of Bihar.

For convenience and better understanding, the entire research work has been divided into Seven Chapters along with paraphernalia's like foot-notes, tables, graphs, annexure etc. Utmost care has been taken to present each and every detail pertaining to the scheme and also most importantly views of the respondents (who are key persons for highlighting fallacies and successes). The chapter plans for the present research study has been planned with a view to provide detailed information on the subject.

The Thesis begins with Introduction, which gives the entire overview of the Ph. D work. Small but important details like need, approach, objectives, study plan etc. are put into this chapter. The entire plan of the study is included into this chapter.

Chapter One is *Approach and Coverage of the Study*. This chapter discusses in detail the socio-economic and demographic situation of the Thesis and detailed plan of action demography of the area selected for study and the pattern for which it was conducted. It also gives in detail the methodology and the objective of the study.

SHG is seen as one of the effective means for the socio-economic development, which ultimately leads to empowerment of women. Keeping this in view, it examines the impact of SHGs on marginalized communities *i.e.* the weaker sections of the society in Muzaffarpur district of Bihar. In addition, this study does introspection of the role of Government and non-government organizations keeping in view the role played by the SHGs in developing the micro-enterprise units in various locations with the involvement of socio-economically backward sections of the society.

Muzaffarpur district of Bihar was selected because of its diverse demographic, economic and social conditions prevalent there. Majority of the Panchayats in the area are dominated either by Bhumihars or Rajputs and the others by Yadavas, Paswans; due to political or economic suppression and in some places from Trading Community (Banias) and in some Panchayats by Muslims, who are predominantly in higher proportion. Having such diverse demographic conditions where different communities have domination, the need was felt to study the impact of SHGs for empowering the socially weak and marginalized communities.

A sample of 500 Self-Help Group members, from 47 villages of five different blocks namely Kanti, Sahebganj, Madwan, Kudhni and

Paru was drawn. Apart from this, 20 Bank Officials, 16 were Branch Managers, 3 Field Officers who were concerned with the formation and linkage of SHGs and one Cashier were also interviewed for the present work.

The method of data collection was through Primary and also Secondary sources, which included interview of the individuals and reports from different Ministries and Departments, who are directly and indirectly related with women and SHG scheme. The chapter towards the end also gives brief but succinct history of the Muzaffarpur District.

Chapter Two focuses on *Marginalized Communities*, which includes Schedule Castes, Backward Castes, Women and Muslim Community members. The percentage of Scheduled Tribes is very low infact negligible in some places and thus has not been taken in the present study. This is an important chapter and deals in length their socio-economic status like demographic composition, educational status, health status, work participation ratio, definition of Self Employed and Regular Workers, growth rates and such other related aspects.

The first group taken into consideration for fulfilment of Ph.D Thesis was Muslim community, where their percentage ratio is recorded to be the highest in comparison to all other communities residing in the States of Bihar, Uttar Pradesh and West Bengal. Majority of Muslim population is illiterate and the overall literacy rate is far below the national average. This percentage is substantially high for rural north where it is 85 per cent. Only 3.56 per cent Muslim women are reported to have received higher education. The health services they are getting are inadequate for them and they have least access to basic healthcare facilities, however the infant mortality rate was reported to be lower. Their work participation rate is also found to be quite low which is counted to 14 per cent, which is the average participation rate. Majority of them reported to be unemployed.

The second group studied is Scheduled Caste where its population, as per the Census 2001 was estimated to be 16.2 per cent of the total population. The literacy rate of this community is found to be very low. As regards health issues, anaemia was the most common disease prevalent among them. Their economic and occupational situation is also not good. Majority of them are living below poverty line, hardly able to meet their day to day requirements. They are landless and their main source of income is wage labour, which includes agriculture and casual labour. The tradition of child marriage was found to be because of prevalence of high level of literacy and poverty.

The third social group belongs to Scheduled Tribes (STs). This community belongs to the poorest of the poor but their percentage was negligible or very low in Muzaffarpur district. As per the Census 2001, their population was estimated to be 8.2 per cent. Their concentration is highest in Mizoram (94.5%). Their literacy rate is the same as that of SCs (28%), however it is estimated to be more than SCs in the State of Bihar. The common disease found among them was anaemia.

Chapter Three discusses the concept, definition, method of formation and *origin of SHG and Microfinance*. Different approaches of formation have also been discussed. Account of some successful experiences on members of SHGs has been presented in the form of Case Studies.

Apart from this, the grading criteria of the groups are also dealt in detail. The chapter discusses the procedure of group formation where five different stages of in-group members are taken into account for discussion. Then the concept and activities of Self-Help Groups have been discussed. The roles and functions assigned to these groups were dealt in detail.

In the later part of the chapter, the concept of Federation; *i.e.* the association of small SHGs to pool up their resources in order to address the social and economic issues collectively, is dealt along with the objectives and functions. The intensive investigation has lead to draw a paradigm on the functioning and approach of SHGs which is also part of the Thesis.

Chapter Four discusses the initiatives taken on the part of Government and Non-Government Organisations in the field of social upliftment of the marginalized community through the instrument of SHGs. This chapter deals with the specific Government Schemes and programmes designed specifically to promote SHGs. Different projects and schemes of Government, functioning of banks and NGOs has been taken into consideration.

Swarnjayanti Gram Swaraozgar Yojana (SGSY) is a holistic Programme of self-employment covering all its aspects *i.e.*, organisation of the rural poor into SHGs, their capacity-building, planning of activity clusters, infrastructure build-up, introduction of holistic technologies and marketing support. It is the most important scheme from the point of view of employment generation as it is the single self-employment programme designed for the rural poor. It lays emphasis on formation of groups in order to bring the poor families on one common platform and assist them. Under it, the target groups are selected and then they are associated under one cluster.

The scheme undertakes various activities such as market analysis, selection of key activity, fostering linkages with various groups and their links, organisation of fairs and exhibitions and identification of foreign markets for export purposes.

NABARD, the bank established for providing rural credit to the agriculture and allied activities. Under it the SHGs and bank linkage programme and the initiatives by SHGs have been discussed in length. The bank provides rural credit to various activities connected with the rural areas particularly in the fields of agriculture and allied activities have made a big impact on the people and also on SHGs.

Apart from various Government Schemes, which have been dealt in detail, other Institutions like NGOs too find place in the Thesis. Three prominent NGOs namely Mahila Samakhya, Hanuman Prasad Gramin Seva Samiti, and Nirdesh have been discussed. These NGOs have played an important role in various projects related to women, micro-enterprises, health, education etc. Some of the important projects undertaken by these NGOs are Swa-Shakti, Swawlamban, and Swayamsiddha.

Chapter Five is on *Social Impact* of SHGs on Marginalised Communities. This chapter highlights the social impact of SHGs in detail, i.e. what has been their impact on the society, habit, confidence and life style as a whole.

The study has been conducted in six different blocks of Muzaffarpur district and a total of 500 respondents were interviewed. The chapter begins with the brief profile of the respondents defining their demographic, social and economic composition in terms of their age, religion, sex, education, marital status, educational background, family composition etc. Of the respondents interviewed, religion-wise, the percentage of Hindu respondents was more in comparison to the Muslim respondents. Apart from Hindu and Muslim community, other social groups included were Scheduled Castes, Scheduled Tribes and Other Backward Classes. Among the General Category, majority of the respondents belonged to the age group of 30-40 years while the majority of SC, ST and respondents were in the same age group.

Educational composition of the respondents showed that the percentage of illiteracy is much higher in all the blocks both religion and social group-wise. Illiteracy rate was found highest amongst the Scheduled Tribes (though their percentage is almost negligible in the district). The percentage of married respondents was found be on higher side in all the blocks. In one of the blocks under study, 100 per cent of the respondents were married.

The number of family members found was in between 3 to 5 members per family and the family type prevalent was Joint Family System.

One of the main objectives of the Self Help Groups is the organisation of regular and timely meetings through which mobilization is done. It was found that the participation of respondents in the group meetings was regular and the membership composition in some of the groups was slightly high than the average number of members.

The results of the grading; religion-wise and social group-wise did not yield better results as far as performance is concerned, may be due to the reason that the members were not fully aware of the guidelines on which grading of the groups is done so more than 50 per cent of the groups were not graded.

Self-Help Groups were also seen as one of the means of creating awareness regarding education, various other social and economic issues, initiating small-scale business enterprises for augmentation of incomes etc. This scheme has made tremendous impact on various cross-section of the society and has motivated even male members in the family to associate the women at home in SHG scheme. The overall percentage of awareness and acceptance is very high in comparison to any other scheme launched by the Government in recent years.

SHGs role in the area of health and hygiene is also found to be positive, as it has lead to major changes in the personal habits of the respondents such as washing of hands before taking meal and also following personal hygiene habits like bathing, washing hands after using toilet etc.

SHGs have also lead to other aspects of empowerment such as decision-making power among the respondents in the areas of fund management, opinion with regards to dowry and girl's education, political participation etc. The general picture that has emerged indicates that there has been an increasing awareness among them after becoming the group member.

As regards financial autonomy and decision-making in the family is concerned, it was stated by the respondents that their say in these matters have increased considerably.

In the end, it can be concluded that the SHG seen as a means of empowerment, were to a considerable extent, successful in social upgradation of the community specially the marginalized community. It will not be wrong to say here that SHGs have been successful in creating awareness among the women respondents specially and many critical issues were also taken up in these groups about which the women once felt hesitant to discuss about it. Thus, the SHGs have served as a platform for discussion and thereby enhancing the knowledge bank of the respondents.

The Chapter Six is on Economic Impact of SHGs on Marginalized Community. It was found that religion-wise and social group-wise the distribution of land was almost same among all the social groups. Overall pattern of the land distribution showed that the size of land holding has reduced among all communities of the society.

Talking about the occupational pattern, majority of the respondents (74%) were found to be unemployed and were housewives. They were engaged in various agriculture and related activities. The percentage of women in the service sector was almost negligible.

Income distribution was also found unequal among the respondents. There was wide range of disparity among them. There were several reasons for it but the main reason was unskilled labour force, where the need of the hour was to earn in order to survive.

The respondents had a number of activities to undertake but the funds required in these activities varied. Bidi making was the most economic activity found by the respondents which had an investment of Rs. 5,000 only. Dairy farming was the most preferred economic activity but it required large investment to be made.

Training is demanded by majority of the respondents for skill up-gradation, group dynamism and book keeping for effective performance of the group.

Most of the respondents hold the view that SHGs are beneficial for them. They are of the view that SHGs leads to cooperation among the members keeps the stakeholders/members away from the money-lenders. In addition, some of them hold the view that SHGs have lead to expansion of knowledge in areas of social, political and economic aspects.

Eight banks were taken for study. Central Bank of India has given first grading to nearly 50 per cent groups while U.B.K.G.B and State Bank of India have given first grading to 81 and 79 per cent groups respectively. However, it is disappointing that very less number of groups have been graded through Regional Rural Banks. A high of 67 per cent of groups have received their second grading through United Bank of India.

Year 2006 had been better in terms of opening of accounts by the groups was concerned. Nearly 91 per cent of the groups opened account in banks. Central Bank of India opened maximum number of accounts of groups. That means on an average, 68 per cent of the groups opened their account in banks.

On being inquiring about the causes of delay in loaning procedure and processing of application forms with the bank officials, it came out that more than fifty per cent of delay happens due to mismatch of signatures of the members.

Then there are the formalities, which do not speed up the processing of the forms. Least delay was reported to be caused because of unmaintained or not properly maintained by the groups.

Recommendation

Capacity-Building

There is a great transformation that is taking place over the world. Speculations are on for a unified market otherwise popularly known as "global market" and India with abundance of raw material and manpower is looked up as leader in the Asian Region as well as in other regions of the world. This transformation is not only demanding but also asks for a perfection that will help them to assume a role model for smaller and upcoming nations. For this, capacity-building is a mechanism which will help in resolving and facilitating in various areas like group dynamism, bookkeeping, marketing and the skill up-gradation for the new enterprise taken up by new rural entrepreneurs. There is mushrooming of entrepreneurs due to easy finances, material and manpower. Most of them are moving without a sense of direction and thus there is urgent requirement of blue print. The following section will spell the agenda, which will throw light on the new strategy for attaining global leadership.

In the First Stage, Training and capacity-building are two important tools required for PRI members, NGO activist, social activist, block and bank officials and field employees.

Involvement of members of Panchayati Raj Institutions:

- Involvement of better NGOs as motivator and facilitator.
- Easier policy for grading of products, by and large, with parameters like range of products, packaging, promotion, sale within the country and outside the country.
- Identification of new products, which are in demand and its requirement within and outside country.
- Easy and trouble-free trade policy and encouragement for medium and small traders and entrepreneurs.

Bank Linkages

Easy Loan Policy and Disbursement: Since the nationalisation there has been downfall of money-lenders in the villages. This can still be removed by full involvement of the financial institutions in providing easy and quick loans of any amount to the SHGs and even individual. Since there is lot of paper work and stringent procedures, people shy off from the banks and prefer local money-lenders. Thus banks can act on the following guidelines for removing the inhibition from the people belonging to backward castes/classes:

Security Free Loan Disbursement: The collateral security in itself is an assurance for the security of the money. There should be no paper work or hassles in providing loan to SHGs. It has been observed that a lot paper work create confusion, corruption and hindrance for poorest of the poor who are mostly illiterate for getting full benefit of such schemes.

Interest Subsidy or Interest Free Loans: The subsidy has become source of corruption. Moreover, for a sizeable portion of our society 'interest' is a taboo, therefore if Government provides either interest free loan or interest subsidy it will be better in place of loan subsidy.

Marketing

This is most important area for sale of finished products. It has been generally observed that many traders or cooperatives do not conduct proper and in-depth feasibility studies before launching their products, which most times utterly backfires at them. For this, following aspects need to be borne into mind prior to selling their products:

- *Products:* An appropriate and saleable range has to be decided after intensive market survey. The choice and taste of the people vary from area to area and certain criteria have to be followed in manufacturing of the products. There should be a wide range of products to suit all communities and classes. Area-specific products have to be put up for sale in the market.
- *Market Locations:* Other then the local markets, markets within a vicinity of 250-300 kms. may be tapped with the new and attractive product for sale. The unit must be located on the all-weather road for easy transportation of raw material and finished products.
- *Quality-control/License:* This is essential for all food products and FPO is issued from the Food Licensing Authority, which has Regional Offices in all major cities. All food products must bear the number alongwith date of expiry and ingredients. For dry and wet products, the license is different.
- *Packaging:* This is very fast assuming an important aspect in the sale of products. Attractive and colourful packaging is very essential for high sales. It should also be born that product and packaging match, otherwise the resulting could be just disastrous.
- *Branding of the Products:* Branding is an important activity for promotion of product. For instance, brands like Colgate and Pond's are associated with dental and utility and make-up items and thus, are popular. Similarly brand gimmick has

to be done for the products depending on the items like food, cosmetics, dresses etc. in the new environment of business every product has to compete with the products of multi-national companies and the above-mentioned aspects, if properly taken care, will go in long way in bringing popularity and profits. The consumer is attracted to the brand and his daily routine associated with it. Quality maintenance is an integral component of the branding. There should be a proper system to check and control of the quality of products.

- *Promotion and Advertising:* Off late this is gaining popularity and also importance to reach the masses. Advertisement and products must match each other and message should properly spell out the utility of the products. The agency may also pursue the effective advertisement policy to compete with the products of the factories and MNCs.
- *Sale and Market Locations:* A nation-wide rural marketing facilitation network has to be created for sale of various products prepared by SHGs and other small and medium level entrepreneurs. This package includes infrastructure like *haat,* places in running malls/shopping complexes having large footfalls, cold-storages/warehousing facilities, facilitation for obtaining and executing export orders, follow-up of the major leads obtained in exhibitions etc. The present implementing agencies, DRDAs, do not have the requisite capacities and are unable to fulfil the demands of new and competitive market network. There should be a plan for creation of a nation-wide rural marketing facilitation network on partnership model, which will help small and medium level entrepreneurs.
- *Coordination with Key Players:* Marketing of the products is essentially a coordinated and concerted effort not only by the entrepreneur but also by various intermediate agencies like advertisers, Government departments and export agencies. The said coordination can be achieved by proper promotional schemes and special emphasis will have to be given to Public-Private Partnerships for sale of the products.
- *Marketing Strategists:* Marketing is a very broad discipline and it generally operates on aspects like product, promotion,

packaging, etc. Large-scale knowledge-management in terms of market information has to be done to empower rural poor producers so that they can exploit opportunities and protect themselves from various threats. A sectoral approach has to be taken for market and value-chain analysis. It has been seen that, very often, more than the resources, anti-poor sectoral policies are responsible for poverty in sectors. Such policies have to be identified and appropriate actions taken to correct the imbalances in the policies. The relevant nation-wise marketing infrastructure and post-project sustainable systems in terms of both finance and institutions have to be created.

- *SWOT of Marketing*: This is basically the approach in terms of professional and identifying economic opportunities with special focus on marketing has to be there. Large economic opportunities have to be identified in which rural producers have some intrinsic advantage so that a large number of people can be accommodated in these activities. The new emerging sectors have to be kept in mind.

    - A minor problem faced in integration of rural producers in the supply chains is the lack of discipline and market-oriented attitudes of the producers. There has to be awareness among the poor producers to honour contracts and mechanisms have to be put in place to ensure them.
    - There are a large number of organisations in public and private sectors, which can have synergy with the efforts of marketing of rural products. A partnership approach has to be adopted with these agencies to add value to rural products and their marketing.
    - To carry out all these activities, a mission approach and committed leadership is needed which is not possible in the present National, State level and district level setups. A new mechanism has to be thought-of. The best way is to create a national level agency, which will create and implement a National Rural Marketing Plan in mission-mode. This Agency may be called 'the National Rural Marketing Agency'.

Appendix

Economic Activities of Groups

Sl.No.	Group Name	Address	Occupation Undertaken
1.	Deepak	Saramsapur	Agriculture and Water Harvesting
2.	Suryamukhi	Mithan Sarai	Cattle
3.	Kamni	Pakadi	Cattle
4.	Shragani	Pakadi	Cattle
5.	Yuva Mahila	Pakadi	Cattle
6.	Gulab	Kaparpur	Cattle
7.	Noor	Narsanda	Cattle
8.	Tegia	Kaparpur	Cattle
9.	Taj	Kaparpur	Cattle
10.	Champa	Pakadi	Cattle
11.	Rupa	Pakadi	Cattle
12.	Swa Shakti Deepak	Saramsapur	Cattle
13.	Swa Shakti Bharti	Saramsapur	Cattle
14.	Swa Shakti Phool	Saramsapur	Cattle
15.	Swa Shakti Chameli	Chapra	Cattle
16.	Swa Shakti Sona	Chapra	Cattle
17.	Swa Shakti Tara	Saramsapur	Cattle
18.	Jai Mata Di	Pakadi	Cattle
19.	Maa Bhagwati	Pakadi	Cattle
20.	Lakshmi	Laskripur	Cattle
21.	Saraswati	Laskripur	Cattle
22.	Basant	Chapra	Cattle
23.	Bahar	Chapra	Cattle
24.	Shweta	Chapra	Cattle
25.	Gulab	Laskripur	Cattle
26.	Roop-Rekha	Narsanda	Cattle
27.	Maa Tara	Bhagwanpur	Cattle
28.	Sarojini Naidu	Bhagwanpur	Cattle
29.	Prakash	Madhukar, Chapra	Cattle

(*Contd.*)

(Contd.)

Sl. No.	Group Name	Address	Occupation Undertaken
30.	Swa Shakti Juhi	Soti Bhediyahi	Cattle
31.	Swa Shakti Sona	Soti Bhediyahi	Cattle
32.	Swa Shakti Shahjadi	Soti Bhediyahi	Cattle
33.	Swa Shakti Chameli	Balaha	Cattle
34.	Swa Shakti Sonia	Soti Bhediyahi	Cattle
35.	Saraswati	Godai Phulkaha	Cattle
36.	Shakti	Shahpur	Cattle
37.	Aadarsh	Shahpur	Cattle
38.	Chameli	Shahpur	Cattle
39.	Indira	Shahpur	Cattle
40.	Sangam	Shahpur	Cattle
41.	Kamal	Manikpur	Cattle
42.	Prabhat Kiran	Bariyarpur	Cattle
43.	Sangam	Manikpur	Cattle
44.	Razia	Manikpur	Cattle
45.	Maa Bhawani	Chapra Manorath	Cattle
46.	Ganga Maaiya	Chapra Manorath	Cattle
47.	Durga	Chapra Manorath	Cattle
48.	Sita	Serena	Cattle
49.	Bibi Fatam	Serena	Cattle
50.	Lakshmi	Dadar	Cattle
51.	Saraswati	Dadar	Cattle
52.	Soni	Dadar	Cattle
53.	Aarti	Dadar	Cattle
54.	Gayatri	Dadar	Cattle
55.	Kalayani	Dadar	Cattle
56	Shakti	Dadar	Cattle
57.	Swa Shakti Durga	Dadar	Cattle
58.	Swa Shakti Narikalyan	Dadar	Cattle
59.	Swa Shakti Sangam	Kolhua	Cattle
60.	Swa Shakti Priya	Kolhua	Cattle
61.	Swa Shakti Saakhi	Kolhua	Cattle
62.	Swa Shakti Pooja	Dadar	Cattle
63.	Shahjahan	Bariya	Cattle
64.	Bajrang	Kothia	Cattle
65.	Maharani	Kothia	Cattle
66.	Shiv	Kothia	Cattle
67.	Kamani	Kothia	Cattle
68.	Kadam	Kothia	Cattle
69.	Swa Shakti Gauri	Kaanti	Cattle
70.	Swa Shakti	Kaanti	Cattle
71.	Swa Shakti	Kaanti	Cattle
72.	Swa Shakti	Kaanti	Cattle
73.	Swa Shakti	Kaanti	Cattle
74.	Swa Shakti	Devaha	Cattle

(Contd.)

(*Contd.*)

Sl. No.	Group Name	Address	Occupation Undertaken
75.	Swa Shakti	Devaha	Cattle
76.	Swa Shakti	Devaha	Cattle
77.	Swa shakti	Devaha	Cattle
78.	Genda	Dhamoli Ramnath	Cattle
79.	Prakash	Dhamoli Ramnath	Cattle
80.	Pooja	Madhuban	Cattle
81.	Jagdamba	Devaha	Cattle
82.	Juhi	Kaanti	Cattle
83.	Sonia Gandhi	Narullahpur	Cattle
84.	Indira Gandhi	Chakbarkurva	Cattle
85.	Chanda	Narsanda	Cattle and Bangle Making
86.	Lakshmi	Sadatpur	Cattle and Fruit Trading
87.	Prerna	Pakadi	Cattle and Readymade
88.	Ekta	Sadatpur	Cattle and Vermi Compost
89.	Bhagya Lakshmi	Bariyarpur	Cattle and Vermi Compost
90.	Mangal	Rasulpur	Cattle for Dairy
91.	Rajasailes	Panapur Kariat	Cattle for Dairy
92.	Yadav	Harchanda	Cattle for Dairy
93.	Maa Saraswati	Narullahpur	Cattle for Dairy
94.	Mahila Vikas	Bangra Choupaan	Cattle for Dairy
95.	Jai Mata Di	Narullahpur	Cattle for Dairy
96.	Swashakti Surbhi	Saramsapur	Cattle, Fruits and Vegetable Farming
97.	Sooraj	Kaparpur	Fruits Marketing
98.	Rupali	Dadar	Fruits Marketing
99.	Swashakti	Kaanti	Fruits Marketing
100.	Gausia	Harchanda	Goatry
101.	Garib Nawaz	Harchanda	Goatry
102.	Rambha	Pakadi	Goatry
103.	Swashakti Sitara	Chapra	Goatry
104.	Indira Gandhi	Manikpur	Goatry
105.	Lakshmi	Manikpur	Goatry
106.	Saraswati	Manikpur	Goatry
107.	Sarojini Naidu	Manikpur	Goatry
108.	Safina Begam	Manikpur	Goatry
109.	Razia	Manikpur	Goatry
110.	Champa	Sahavajpur	Goatry
111.	Janki	Sahavajpur	Goatry
112.	Gulab	Gangapur	Goatry
113.	Tegia	Harchanda	Lac Bangle Making
114.	Swashakti	Devaha	Lac Bangle Making
115.	Swashakti	Devaha	Lac Bangle Making
116.	Swashakti	Devaha	Lac Bangle Making
117.	Swashakti	Devaha	Lac Bangle Making
118.	Roshan	Chakmurmur	Readymade Garments

(*Contd.*)

(Contd.)

Sl. No.	*Group Name*	*Address*	*Occupation Undertaken*
119.	Swashakti Shanti	Kaparpur	Sattu Masala
120.	Swashakti Janki	Sirsiya	Sattu Masala
121.	Chandni	Dadar	Sattu Masala and Business
122.	Suraksha	Chakbarkurva	Sattu Masala and Cattle
123.	Sooraj	Narsanda	Stitching and Vegetable Farming
124.	Sita	Kothia	Vegtable Farming
125.	Aadarsh	Manikpur	Vegetable and Cattle
126.	Utprerna	Pakadi	Vegetable and Pan Farming
127.	Maa Santoshi	Pakadi	Vegetable Farming
128.	Rekha	Pakadi	Vegetable Farming
129.	Nisha	Pakadi	Vegetable Farming
130.	Nikki	Pakadi	Vegetable Farming
131.	Lakshmi	Kothia	Vegetable Farming
132.	Chameli	Kothia	Vegetable Farming
133.	Chand	Kothia	Vegetable Farming
134.	Kasturba	Pakadi	Vegetable Farming and Cattle
135.	Sawarmati	Pakadi	Vegetable Farming and Cattle
136.	Kabir	Pakadi	Vegetable Farming and Cattle
137.	Mother Teresa	Pakadi	Vegetable Farming and Cattle
138.	Vaishnavi	Kothia	Vegetable Farming and Vermi Compost
139.	Vishwakarma	Suratpur	Vegetable Growing and Marketing
140.	Mahila Vikas	Pakadi	Vegetable Growing and Marketing
141.	Swashakti Champa	Haridaspur	Vegetable Production

Bibliography

Aliber, M. (2001). Study of the Incidence and Nature of Chronic Poverty and Development Policy in South Africa: An Overview. CPRC Working Paper No. 3, IDPM, University of Manchester (available online www.chronicpoverty.org).

Alternative Survey Group, (2001). Alternative Economic Survey. Delhi: Rainbow Publishers.

Amis, Phil. (2001). Thinking about Chronic Urban Poverty. Draft CPRC Working Paper.

Annual Reports of Ministry of Rural Development; Government of India; Year 2000-01; 2001-02; 2002-03; 2003-04; 2004-05, 2005-06, 2006-07.

Baliwala, Srilatha (1994). The Meaning of Women's Empowerment: New Concepts from Action in Gita Sen, Adrienne Germain and Lincon Chen (eds), Population Policies Re-considered: Health, Empowerment and Rights. Cambridge: Harvard University Press.

Baulch, Bob and McCulloch, Neil (September, 2001). Being Poor and Becoming Poor: Poverty Status and Poverty Transitions in Rural Pakistan. Draft Paper.

Bhalla, G.S and Hazel, P. (August, 2003). Rural Employment and Poverty: Strategies to Eliminate Rural Poverty within a Generation: *Economic and Political Weekly.*

Bharthi, K.S. Gandhian Approach to Rural Development. New Delhi: Omsons Publications.

"Bihar—Towards a Development Strategy", a World Bank Report. (www.worldbank.org)

Bird, K., Hulme, D. and Shepherd, A. (2001). Chronic Poverty in Remote Rural Areas. Working Paper (forthcoming), IDPM University on Manchester (available online www.chronicpoverty.org).

CARE (2000), State Level Convention on Federations: A Report. New Delhi.

Caste, Ethnicity, and Religion (May 2003), An Overview Paper on Exclusion/Discrimination and Deprivation, Concept Paper for DFID. New Delhi: DFID.

Caste, Exclusion/Discrimination and Deprivation (May 2003). The Situation of Dalits in India, Concept Paper for DFID, New Delhi: DFID.

Census Report (2001). Census of India, Ministry of Home Affairs, Government of India, New Delhi. (available at http://www.censusindia.gov.in).

Census Report of Village Infrastructure, (2001). Census of India, Ministry of Home Affairs, Government of India, New Delhi (available at http://www.censusindia.gov.in).

Chandra, Ramesh (2004). Minority: Social and Political Conflict. Volume 3. Delhi: Isha Books.

Choudhary, Deo Chandra (2000). Changing Structure of Indian Villages. New Delhi: Janaki Prakashan.

Chronic Poverty Research Centre, (2001). Chronic Poverty Research Toolbox. Forthcoming Working Paper (available online www.chronicpoverty.org).

Concurrent Evaluation of Swarnjayanti Gram Swarozgar Yojana (March, 2003). Conducted by Centre for Management Development, Thiruvananthapuram, Tamil Nadu, Sponsored by Ministry of Rural Development.

Country is less poor; levels shrink 10 per cent since 1993-94: (February, 2001), *Economic Times*, New Delhi.

Dahloan, Carl and Utz Anuja. India and the knowledge economy leveraging strengths and opportunities. New Delhi: World Bank Institute.

Debroy, Bibek and Bhandari, Laveesh (2003). District Level Deprivation in the New Millennium, edited by Rajiv Gandhi Institute for Contemporary Studies, Rajiv Gandhi Foundation, New Delhi, International Development Enterprises (India). New Delhi: Konark Publisher Limited.

Deichmann, Uwe and *et al.* (October, 2002). Economic Structure, Productivity and Infrastructure Quality in Southern Mexico. World Bank Policy Research Paper No. 2900.

Dohorty and Jodha (1977). Conditions of Group Action, Occasional Paper 19, ICRISAT, Douglas North: Institutions and Institutional Change.

Dreze, Jean (February, 2001). Starving the Poor. *The Hindu.*

Dreze, Jean and Sen, Amartya (1995). India: Economic Development and Social Opportunity. New Delhi: Oxford University Press.

Duflo, Annie (September, 2005). Health Shocks and Economic Vulnerablity in Rural India: Break the vicious cycle, Centre for Micro Finance Research Working Paper Series.

Fan, Sheggen and Peter, Hazell (April-June, 2000). Should Developing Countries Invest More in Less Favoured Areas? "An Empirical Analysis of Rural studies", *Economic and Political Weekly*.

A Workshop Report on Best Practices in Group Dynamics and Micro-Credit (2000). New Delhi: Department of Women and Child Development, Government of India and Gender Equality Fund, Canadian International Development Agency, (DWCD and CIDA).

Final Report of Research Work, (2007). Micro Finance and Empowerment of Scheduled Caste Women: "An Impact Study of SHGs in Uttar Pradesh and Uttaranchal", conducted by: BL Centre for Development Research and Action, Sponsored by: Planning Commission, Government of India, New Delhi.

Foundation for Micro-Credit: A Profile, SIDBI. Lucknow: SIDBI.

Ghosh, B. and P., De. (October, 2004). How do Different Categories of Infrastructure affect Development? Evidence from Indian States. *Economic and Political Weekly.*

Ghosh, P.K., Kundu, Amitabh and Shariff, Abusaleh (2002). Indexing Human Development in India: Indicators, Scaling and Composition. National Council of Applied Economic Research, Working Paper series No. 83. New Delhi: NCAER.

Gopalan, Sarala (2002). Towards Equality—The unfinished Agenda-Status of Women in India 2001. National Commission for Women, Government of India: NCW.

Government of India (2000-01). Mid-Term Review of Ninth Five Year Plan (2002-07). New Delhi: Planning Commission.

Government of India (2001). Economic Survey 2000-2001. Ministry of Finance. New Delhi: Ministry of Finance.

Government of India (February, 2001). Poverty Estimates for 1999-2000. Press Release, Press Information Bureau. New Delhi: PIB.

Government of India (2006). Towards Faster and More Inclusive Growth: An Approach to the 11th Five Year Plan. New Delhi: Planning Commission.

Government of India (1996). Expert Group on the Commercialisation of Infrastructure Projects, The India Infrastructure Report: Policy Imperative for Growth and Welfare, New Delhi: NCAER.

Gowda, G.S. (1998). Women in Panchayati Raj Institutions: A Case Study in Karnataka. Volume 17 (4). *Journal of Rural Development.*

Human Development Report (2005). International Cooperation at a cross road: Aid, trade and Security in an Unequal World. New Delhi: Oxford Publication.

Hussain, Monirul and Ghosh, Lipi (2002). Religious Minorities in South Asia: Selected Essays on Post Colonial Situations, Vol. 2. New Delhi: Manak.

IBRD (2001). World Development Report: Attacking Poverty. Delhi: Oxford University Press.

"Industrial Development Imperative for Bihar and Jharkhand—A Report"; Bihar Industries Commission—Chairman, Dr. Jamshedji.

Isolation and Deprivations (2000). Economic Situation of Tribals in India, in Development Issue in India, Edited, Dr. Solanki, Department of Economics, Dr. Babashaheeb Marathwada University, Aurangabad, Maharashtra.

James, K.S. and Sajini, B. Nair (2005). Accelerated Decline in Fertility in India since the 1980s—Trends among Hindus and Muslims. *Economic and Political Weekly*, Volume 40, No. 5.

Jha, D. (August, 2000). Strategies for Rural Development: Strategies for Rural Development in Ninth Plan, edited by R. P Singh, Hyderabad, NIRD.

Kabeer, N. (2000). Inter-generational contracts, demographic transitions and the 'quantity and quality' trade-off: parents, children and investing in the future. *Journal of International Development*, Vol. 12, No 4.

Karmakar, K.G. (1999). Rural Credit and Self Help Groups: Microfinance Needs and Concepts in India. New Delhi: Sage Publications.

Kay, Thelma. Gender and Development Section, Emerging Social Issues Division: Empowering Women Through Self-Help Micro-credit Programmes. New Delhi: ESCAP.

Kozel, Valeria and Parker, Barbara (2001). Poverty in Rural India: The Contribution of Qualitative Research in Poverty, Draft Paper.

Kundu, Amitabh, Abusaleh Shariff and P.K Ghosh (July, 2002). Indexing Human Development in India: Indicators, Scaling and Composition. Working Paper 83, New Delhi: NCAER.

Lalitha, N. and Nagarajan B.S. (2002). Self Help Groups in Rural Development. New Delhi: Donimant Publishers and Distributors.

Louis, Prakash (2001). Nai Arthik Niti Aur Dalit. New Delhi: Indian Social Institute.

Malhotra, Rakesh (2000). Swarnjayanti Gram Swarozgar Yojana: An Improvisation in Anti-Poverty Programme. NABARD: Mumbai.

Mandal, Amal (August, 2003). Poverty Eradication in Rural India: Reflection on Methodology. *Kurukshetra.*

Marjit, S. and Ghosh, B. (June, 2005). Educating the Poor in India—A Re-statement of the Problem, International Conference on Education, Kolkata: CSSS.

Massey, James (2003). Minorities and Religious Freedom in a Democracy, New Delhi: Manohar.

McKay, A. (2001). A Comparative Review of Quantitative Studies of Chronic Poverty. CPRC Working Paper (forthcoming), IDPM, University on Manchester (available online www.chronicpoverty.org)

McLluraine, C. and Moser, C.O.N. (2001). Violence and social capital in urban poor communities. *Journal of International Development*, Vol. 36, No 6.

Mehta, Aasha Kapur and Shah, Amita (2002). Chronic Poverty in India: Overview Study. CPRC Working Paper.

Mehta, A.K. and Shah, A. (2002). Chronic Poverty in India: Incidence, Causes and Policies, CPRC Working Paper.

Menon, G.A. and Gupta, S. From Margin to Mainstream: Building Stakes in the SHG-Bank Linkage Programme. Swayam Shikshan Prayog.

Mishra, J.P. (August, 2000). Policy Imperatives for an Effective Rural Credit System: Strategies for Rural Development in Ninth Plan edited by R. P Singh. Hyderabad: NIRD.

Mitra, Siddhartha (2003). Financing Rural Infrastructure: Trends and Alternatives to Public Finance. Unpublished Report, New Delhi, NCAER.

Moore, K. (2001). Frameworks for understanding the inter-generational transmission of poverty and well-being in developing countries. CPRC Working Paper (forthcoming), IDPM, University on Manchester (available online www.chronicpoverty.org)

MYRADA (2001). The MYRADA Experience: A Manual for Capacity Building of Self-Help Affinity Groups.

Narayan. D. and Patti, Petesch (2002). Voices of the Poor: From many lands. U.S.A.: The World Bank and Oxford University Press.

Narayanan, P. (June, 2003). Empowerment through Participation: How Effective is this Approach? *The Economic and Political Weekly,* 38(25).

National Bank for Agriculture and Rural Development. (July, 1999a). Handbook on Self-Help Groups Linkage Programme, NABARD, Ahmedabad.

National Bank for Agriculture and Rural Development (May, 1999b). Micro Finance and NABARD: Role and Perspectives, NABARD, Mumbai.

National Bank for Agriculture and Rural Development. (1999c). Task Force on Supportive Policy and Regulatory Framework on Microfinance: Summary and Recomendadtions. NABARD, Mumbai.

Nehru, Jawaharlal. Social Welfare in India—Ministry of Information and Broadcasting, Government of India, New Delhi.

NSS 38th, 50th and 55th Round, Differences in level of consumption among socio-economic group, Ministry of Statistics and Programme Implementation, Government of India, 1983-84, 1993-94 and 1999-2000.

NSSO, (2000-01). "Unorganized Manufacturing in India—Key Results", Ministry of Statistics and Programme Implementation, Government of India, 56th Round. New Delhi: NSSO.

Pathusha, K.M. Enrollment of Women in Distance Education with Special Reference to Muslim Women. All India Muslim Women's Education Confrence, Chennai.

Pattanaik, B.K. (2004). Muslims or Dalit Muslims: To Whom Need Protective Discrimination? Young India, Vol. 15, No. 17.

Persistence of Poverty (2004). Why Do Scheduled Caste and Scheduled Tribes Stay Chronically Poor? (Paper presented in Seminar on Chronic Poverty in India), IIPA, Delhi and DFID, London, Centre for Studies on Chronic Poverty.

Prasad, B.K. (2003). Rural Development Concept Approach and Strategy. New Delhi: Sarup & Sons.

Prasad, B. Devi and Haranath, S. (July-September, 2004). Journal of Rural Development: Participation of Women and Dalits in Gram Panchayat. Volume 23, No. 3. Hyderabad, National Institute of Rural Development.

Prasad, Hemlata (2006). Social Mobilisation, Employment and Empowerment of Women through SHGs. Hyderabad: National Institute of Rural Development (NIRD).

Rajan, S. Irudaya (2005). District Level Fertility Estimates for Hindus and Muslims. *Economic and Political Weekly*, Volume 40, No. 5.

Rajgopalan, S. (2000). Good Practices of NGOs in Setting up Alternative Development Financial Institutions. AIAMED (All India Association for Micro-Enterprise Development).

Rajneesh, Shalini, Rural Development through Democratic Decentralization. New Delhi: Deep & Deep Publication Pvt. Limited.

Rajshekhar, D. (1994). Savings and Credit Systems of Poor: Some Non-Governmental Organization (NGO) Experiences: NOVIB and HIVOS.

Rangacharyulu, S.V. (2005). Guaranteed Employment for the Rural Poor. Volume II. Hyderabad: National Institute of Rural Development.

Rao, Hanumant K. and Durgaprasad, P. (April 2003). Social Mobilisation and Empowerment and Poverty Alleviation, (Occasional Paper). Hyderabad: National Institute of Rural Development.

Rashtriya Mahila Kosh, (1998). Features of the Main and Sub-schemes. New Delhi: RMK.

Reddy, Y. Gangi (April-June, 2004). The Indian Journal of Public Administration: Innovative Approaches to Weaker Sections Development: A Case of Janmabhumi. Volume L, No. 2. New Delhi: Indian Institute of Public Administration (IIPA).

Report of the XI Plan Working Group on Poverty Elimination Programmes (2006). New Delhi: Planning Commission.

Rural Development Statistics 2002-2003. National Institute of Rural Development (NIRD): Hyderabad.

Sankar, D. and Kathuria, V. (March 2004). Health System Performance in Rural India: Efficiency Estimates Across States. *Economic and Political Weekly*.

Sen, Amartya (2000). Social Exclusion: Concept, Application and Scrutiny. Asian Development Bank Working Paper.

Shah, A. (2002). Spatial Poverty Traps in Rural India: An Explanatory Analysis of the Nature of the Causes. *Journal of Social and Economic Development*.

Shah, A. (2002). Spatial Poverty Trap in Rural India: An Exploratory Analysis of its Extent and Clauses, Mimeo.

Shah, Tushaar (1995). Making Farmers' Cooperative Work-Design, Governence and Managemant. Sage Publication.

Sharma, Aruna (2005). Resource Convergence Mantra: Holistic Planning Approach through Resource Convergence, United Nations Development Programme (UNDP). New Delhi: Ministry of Rural Development, Government of India.

Sharma, Jay and Parthasarthi, K. (2007). A Quantitative Study. New Delhi: Nirantar Publications.

Sharma, K.L. (2001). Caste, Class and Tribe. Jaipur and New Delhi: Rawat Publications.

Sikligar, P.C. (2005-06). Economic Upliftment of Minorities through Micro-Credit Finance: An Evaluation. Hyderabad: NIRD.

Singh, Ajit Kumar (August, 2000). Improving the Effectiveness of IRDP: Suggestive bases on a field study in Uttar Pradesh, Strategies for Rural Development in Ninth Plan edited by R. P Singh. Hyderabad: NIRD.

Singh, Katar (1999). Rural Development Principles, Policies and Management. New Delhi: Sage Publications.

Singh, Naresh (December, 2003). Perspectives on Emergence and Growth of Microfinance Sector. *Asia-Pacific Journal of Rural Development*, Vol. XIII, No 2, CIRDAP.

Singh, R.P. (1997). New Economic Policy and Prospective to Rural Development. Hyderabad: NIRD.

Singh, S.N. (2003). Muslim in India. New Delhi: Anmol Publications.

Sinha, Archana. (April 2004). Micro-Finance for Women's Empowerment. *Kurukshetra*.

Social, Economic and Educational Status of the Muslim Community of India. (November, 2006). A Report of Prime Minister's High Level Committee, Cabinet Secretariat. New Delhi: Government of India.

Sundaram, and Tendulkar (2002). Poverty among social and economic groups in India in the nineties. Working Paper No. 118. Delhi: CDE.

Tamil Nadu Corporation for Development of Women Ltd. (DeW), (1999). A Guide to SHG Federations.

Tankha, Ajay. (2002). Self-Help Groups as Financial Intermediaries in India: Cost of Promotion, Sustainability and Impact. Unpublished Report prepared for Sa-Dhan.

Thomas, Fisher and Sriram, MS. (2002). Beyond Micro-credit: Putting Development bank-finance, originally published by New Economics Foundation, London (Oxford). New Delhi: Vistaar Publications.

Sriram Herperenal Colm; Ajit Kanikat; Frances Simla SAN. United Nations Development Project (2006), Asia Pacific Human Development Report, 2006.

United Nations Development Programme (2001). Human Development Report, 2001. New York: Oxford University Press.

Vaidynathan, A. (August, 2000). Poverty allocation programmes: Some lessons from Indian experiences—Strategies for Rural Development in Ninth Plan; Strategies for Rural Development in Ninth Plan edited by R. P Singh, Hyderabad: NIRD.

Vempeny, Sebastian (2003). Minorities in Contemporary India. New Delhi: Kanishka.

Verma, B.M. (2000). Welfare Measures for Weaker Section (A Policy Analysis). New Delhi: IIPA.

Vijapur, A.P. (2000). Plight of Education Among Indian Muslims: A Case Study of some Aspects. Delhi: Devika Publications.

Vyas, V.S. (December, 2004). Agrarian Distress: Strategies to Protect Vulnerable Sections. *Economic and Political Weekly.*

Waqif, A. (August, 2000). Social Mobilization and Empowerment: A Vote on Concept and Application in South Asia, Strategies for Rural Development in Ninth Plan. Hyderabad: NIRD.

Wilson, Kim (2002). The New Micro Finance: An Essay on Self-Help Group in India. *Journal of Micro Finance*. Vol. 4(2).

World Bank (October, 2008). World Development Report, 2008: Agriculture for Development. Oxford University Press.

World Bank (September, 2007). World Development Report, 2007: Development and the next Generation. Oxford University Press.

World Bank (September, 2006). World Development Report, 2006: Equity and Development. Oxford University Press.

Yeo, R. (2001). Chronic Poverty and Disability. CPRC Working Paper (forthcoming), IDPM, University on Manchester (available online www.chronicpoverty.org).

WEBSITES

i. www.abc.net.au
ii. http://www.careindia.org/ManageProgramKey/VisitProgramDetail
iii. http://www.censusindia.gov.in
iv. www.chronicpoverty.org
v. http://education.nic.in/ms/10th Plan-MSL.pdf. Retrieved May 25, 2006.
vi. www.en.wikipedia.org
vii. www.grameen-info.org
viii. ORG Marg, Muslim Women's Survey, (2002). Muslim Women's Survey. Retrieved on August 25, 2007 from
ix. www.infochangeindia.org/bookandreportsst22.jsp. Retrieved July 25, 2007.
x. http://megapib.nic.in/mselfhelpgroup_geninf.htm
xi. http://megapib.nic.in/mselfhelpgroup_linksbi.htm
xii. http://megapib.nic.in/mselfhelpgroup_rbicir.htm
xiii. http://megapib.nic.in/mselfhelpgroup_sbishakti.htm
xiv. www.microcreditsummit.org
xv. www.mospi.gov.in/mospi_cso_rept_pubn.htm. Retrieved on August 15, 2007.

xvi. http://www.mospi.gov.in/mospi_nsso_rept_pubn.htm
xvii. http://www.nabard.org/introduction.asp
xviii. http://www.nabard.org/development&promotional/developmentalinitiatives.asp
xix. http://www.nabard.org/investmentcredit/govt_sponsered.asp
xx. http://www.nfhsindia.org/pdf/BH.pdf
xxi. http://www.nird.org.in/RDS26/RDSINDEX.htm
xxii. www.planningcommission.nic.in/data/dataf.htm
xxiii. www.rmaf.org.ph
xxiv. www.rural.nic.in. Retrieved on May 6, 2007
xxv. www.rural.nic.in/sgsy.htm. Retrieved on July 13, 2007.
xxvi. www.unescap.org/drpad
xxvii. http://web.worldbank.org/WBSITE/EXTERNAL/DATASTATISTICS/
xxviii. http://www.who.int/mdg/en/
xxix. http://www.who.int/topics/pregnancy/en/

End of The Book

Index